BRET HARTE

Opening the American Literary West

The Oklahoma Western Biographies
Richard W. Etulain, General Editor

BRET HARTE

Opening the American Literary West

By Gary Scharnhorst

UNIVERSITY OF OKLAHOMA PRESS : NORMAN

Also by Gary Scharnhorst

The Lost Life of Horatio Alger (Bloomington, Ind., 1985)
(editor) *Bret Harte's California: Letters to the* Springfield Republican *and* Christian Register, *1866–67* (Albuquerque, 1990)
Bret Harte (New York, 1992)
(editor) *Critical Essays on* The Adventures of Tom Sawyer (New York, 1993)
(editor, with Tom Quirk) *American Realism and the Canon* (Newark, Del., 1994)
Bret Harte: A Bibliography (Metuchen, N.J., 1995)
(editor) *American Literary Scholarship: An Annual* (Durham, N.C., 1993, 1995, 1997, 1999)
(editor) *Selected Letters of Bret Harte* (Norman, 1997)

Library of Congress Cataloging-in-Publication Data

Scharnhorst, Gary.
    Bret Harte : opening the American literary West / by Gary Scharnhorst.
        p.   cm. — (The Oklahoma western biographies ; v. 17)
    Includes bibliographical references and index.
    ISBN 0–8061–3254–X (alk. paper)
    1. Harte, Bret, 1836–1902.   2. Harte, Bret, 1836–1902—Knowledge
—West (U.S.)   3. Authors, American—19th century—Biography.   4.
Western stories—History and criticism.   5. West (U.S.)—In literature.
I. Title.   II. Series.
PS1833 .S38 2000
813'.4—dc21
[B}   00–022412
                                                                        CIP

Bret Harte: Opening the American Literary West is Volume 17 in The Oklahoma Western Biographies.

The paper in this book meets the guidelines for permanence and durability of the Committee on Production Guidelines for Book Longevity of the Council on Library Resources, Inc. ∞

1   2   3   4   5   6   7   8   9   10

To Sandy,
whose gift I accept every day
with untold thanks I have been chosen to receive it.

Contents

Illustrations

Series Editor's Preface

STORIES of heroes and heroines have intrigued many generations of listeners and readers. Americans, like people everywhere, have been captivated by the lives of military, political, and religious figures and of intrepid explorers, pioneers, and rebels. The Oklahoma Western Biographies endeavor to build on this fascination with biography and to link it with two other abiding interests of Americans: the frontier and the American West. Although volumes in the series carry no notes, they are prepared by leading scholars, are soundly researched, and include a list of sources used. Each volume is a lively synthesis based on thorough examination of pertinent primary and secondary sources.

Above all, the Oklahoma Western biographies aim at two goals: to provide readable life stories of significant westerners and to show how their lives illuminate a notable topic, an influential movement, or a series of important events in the history and culture of the American West.

In this biography of Bret Harte, Gary Scharnhorst, a well-known American literary historian, provides a balanced study of a notable writer of the nineteenth century. As the country's leading specialist on Harte, Scharnhorst draws on his extensive research and previous writings to fashion a biography that is fair-minded and thorough as well as smoothly written. His life story of the writer overflows with apt quotations from a wide variety of primary sources.

Scharnhorst emphasizes Bret Harte's role as a famous man of letters. We learn about Harte's early struggles as an editor/author in California, his difficulties in breaking into eastern literary

markets and salons, and his successful failures in his final years in
Europe. Scharnhorst focuses on his subject's life as a writer, but
not at the expense of Harte's personal life, especially his painful
limitations as a husband and father. While describing Harte's
achievements as an internationally recognized author of local-
color stories, Scharnhorst also honestly confronts Harte's human
weaknesses.

In this important addition to the Oklahoma Western Biographies series, a major literary scholar utilizes the life of a noted
westerner, in this case a western American writer, to illuminate
American and European literary cultures of the late nineteenth
century. Scharnhorst's appealingly written biography will draw
both readers interested in the American West and those wishing
a brief but authoritative life story of a well-known American literary figure.

RICHARD W. ETULAIN

University of New Mexico

Preface

HENRY Seidel Canby asserted in 1926, with pardonable hyperbole, that "the literary West may be said to have founded itself upon the imagination of Bret Harte." To be sure, Harte was not the first writer to stake a claim to the California mining camps, but with the completion of the transcontinental railroad in 1869 he was perfectly positioned to exploit the burgeoning popular interest in the American West. A pioneer in the use of California local color, Harte in his story "The Luck of Roaring Camp," first published in the *Overland Monthly* in July 1868, "reached across the continent and startled the Academists on the Atlantic Coast," as Kate Chopin later opined. Harte's subsequent *Overland* tales and verse, so different in tone and texture from the polite pontifications of Cooper, Hawthorne, and the Fireside Poets, challenged genteel assumptions about literary production and helped to open the pages of the *Atlantic Monthly* and other eastern papers to such western writers as Mark Twain, Ambrose Bierce, Ina Coolbrith, and Joaquin Miller. Lured east by the promise of wealth and celebrity in 1871, Harte signed the most lucrative contract to that date in the history of American letters—ten thousand dollars for all fiction and poetry he might write over a twelvemonth. For one year he was both the highest paid and the best-known writer in America.

For better or worse, moreover, Harte was a prototype of the modern man of letters as man of business. As his career spiraled downward over the next decade—the joke made the rounds that he had reversed the path of the sun, rising in glory in the West and setting in darkness in the East—his professional life consisted largely of negotiations with the middlemen of literary production (publishers, editors, theatrical producers, managers, and so forth), whose interests never quite coincided with his own. His coauthorship with Samuel Clemens of the play *Ah Sin* in 1877 was arguably the most disastrous collaboration in the history of American letters. To the end of his life he was haunted by the specter of the hardscrabble winter of 1877–78, when he lived literally hand to mouth. "Few American writers," Newton Arvin averred, "have ever passed so melodramatically from the sunshine of adulation into the darkness of disreputability." His later tales were mostly written according to the same tested and tired formula. "I grind out the old tunes on the old organ and gather up the coppers," he privately allowed in 1879. Less a craftsman by then than a literary celebrity who traded on his name, he gauged the market for his writings with a calculating eye and, as W. D. Howells put it, "wrote Bret Harte over and over again as long as he lived."

The commonplace assumptions about Harte notwithstanding, his career was neither short-lived nor punctuated by repeated failures. In fact he published dozens of stories over the last twenty years of his life, a collection of them every year between 1883 and 1902. Fully two-thirds of the stories in his *Complete Writings* appeared after he left the United States for Europe, never to return, in 1878. First in Germany and then in Great Britain, he steadily worked as a magazinist until his death, and his stories were regularly translated into German, French, Italian, Swedish, Russian, and other languages. When he died, his friend Henry Adams pronounced him one of "the most brilliant men of my time." He was also, in truth, one of the most fortunate. At no less than five critical junctures in his career he enjoyed "the luck of the draw": his initial discovery by Jessie Frémont in 1860; his selection as founding editor of the *Overland Monthly* in 1868 and the fortuitous publication of "The Luck of Roaring Camp" in its second issue; the offer he received in 1871, at the height of his fame, to contribute to the *Atlantic Monthly* when its publishers desperately needed to recruit a marquee name; his unexpected appointment to a diplomatic post in 1878 at the nadir of his literary career; and his contract with A. P. Watt, the first professional literary agent, and the coincident growth of the first newspaper syndicates in the United States and England after his dismissal from the diplomatic corps in 1885.

This biography describes both the literary construction of the American West and its commodification as a literary property during the late nineteenth century. It also details the extent to which Harte became a creature of the literary and theatrical market, accommodating the demands of his audience (especially those who commissioned and paid him for his piecework) that he write about the West long after he left it. Obviously, these two narratives often intersect. My fundamental assumption is that literary popularity in general and Harte's popularity in particular were less ideological or political than market driven and that markets for "the western" in its various incarnations were deliberately *made* by publishers and theatrical producers. Whereas in *Virgin Land* Henry Nash Smith chronicled the appropriation of the American West in symbol and myth, in this book I trace the growing commercial appeal of western fiction and drama on both sides of the Atlantic during the final third of the nineteenth century.

In quoting from Harte's letters in this biography, for the record, I retain their original spelling and punctuation.

Once again, I am indebted to the many kindnesses of strangers and friends for assistance in the completion of this project. I thank my friend and colleague Dick Etulain for entrusting me with the project and allowing me free rein. I also appreciate the help and encouragement of Paul Sorrentino, Stanley Wertheim, Bob Fleming, Andy Smith, Alice Wallace, Harriet Elinor Smith, Alice Hall Petry, Tom Quirk, Jim and Connie Thorson, and Dick Winslow; the members of the Research Allocations Committee of the University of New Mexico; my many friends in the Western Literature Association, including Deb and Edith Wylder, Larry Berkove, Glen and Rhoda Love, and Joe and Christine Flora; and my many friends at Scalo, including Tim Conway, Charlie LeBlanc, Steve Paternoster, Michael Daly, Colleen Langan,

Susie Smith, Jenni Kain, Marc Champoux, Nicole Gabel, Jason Gable, Tom White, Nik Fioretti, Greg Atkin, Paul Ariaza, Harris "Yummy" Moskowitz, Javier Leal, and Roy Courtright. For the record, too, I have deposited a fully documented copy of the manuscript of this biography in the UNM English Department library, should interested scholars wish to consult my sources.

GARY SCHARNHORST

University of New Mexico

BRET HARTE

Opening the American Literary West

CHAPTER I

"I am Fit for Nothing Else"

ON the last day of 1857, scarcely four months after his twenty-first birthday, Francis Brett Harte penned a note in the end pages of his diary for the year: "The conviction forced on me by observation and not by vain enthusiasm, that I am fit for nothing else—must impel [me] to seek distinction and fortune in literature. Perhaps I may succeed—if not I can at least make the trial." Harte's heady ambition seems all the more remarkable under the circumstances: largely self-educated, he lived at the time in a single room of a rustic cabin in rural Humboldt County, California, where he tutored the sons of a ranching family. Not only was he far from the publishing centers of Boston and New York when virtually all mail between California and "the States" still traveled by ship around Cape Horn, but there was, for all practical purposes, no local literary market in this barren outback. To be sure, George H. Derby ("John Phoenix") had earned modest celebrity as a California humorist before he died at age thirty-eight in 1861, and Louise A. K. Smith Clappe had published a memorable nonfictional account of the gold-rush mining camps in *The Shirley Letters* (1854) a few years earlier. But in 1857, when Harte's ambition to succeed as a writer was fired, there were no daily newspapers on the Pacific slope outside San Francisco, Sacramento, and Stockton, and there was only a single literary paper, the weekly San Francisco *Golden Era*.

His literary prospects would have been better, that is, had he remained in the East, where he spent most of his first seventeen years. Born in Albany on August 25, 1836, the third of four children, Harte was, to judge from all available evidence, a precocious child. His father, Henry Harte, was an improvident teacher

3

and sometimes principal at a number of small academies around the Northeast. A scholar gypsy and former student at Union College who spoke French, Spanish, and Italian and read Greek and Latin, he moved his family from Albany to Hudson early in 1837, then to New Brunswick, Philadelphia, Providence, to Lowell and Boston and New York City before his death in 1845. As Harte later reminisced, his "dear old father" was "barely able to eke out a living" at such schools as the Albany Female Academy, the Hudson Academy, and the Ellington Institute, but "he would not give up a vocation which enabled him to cultivate literary graces, even though by so doing he could have earned a little more money." Harte's mother, Elizabeth Rebecca Ostrander, a descendant of old Knickerbocker families and Revolutionary War heroes, had married Henry Harte in 1827. After her death in 1875 Harte remembered that "my mother had often talked of her Revolutionary ancestors," and he adapted this family lore in such stories as "Thankful Blossom" (1876) and "Two Americans" (1897).

Henry Harte took to his grave a family secret, moreover: he was in fact the son of Bernard Hart, an Orthodox Jew and one of the founders of the New York Stock Exchange, who had briefly been married at the turn of the century to a gentile woman, Catherine Brett. Among his immediate family, it seems, Bret Harte made no secret of his Jewish grandfather. He sometimes mentioned a visit he made as a small child to the floor of the stock exchange, where his father pointed Bernard Hart out to him, though "he never spoke to him nor saw him again." In public, however, Harte was more circumspect. Though a reviewer in the *Overland Monthly* in January 1883 also remarked on Harte's "English, German, and Hebrew blood," his sometime friend and eventual enemy Samuel Clemens once complained that "he conceals his Jewish birth as carefully as if he considered it a disgrace." Certainly Harte lied about his bloodlines in a letter he sent the British psychologist Havelock Ellis in 1889: "to the best of my knowledge," he claimed, "my *mother* and her immediate ancestors were descended from the Early Dutch (Holland) settlers in America, while my *father* and his immediate ancestors were as distinctly English in origin."

From all reports—mostly his own testimony in later life—young Harte was "an omniverous reader" whose delicate health often confined him to bed and books. He claimed in 1894, in one of his rare interviews, that while still a child he read "Froissart's 'Chronicles of the Middle Ages,' 'Don Quixote,' the story of the Argonauts," and other volumes his father owned. He once bragged to Annie Fields, wife of the Boston editor and publisher James T. Fields, that he had read Shakespeare at the age of six, Dickens at seven, Montaigne at eight. On the other hand he ridiculed a religious tract, entitled *Conversation between a Converted Heathen and a Missionary,* that he had been assigned to read in Sunday School: "Had I any respect for an imbecile black being who groveled continuallly, crying 'Me so happy—bress de lor! send down him salvation berry quick,' in uncouth English? Believed I in his conversion?" He also allowed near the end of his life that as a boy he had been unable "to take John Bunyan seriously. The 'Pilgrim's Progress' affected me very much in the same way as the converted Africans or Indians who were introduced to me at Sunday School by their missionary showmen, and who talked 'baboon' or 'pigeon' English. . . . I know I used to roar with laughter over 'Mr. Facing-both-ways' and 'Mr. By-ends,' to the great detriment of my spiritual education."

According to T. Edgar Pemberton, his friend, collaborator, and official biographer, Harte gleaned his "spiritual education" instead from more contemporary sources. He read Dickens's *Dombey and Son* in monthly parts in 1846, then "made himself master of the glorious works from the same pen which had preceded it." He then "proceeded to Fielding, Goldsmith, Smollett, Cervantes, and Washington Irving," as his older sister Eliza remembered. Not that he seemed destined from childhood to literary fame and fortune. At the age of eleven Harte published a satirical poem, now lost, entitled "Autumn Musings" in the New York *Sunday Atlas,* which his family mocked. "It was a terrible experience," he remembered years later. "Sometimes I wonder that I ever wrote another line of verse."

Harte's formal schooling ended in 1849, at the age of thirteen, when he went to work as a clerk, first for a lawyer and later for a merchant in New York. He enlisted in one of the military companies deployed in quelling the Astor Place theater riots in May 1849. While in his mid-teens, he also wrote a long poem, "The Hudson River," which was never published. In late January 1854 he attended a lecture on Japan by Bayard Taylor, whose travel letters he had read in the *New York Tribune*. Taylor seemed to him a "romantic, handsome presence," a veritable "Robinson Crusoe incarnate, a Sinbad come to life." In stark contrast, Harte's family lived in genteel poverty, unable to send its sons to college, dependent for its livelihood on Bernard Hart's charity. In late 1853 his widowed mother moved to California, where she married the lawyer Andrew Williams, a future mayor of Oakland, and Harte and his younger sister Maggie soon followed. Embarking from New York on February 20, 1854, they crossed the isthmus of Panama in early March and arrived in San Francisco aboard the steamer *Brother Jonathan* on March 26. Their passage along the Pacific coast had been delayed when a boiler burst, causing "a little alarm among green passengers." At the age of seventeen, Harte went to California partly out of filial duty, partly from a sense of adventure, partly because he had no alternative. He would spend the next seventeen years there; after he left in 1871 he would never return.

Harte's early years in the West, largely obscured in a biographical blind spot, seem to have been unremarkable. He worked briefly as a druggist's assistant in Oakland, an experience he recreated in his late story, "How Reuben Allen 'Saw Life' in San Francisco" (1900). He was eventually hired to tutor the four "tractable and docile" sons of the cattle rancher Abner Bryan, who lived near Alamo, a half-day's ride from Oakland. He wrote his earliest extant letter (the only known documentary evidence about his life between his arrival in California in March 1854 and the publication of his first poem in the *Golden Era* over three years later) to his "peerless sister" Maggie on October 8, 1856, saying that the Bryan homestead was "stuck in a deep canyon with high hills on either side, a mere shanty that might be a hunter's cabin in the wilderness. . . . As Mr. Bryan is not a farmer, but a drover, there is nothing of the rural character of a

Bret Harte at the age of seventeen in Boston, shortly before leaving for California. (Courtesy of Cathy Gardner and Paul Deceglie)

farm, saving the corral at the bottom of the field and the haystack at the top, and the whole place is as wild as the God of Nature made it." He later worked his reminiscences of these months into his sketch, "Notes 'By Flood and Field'" (1862). His friend Charles Murdock, whose testimony is probably more reliable than Harte's own later comments, reported that Harte "found the experience agreeable and valuable" but that he left the San Ramon valley that winter or early spring. The rancher apparently could no longer afford the luxury of a private tutor for his boys.

Walking to Tuolumne County by way of Sacramento, Harte opened a school in a "little bark-thatched" building on Dry Creek near Sonora, which he soon closed for lack of students. He explained to an interviewer in 1870 that some parents withdrew their children from the school after he expelled a particularly recalcitrant boy. In 1899, in his semiautobiographical essay "How I Went to the Mines," however, Harte claimed he lost his teaching job in the "little pioneer settlement school" when a pair of families "announced their intention of moving" to a more prosperous district and "the school was incontinently closed." He then spent a few weeks at placer mining "but met with indifferent success," the gold he found "barely paying expenses." "I took my pick and shovel and asked where I might dig. They said 'Anywhere,'" he remembered later, but "I was not a success as a gold-digger." In truth, Harte "was not a man to go to work and rustle around and mix with the miners," the publisher Anton Roman reminisced. While he may have enjoyed a reputation during his lifetime as a former redshirt miner, as Patrick Morrow has suggested, Harte likely "spent less time in the Mother Lode than many of today's enthusiastic tourists." According to Clemens's friend Steve Gillis, Harte appeared on foot one day "carrying a roll of blankets" at the Gillis brothers' claim on Jackass Flat in Tuolumne. "He came upon my brother Jim," Gillis recalled, just as he was "taking out a rich pocket of gold. Poor little Bret stood in the trail, dusty and tired and hungry and dead broke and looked down into my brother's pan which contained a good pile of free gold. Well, Jim took him in and kept him for four days."

Harte also worked briefly in the spring of 1857 as an agent and messenger for the Wells, Fargo Express Company in Tuolumne. He noted in his diary at the end of the year that he had "taught school, played the Expressman for a brief delightful hour" and "travelled some." He later claimed, in the full bloom of his fame, that he had worked "for some months" as a Wells, Fargo messenger and that his predecessor in the job had been "shot through the arm" and his successor killed. As with many of his comments about his early life in California, however, these assertions are more myth than fact. Returning briefly to San Francisco, he began to contribute occasional verse to the *Golden Era*—a total of ten poems over the next few months—none of them particularly memorable, none of them gathered by him into a later collection of his writings.

In May 1857 he surfaced in Eureka near his sister Maggie, who had married and settled in Uniontown (now Arcata) on the northern side of Humboldt Bay. He sent a sketch about his journey up the coast to Joseph Lawrence, editor of the *Golden Era*. "I resolved to leave San Francisco," he explained, because he had grown weary of the "dirty streets, sand hills, bricks and mortar" of the city and its weather "had become contemptuously familiar. I sought a change of clime" in Humboldt country, which "possesses a certain stamina and stability" unusual for California. "This is a right down smart town," Harte wrote in the first of six columns he published under the pseudonym "Icabod" in the weekly *Humboldt Times* that spring and summer. It enjoyed "a degree of substantial prosperity that is not found in every town in the State," though he added that the local citizens "are suffering for want of preaching of the gospel." Clemens visited the town four years later; as he described it in chapter twenty-eight of *Roughing It,* it consisted of "eleven cabins and a liberty pole." Murdock remembered, too, that Harte "liked little Humboldt, or else he had no call elsewhere. He stayed and took life easily." Like many another young man, he fell in love, or so he wrote in the last of his "Icabod" letters. The object of his affection was a "pert" young lady, a "sweet creature" who "makes herself useful as well as ornamental, and has no doubt been fed on violets and sleeps on a bed of roses"— perhaps young Cassie Martin, whom he once apotheosized in his diary (only one of two he is known to have kept) as "the prettiest, best behaved girl" he knew.

In the fall he began to tutor the two teenaged sons of the rancher Charles Liscomb and moved into their ranchero near Uniontown. As he noted in his journal, he "commenced school" on October 19, 1857. Almost every morning except Sundays until the following March 5, Harte instructed the boys in reading and spelling, geography, and arithmetic. He read to them such books as the *Arabian Nights,* and in the afternoons he often took them bird hunting in the marshes or along the slough, usually with little game to show for it. He was an inept marksman, to judge from his diary entries. One winter day, for example, he went shooting but had "no success." He even "broke one of my good revolvers."

Murdock thought him "a somewhat pathetic figure, for he was evidently a gentleman of refined tastes with no means of support. He was willing, but helpless," and he "held himself somewhat aloof from the common run of his fellows." Sophie Whipple Root, who also knew Harte in Uniontown, recalled later that he "did not mix very well with the rougher element which formed a great part of the population," who "considered him quite a snob." Though some thirty years later, by then a darling of the English leisure class, Harte bragged that he had been "obliged in California to get his dinner by depending upon his *rifle* for it," he apparently stretched the point. The incongruity between his modest station and his grandiose aspirations was not altogether lost on him. In a moment of despair on Christmas Day 1857, Harte pondered his future: "What the d——l am I to do with myself—the simplest pleasures fail to please me—my melancholy and gloomy forboding stick to me closer than a brother. I cannot enjoy myself rationally like others but am forced to make a gloomy spectacle of myself to gods and men."

Within a week he had framed an answer to this anguished question. As he wrote in his diary on New Year's Eve,

Before I close this Journal containing but a small portion of last years doings let me indulge in a retrospect. I am at the commencement of this year—a teacher at a Salary of $25 per mo—last year at this time I was unemployed. Last year I thought I was in love—this year I think the same tho the object is a different one. . . . I have added to my slight stock of experiences and have suffered considerable. Ah! well did the cynical Walpole say life is a comedy to those who think—a tragedy to those who feel.—I both think and feel. My life is a mixture of broad caricature and farce when I think of others, it is a melodrama when I feel for myself. In these 365 days I have again put forth a feeble essay toward fame and perhaps fortune.—I have tried literature albeit in an humble way—successfully—I have written some poetry: passable and some prose (good) which have been published. . . . Therefore I consecrate this year or as much as God may grant for my service—to honest heartfelt sincere labor and devotion to this occupation.—God help me—may I succeed.

He read eagerly—Douglas Jerrold's *History of St. Giles and St. James,* Irving's *Life of Washington,* Elisha Kane's *Arctic Voyage,* William Prescott's *The Conquest of Peru*—as part of his literary self-education. He also wrote and repeatedly revised a story entitled "What Happened at Mendocino," which he apparently failed to place with an editor. But he enjoyed a signal triumph when, barely past his majority, he placed his satirical poem "Dolores" in the New York *Knickerbocker* for January 1858—his first appearance in a national magazine. With its artificial tone, stilted rhyme, and inflated diction, the lyric exhibits few of the vernacular or humorous qualities that earned him fame and fleeting fortune a decade later. The poet adjures a "Hooded Nun" to

> Turn that pensive glance on high:
> Seest thou the floods in yon blessed sky. . . .
> E'en as thou gazest, lo! they fade:
> So doth the world from these walls surveyed.

In the end the nun flees the convent and the ascetic life to satisfy the "languid fires" of passion, much as Harte abandoned his early religious faith and surrendered to what he called, in a later poem, the "aimless loves" and "idle pains" that "shook my youth." Clemens claimed some fifty years later that Harte told him "in his early days in California when he was a blooming young chap" he had "kept a woman who was twice his age—no, the woman kept him." Might "Dolores" betray the poet's own conflicted desires? By questioning the pieties of Christian orthodoxy, the poem seems to anticipate Harte's mature religious nonconformity and the parodies of biblical text in several of his *Overland* stories a decade later. In any event, Harte finished his teaching stint at the Liscomb homestead in early March, then kept store in town for two weeks at a salary of fourteen dollars a week and board.

And he no doubt remained in the neighborhood of Uniontown throughout the summer and fall. He probably suffered a bout of smallpox at the time; certainly his face was pitted with smallpox scars as a young adult, and he told the poet Ina Coolbrith in the late 1860s that he had stopped teaching school after "a bad attack of smallpox, which rendered it, at least temporarily, advisable." Though his whereabouts during these months cannot be ascertained for a certainty, partly because he published nothing more than one poem in the *Golden Era,* Harte was hired in December 1858 to be a printer's assistant on the staff of the *Northern Californian,* a Uniontown weekly paper, for sixteen dollars a month. "As a practical man he was not a success," according to Murdock, whose father was one of the co-owners of the paper, "and I imagine that 'grass was pretty short' about the time the Northern Californian was started." Harte remained in this "very dirty job," sometimes contributing to its columns and even substituting for its editor during his absences, for over a year. Most of the articles, virtually all of them unsigned, which have been attributed to him are brief and innocuous (e.g., reports about the local judicial term or the lyceum season). He published nothing in the *Golden Era* during this year.

In one respect only was Harte's tenure as a printer's devil and editor pro tem of a rural newspaper at all remarkable: he consistently championed the rights of Native Americans in his editorials. In "Cruelty to Indians" in the issue for September 7, 1859, for example, he described "an assault upon a squaw at Trinidad" who was stabbed by a white man "so severely that her life was despaired of." Harte believed so-called "Indian outrages" were in fact precipitated by white aggression: "It is a painful reflection that the provocation is usually the work of the white civilizer." To be sure, Harte likely served at the time in a volunteer militia charged with protecting the property of white ranchers. He referred in 1879 to his "year's service against the Indians on the California frontier," and Pemberton later claimed that "in the warfare with the Indians he fought through two campaigns to a staff appointment." He had been "escorted to the recruiting officer by indignation and hunger," Harte explained.

Still, he freely voiced his anger and frustration when racial tensions in Humboldt erupted into bloodshed. Early in the morning of February 26, 1860, over sixty Wiyot Indians—most of them women and children—were murdered in cold blood by white settlers on an island in Humboldt Bay. Temporarily in charge of the *Northern Californian,* Harte condemned the killings in unequivocal terms. He headlined the story in the next issue "Indiscriminate Massacre of Indians/Women and Children Butchered" and declared that "Our Indian troubles have reached a crisis. Today we record acts of Indian aggression and white retaliation. It is a humiliating fact that the parties who may be supposed to represent white civilization have committed the greater barbarity." Harte apparently saw the bodies of the victims when they were brought to Uniontown, for he reported that

a more shocking and revolting spectacle never was exhibited to the eyes of a Christian and civilized people. Old Women wrinkled and decrepit lay weltering in blood, their brains dashed out and dabbled with their long grey hair. Infants scarce a span long, with their faces cloven with hatches and their bodies ghastly with wounds.

Not too surprisingly, a "violent minority" in the town objected to Harte's characterization of the massacre. No one was ever prosecuted for the crimes. According to Murdock, Harte "was seriously threatened and in no little danger" from a mob of

outraged citizens when he quit both his job and the community. Newton Arvin has remarked that "this is the only incident
in his life in which Harte defied public sentiment for an imper-
sonal cause." As late as 1890, during the Ghost Dance excitement in the West, in a letter to the liberal politician Robert
Boutine Cunninghame Graham, he referred derisively to "the
old story of our Anglo Saxon civilized aggression" against the
Indians, which he had hoped "was of the Past. Of course, the
desire to 'improve' people off the face of the earth with a gun,
and then to punish them for learning how to use the weapon
will continue to exist." Harte later wove the events surrounding
the Humboldt Bay massacre into his story "Three Vagabonds
of Trinidad" (1900), a forceful denunciation of the doctrines of
Manifest Destiny and racial extermination written in oblique
response to the Spanish-American and Boer Wars. While Harte
rarely romanticized Indians, he often identified with them, particularly with mixed-bloods. As his biographer George Stewart
observes, Harte's own mixed ethnicity prompted him to portray characters of mixed white and Indian blood sympathetically
in such stories as "In the Carquinez Woods" (1883) and "The
Ancestors of Peter Atherly" (1896).

Harte beat a hasty retreat from Uniontown for San Francisco
aboard the steamer *Columbia* in early March 1860. Forty years
later, in "Bohemian Days in San Francisco" (1900)—a narrative
so glib and fanciful its accuracy must be questioned—he described
his first "idle week" back in the city of some sixty thousand
souls. He loitered along the wharves and waterfront warehouses,
wandered through the Spanish quarter "where the proverbs of
Sancho Panza were still spoken in the language of Cervantes,"
and "experienced a more fearful joy in the gambling saloons"
among "the gaudily dressed and painted women."

By late April he had rejoined the staff of the *Golden Era* as a
typesetter, a job that enabled him to begin his literary career in
earnest. To paraphrase Herman Melville, the printshop became
his Harvard and his Yale. There he chastened and refined his
style, like two other scions of newspaper families, Samuel Clemens
and W. D. Howells. In addition to the ten dollars per week he

Telegraph Hill, San Francisco, in 1865. Photo by T. E. Hecht. (Bancroft Library, Berkeley)

was paid as a compositor, he earned a dollar a column for his own contributions to the eight-page weekly. Joe Lawrence did not edit Harte's manuscripts because, as Clemens remembered, "there weren't any. Harte spun his literature out of his head while at work at the case, and set it up as he spun." Or as Harte himself reminisced, "I was very young when I first began to write for the press. I learned to combine the composition of the editorial with the setting of its type" and so "to save my fingers mechanical drudgery somewhat condensed my style." To be sure, he loitered at his case. He "would waste more time over a two-stick item than I would take for a column," as his coworker H. K. Goddard recalled in 1908.

Between April 29, 1860, and May 5, 1861, Harte published a total of eleven poems and seventy-four sketches, stories, and serials in the *Golden Era*. The first of these pieces, "My Metamorphosis," a story about a European traveler who poses as a statue to avoid embarrassment while swimming in the nude, was also the first article the author signed with his nom de plume "Bret Harte." (As if to concede his poverty of invention, Harte would essentially rewrite this story forty years later in "A Vision of the Fountain," one of his last tales.) For the most part the earliest of these writings are utterly unremarkable (e.g., a humorous "story of the Revolution," hackneyed love poems, a paean to the Pony Express in heraldic verse). Still, by late May 1860, Harte was contributing a regular topical column to the *Golden Era* entitled "Town and Table Talk" that he signed "The Bohemian."

Even as a novice he began to adjust his writing to the demands of the local literary market, to spurn the foreign for the familiar. Quickly discovering at the age of twenty-four the fictional vein he would mine the rest of his life, he published a pair of sketches in the fall of 1860 that contain generous dollops of local color about the California gold fields. He subsequently gathered both "The Man of No Account" and "A Night at Wingdam" in his collected works. Over the years, one or both of these sketches would also be translated into Danish, Spanish, German, Swedish, French, Italian, Russian, Finnish, Serbo-Croatian, and Romanian.

Harte published his first important mining-camp story, "The Work on Red Mountain," the original version of his classic "M'liss," in the *Golden Era* in December 1860, only nine months after returning to San Francisco with neither job nor prospects.

During the months he began to mature as a writer, not coincidentally, Harte also became the protégé of Jessie Benton Frémont, wife of "the Pathfinder" John Frémont, a military hero and the Republican candidate for president in 1856. Like a sentry alert for promising young artists and writers, Jessie Frémont had started a salon of sorts in Black Point, her home overlooking San Francisco Bay. Impressed by one of Harte's sketches in the *Golden Era* that she read while on a steamboat en route to Stockton, California, Frémont invited the author to join her circle of antislavery intellectuals in the fall of 1860. "I had to insist this very shy young man should come to see me," she remembered later,

> but soon he settled into a regular visit on Sunday, his only time of leisure, and for more than a year dined with us that day, bringing his manuscripts; astonished by the effect of some, at times huffed by less flattering opinion on others, but growing rapidly into larger perceptions as he saw much of various people to whom I made him known.

As she wrote one such friend, the local Unitarian minister Thomas Starr King, "As my hands are empty I have taken a young author to pet." Her teenaged daughter, Elizabeth Frémont, also thought him "brilliantly clever."

Among the distinguished men of letters Harte may have met at her home was Melville, who passed through San Francisco in mid-October 1860 and spent an afternoon with the Frémonts. (In any event, Harte probably wrote the unsigned review of Melville's *Battle Pieces and Aspects of the War* printed in the San Francisco *Evening Bulletin* in September 1866.) At Frémont's urging, Harte punctuated a rousing antislavery speech at the American Theatre by Senator Edward Baker of Oregon in late October 1860 by rushing the stage and waving the Stars and

Stripes to excite the crowd. He also enlisted in the Volunteer
City Guard in San Francisco soon after the Civil War erupted—
not that he was liable to join the hostilities. With the help of his
sister Maggie he made a huge American flag, which they flew
over the house they shared on Rimcon Hill. This flag still survives among family memorabilia in the Bancroft Library at the
University of California, Berkeley.

Through Frémont's patronage Harte was eventually awarded
a series of sinecures, all of them federal government jobs. In
May 1861, shortly before she left San Francisco and as Harte was
about to start for Oregon to edit a newspaper there, she arranged
for her friend Edward F. Beale, the new U.S. surveyor-general
of California, to hire him to work in his office at a salary of $100
a month. In the fall of 1862, as Beale was about to leave the
state, Harte was hired by U.S. Marshal Rand, and in the summer
of 1863, when Rand resigned, Robert B. Swain, the Superintendent of the San Francisco Mint, "took up the chain of good
will," as Frémont later explained, "and again a good salary
secured leisure and a quiet mind to the young writer." Harte
was hired as secretary to the superintendent at a starting salary
of $180 a month and he held the job for six years. By 1868 he
was drawing $270 a month and directing a staff of twelve. The
joke went the rounds that he was paid a salary merely for
signing his name once a day. "If I were to be cast away on a
desert island," he wrote Frémont before she left the state and
his life forever, "I should expect a savage to come forward with
a three-cornered note from you to tell me that, at your request,
I had been appointed governor of the island at a salary of two
thousand four hundred dollars." Significantly, after Frémont
closed her salon and moved to St. Louis, Harte quit his job with
the *Golden Era* to work in the surveyor-general's office and
published no new literary work for over a year.

Not that he was idle, nor Frémont his only patron. Starr King
and Harte met at Frémont's house in 1860, not long after each
of them settled in San Francisco, and soon Harte began to
attend King's church on Stockton Street. King was indefatigable
on behalf of the Union and abolition, and he enlisted Harte in

these causes as well. In August 1861, for example, Harte was appointed to a committee at King's church charged with raising money for the families of Northern war casualties. King routinely read Harte's patriotic poetry—e.g., "The Reveille," "Our Privilege," "The Goddess," "The Copperhead"—at the close of his pro-Union speeches around the state. "I shall probably avail myself of Mr. King's proffered courtesy to read for me," Harte once replied to an invitation to declaim his own verse, "not only because I am an indifferent reader, but that in the charm of the Orator's voice Criticism may overlook the demerits of the Poet." King helped to arrange Harte's appointment in the Mint— Swain chaired the board of trustees at the First Unitarian Church of San Francisco—and as early as November 1862 he predicted in a Boston newspaper that young Frank Harte "will yet be known more widely in our literature."

In fact, in January 1862 King wrote his Boston friend James T. Fields, editor of the *Atlantic Monthly,* on Harte's behalf, specifically to recommend his story "The Legend of Monte del Diablo":

> Mr. F. B. Harte, a very bright young man who has been in literary ways for a few years, has written a piece, wh[ich] I have not yet seen, but feel sure it is good. He is a particular friend of Mrs. Jessie Fremont, who has a very high opinion of his powers, & obtained for him a situation as clerk in the Land Surveyor's office here. I shall read the piece before this note goes. I hope the editors will accept it if it is worthy, for I am sure there is a great deal in Harte, & an acceptance of his piece would inspirit him, & help literature on this coast where we raise bigger trees & squashes than literati & brains.

Frémont also wrote Fields to praise the story, which both celebrated Spanish colonialism and satirized the "swaggering Saxons" lured west during the gold rush. She presumed that Harte "pleases you as he does Mr. King and myself. But of that there can be no doubt for his is a fresh mind filled with unworn pictures." She anticipated that Fields would respond as she had, with "a calm well founded admiration for the Mt. Diablo legend." Fields eventually accepted the story, which was published in the

October 1863 issue of the *Atlantic,* immediately preceding Henry David Thoreau's essay, "Life Without Principle." Despite King's and Frémont's appeals on Harte's behalf, however, Fields was not particularly impressed. As he eventually wrote Frémont, "Your young friend fails to interest. He is not piquant enough for the readers of the *Atlantic.*" Five years later, of course, Fields would eat his words.

On his part, Harte admired the minister as he admired few other men. King was a "true apostle" of humanity, Harte believed, with a "flashing genius and personal magnetism," who as a fund raiser for the U.S. Sanitary Commission (a type of forerunner of the American Red Cross) during the Civil War "infused into this hard money-loving community something of his own tenderness and magnanimity." King's most popular orations, he thought, were "remarkable for their precision of epithet, artistic construction of sentence, and felicity of illustration conveyed in an English often as exquisite as Hawthorne and as genial as Irving." Harte readily allowed in 1865, a year after King's sudden death from diphtheria, that he may have "lost sight of the heroic proportions of my friend, in the familiar contemplation of his exquisite details." Harte wrote three obituary poems about King: "Relieving Guard," "At the Sepulchre," and "His Pen." In the second of them, the poet contemplated King's grave on the grounds of his church in San Francisco in the formal or conventional manner he would gradually abandon:

> And greener yet that spot shall grow,
>   For thy dear dust within it laid,
> And brighter yet the sunlight glow—
>   And dim and grateful seem the shade.

Harte was convinced, like many of his contemporaries, that by battling the infestation of copperheads, or Southern sympathizers, in the state, King almost single-handedly saved California for the Union.

At least indirectly through King, Harte also met his wife. Anna Griswold sang in the choir at the First Unitarian Church and performed in concert with the local Motet and Madrigal Society. As one critic remarked, her "contralto is pure, soft and finely modulated, exhibiting a nice cultivation." Little is known about their courtship—unfortunately, no letters she wrote him before or during their forty-year marriage are known to survive—except what Harte remarked later in jest: "It was a mule that eventually delivered me into the hands of Mrs. Harte." They were married in the Methodist church in San Rafael on August 11, 1862. Their first child, a son they named Griswold, was born a year later, and their second, named Francis King after his father and Starr King, on March 5, 1865. The granddaughter of David Dunham, a prosperous New York merchant, the daughter of Daniel and Mary Griswold of New York, and older than her husband by almost two years, Anna Harte was, according to Elinor Mead Howells, "stylish, dignified and sensible" albeit "positively plain" looking. Howells also thought she was "a most admirable woman," and, some thirty years after he last saw her, Clemens praised her in his autobiographical dictation as "a good woman, a good wife, a good mother, and a good friend."

By all accounts, however, the marriage was rocky from the start. Josephine Clifford, one of Harte's friends in San Francisco, believed he was a victim of petticoat tyranny, of "allowing his wife to rule him." Anna Harte "never seemed a lovable woman to me," Clifford reminisced later. "There was a morose, stubborn expression on her face which invited neither cordiality nor sympathy." H. K. Goddard, Harte's coworker at the *Golden Era,* noted diplomatically that "the married life of F. B. Harte and Anna Griswold" was "not happy." The rumors flew after they had been married a few years that he "was handicapped by a jealous spouse—jealous of his fame and jealous of the attention he attracted." Harte's early biographer, Henry C. Merwin, privately conceded to Harte's nephew Ernest Knaufft in 1911 that Anna "was a *virago,*—almost impossible to live with,—but I cannot say *that* while she and her children are living." Bret and Anna's grandson Geoffrey Bret Harte, in a family memoir written in 1941, allowed that "my grandparents had little in

Bret Harte, probably about the time of his marriage in August 1862.
(*Reader* 10 [July 1907], 126)

common. In the final analysis, what my grandfather most wanted was peace in the home and this I believe he never got. In our age this problem would have been solved by divorce; in theirs such a course was unthinkable." As he explained, Anna Harte "belonged to the old school where ladies had to have aristocratic bearing." (Elinor Howells also hinted at her snobbery: "Her family I should say was superior to his.") She also "possessed a fiery temper which when provoked became ungovernable fury." Certainly the union was riven by unusual strains and pressures.

For one thing, Anna Harte was nearly as reckless a spendthrift as her husband. They lived during their first months of marriage in a fashionable neighborhood near Union Square, then moved with their servants to North Beach. "In the days when he could afford it—and in the days when he couldn't," Harte's suits "always exceeded the fashion by a shade or two," Clemens remembered. Harte bought a lot in Berkeley for $2,000 before the University of California was founded there and sold it later for $1,500—perhaps the last time anyone lost money investing in California real estate. Harte's resumption of writing for the *Golden Era* after a lapse of fifteen months "coincided with his marriage, and was the result probably of need for money," as Stewart surmises. Between July 1862 and May 1864, Harte published twenty-one new poems and twenty-three sketches and stories in the *Era* and a dozen more new poems in the San Francisco *Evening Bulletin*. These works mark a considerable advance from his earlier writings. For example, he began to experiment with a comic form he called the "condensed novel," basically a brief parody of a well-known text. "Fantine," after the French fiction of Victor Hugo, was in fact the first piece he wrote for publication in California that was widely copied in the East.

He also contributed a series of "Bohemian Papers" to the *Golden Era* on such topics as the Mission Dolores and Chinese immigration. In his first important book, *The Luck of Roaring Camp and Other Sketches* (1870), he would collect four of these "Bohemian Papers" and two sketches of pioneer California that

Anna Griswold Harte, 1892. (Courtesy of Cathy Gardner and Paul Deceglie)

he wrote for the *Era* during these months ("A Lonely Ride" and "Notes 'By Flood and Field'"). At the request of Joe Lawrence he also revised and more than doubled the length of his earlier serial "The Work on Red Mountain," retitling it "The Story of M'liss," though to his credit Harte soon regretted this misbegotten attempt to exploit his popularity. Rather than polishing and brightening the colors of the original tale, involving a tomboy of "lawless character" who resists domestication, Harte varnished them in the revision, which concludes its weary tangle of subplots of mystery and intrigue with the heroine both wealthy and tastefully dressed. After ten installments, Harte later explained, "I wound it up in disgust. As I always preferred my first conception" or 1860 version of the story, he collected it, not the revision, in *The Luck of Roaring Camp and Other Sketches.* Even in the mid-1860s, Harte was sensitive to the machinations of the literary market.

When, in May 1864, his friend Charles H. Webb launched a new sixteen-page literary weekly, the *Californian,* Harte became its star contributor and occasional editor at a salary of twenty dollars a week. "The 'Californian' circulates among the highest class in the community," Clemens wrote his family back in Missouri, "& is the best weekly literary paper in the United States." Between May 1864 and August 1866, Harte published a total of thirty-five poems and seventy-eight prose pieces in the *Californian,* including a sheaf of Civil War verse (e.g., "John Burns of Gettysburg," "A Second Review of the Grand Army"); burlesques of poems by Spenser, Poe, Scott, and Tennyson; topical humor on the fraudulent discovery of human fossils in Calaveras County ("To the Pliocene Skull"); more of his condensed novels parodying Dumas, Bulwer-Lytton, T. S. Arthur, Wilkie Collins, Charlotte Brontë, James Fenimore Cooper, Dickens, Frederick Marryat, and others; a series of informal essays entitled "Neighborhoods I Have Moved From"; and several book and theatrical reviews.

By far the most important of his contributions to the *Californian* were the condensed novels, which would inspire a host of imitators, among them Webb and, later in the century, Frank

Norris. In the late nineteenth century these literary burlesques (e.g., "Muck-a-Muck," an "Indian novel" after Cooper; "The Haunted Man," a "Christmas story" after Dickens; "Mr. Midshipman Breezy," a naval story after Marryat's "Mr. Midshipman Easy") seemed harbingers of Harte's literary genius. As G. K. Chesterton noted, "Harte had a real power of imitating great authors, as in his parodies on Dumas, on Victor Hugo, on Charlotte Brontë." In "The Haunted Man," the Scrooge-like hero is repeatedly visited by phantoms who transport him to various sites and ask him what he sees. "Don't you think, Charles, you're rather running this thing into the ground?" he finally replies. "Of course it's very moral and instructive, and all that. But ain't there a little too much pantomime about it?"

Apart from some of the poetry and his condensed novels, Harte later collected few of his writings for the *Californian*. The magazine aimed to be more "high-toned" than the *Golden Era,* and as a result what Harte contributed to its pages—virtually none of it fiction except the condensed novels—tended to be either too topical or too local in its appeal. Perhaps predictably, the paper also foundered financially. In May 1866 Webb sailed from San Francisco for New York, where he would write for the *Nation, New York Tribune,* and *Times* and other magazines and newspapers under the pseudonym "John Paul," instructing Harte meanwhile to sell his interest in the *Californian*. In October Harte reported that he had disposed of Webb's share of the magazine for $150 in gold and that the new publisher and editor "have popularized the paper" and "made it pecuniarily successful—more so than under your or my management." The problem, Harte explained later in another context, was "the old trouble of inadequate supply and demand. We have in fact more writers than readers; more contributors than subscribers" to western magazines. Not surprisingly, the *Californian* limped along for only two more years under its new management before finally suspending publication.

Under these circumstances, the hostile reception accorded *Outcroppings,* a collection of California verse Harte compiled for sale during the Christmas season in 1865, is not surprising.

Commissioned by Anton Roman some three years earlier, the volume soon became something of a cause célèbre even though Harte simply inherited the project. As he recalled in his autobiographical essay "My First Book" (1894), he was blithely unconscious of the controversy swirling around the anthology as he winnowed the submissions: "I found myself in daily and hourly receipt of sere and yellow fragments, originally torn from some dead and gone newspaper, creased and seamed from long folding in wallet or pocketbook." Harte sorted through dozens of paeans to the Golden Gate, Mount Shasta, the Yosemite, the state bird and flower, and he rejected the "usual plagiarisms" and "acrostics of patent medicines." He acknowledged later that he had also wrongfully overlooked some deserving poems, among them his friend Clemens's "He Done His Level Best."

Finally the anthology was published—"a pretty little volume typographically, and externally a credit to pioneer book-making," with forty-two poems in it by nineteen poets, among them Webb, Ina Coolbrith, Charles Warren Stoddard, and John Rollin Ridge (Yellow Bird)—when suddenly the bolt fell. In Harte's memoir thirty years later, he cited notices in several facetiously named western papers (e.g., the Red Dog *Jay Hawk*, the Mormon Hill *Quartz Crusher*) that were ostensibly reprinted on the front pages of the "big dailies." In fact, while favorably noticed in such eastern papers as the Philadelphia *Evening Bulletin,* New York *Evening Post, Springfield Republican* ("very elegantly got up"), *Boston Courier* ("a string of gems"), and the *Daily Advertiser* ("welcome and worthy"), *Outcroppings* was ridiculed on the Pacific slope by reviewers for such papers as the Gold Hill, Nevada, *News* (which labeled it "purp-stuff"), the *Pajaro Times* ("the offspring of a mutual admiration society"), and the San Francisco *American Flag* ("a Bohemian advertising medium for Webb, Harte & Co."). A wag in the *Carson Daily Appeal* set his review to verse:

> Have you read the book in muslin bound,
> Compiled by Harte? It's going the round
> Of all the critiques—but here has found
> At the Folio's hands a terrible pound.

Joseph Goodman, editor of the Virginia City *Territorial Enter-prise* and one of the rejected contributors, devoted four and one-half columns to disparaging the book ("the very trashiest of the trash"). And the San Francisco *Evening Bulletin,* exactly as Harte later remembered, reprinted excerpts from many of these hostile reviews over three columns on the first page of its January 6, 1866, issue. The "book has created considerable excitement here," and "the compiler has been abused beyond his most sanguine expectations," he wrote Roman, who was back in New York, two days later. The net effect of this editorial abuse was that the "book sold tremendously," some five hundred copies in the first six weeks.

Still, as Stewart remarks, Harte exhibited "certain unadmirable qualities" in this affair. Though he acknowledged in his preface that he had selected some poems "from material collected three years ago for a similar volume, by Miss M. V. Tingley," Mary Tingley publicly accused him of robbing her. As late as 1929, she complained that Harte was a "thief" who "deliberately broke into my 'Outcroppings of California Early Writers' and . . . dishonestly appropriated them." Harte also wrote Roman a month after publication to negotiate his fee: "I certainly cannot consent to any [amount of remuneration] that is to be *contingent* upon the success of the volume," he explained. He did not want a royalty on sales but a lump sum, which always would be his preferred method of payment. He had never been "sanguine of the success of this venture"—that is, he had edited the book not because he believed in its merit but solely for the cash. Another measure of Harte's modest estimate of its worth: he did not include any of his own verse in the anthology. Clemens joked that, apart from this failure to insert "a single line of his own poetry," Harte had exhibited "rare good taste and ability" in compiling the volume.

They had, in fact, become fast friends after Clemens (a la Harte from Humboldt) beat a hasty retreat from Virginia City in May 1864, settled in San Francisco, and became a beat reporter for the San Francisco *Morning Call.* Despite the famous feud that later destroyed their friendship, Harte and Clemens shared many traits, including spendthrift ways and overweening ambition. They were friendly rivals and collaborators for over a decade before they became implacable enemies. The two were introduced by George Barnes, editor of the newspaper, on the second floor of the *Call* building on Commercial Street, where the superintendent of the Mint and his young secretary had their offices. As Harte related the story in 1894, he was initially struck by Clemens's appearance: "His head was striking." He had "curly hair," an "aquiline nose," and "an eye so eagle-like that a second lid would not have surprised me. . . . His eyebrows were very thick and bushy. His dress was careless, and his general manner one of supreme indifference to surroundings and circumstances." Clemens soon "dropped in on me again" to spin an extravagant yarn, "as graphic as it was delicious," much to the delight of Harte, who urged him to write it up. "He did so," Harte remembered, and "The Celebrated Jumping Frog of Calaveras County" became "an emphatic success," though "it will never be as funny to anybody in print as it was to me, told for the first time by the unknown Twain himself, on that morning in the San Francisco Mint." Harte reprinted the jumping-frog story in the *Californian* in December 1865 as it was originally published in the New York *Saturday Gazette*.

Harte soon hired the "genial humorist" to write an article a week for the *Californian* at a salary of fifty dollars a month. Long before Clemens was known outside the West, Harte championed his genius: "His humor has more motive than that of Artemus Ward," he wrote in 1866, and "he is something of a satirist, although his satire is not always subtle or refined. He has shrewdness and a certain hearty abhorrence of shams which will make his faculty serviceable to mankind. . . . I think I recognize a new star rising in this western horizon." On his part, Clemens wrote his mother and sister in January 1865 that although "I am generally placed at the head of my breed of scribblers in this part of the country, the place properly belongs to Bret Harte."

Two years later, Harte helped Clemens hew and sculpt the manuscript of *The Innocents Abroad* from the mass of dispatches he had sent various New York and California papers during his *Quaker City* voyage. "Harte read all of the MS of the 'Innocents' & told me what passages, paragraphs & chapters to leave out—& I followed orders strictly," Clemens later allowed. "It was a kind thing for Harte to do, & I think I appreciated it." He reiterated that Harte was "the finest writer out there," and as late as 1871 he remarked that Harte "trimmed & trained & schooled me patiently until he changed me from an awkward utterer of coarse grotesquenesses to a writer of paragraphs & chapters that have found a certain favor." In the first blush of their friendship, they planned to work together on a collection of humorous sketches. Harte contacted a New York publisher, Clemens explained, "& if we are offered a bargain that will pay a month's labor, we will go to work & prepare the volume for the press." They also considered another project: a book of burlesque poems, a satire of *Outcroppings:* "We know all the tribe of California poets, & understand their different styles, & I think we can just make them get up & howl." Nothing came of either idea, though a decade later, with Harte's career in a shambles, they would resurrect the plan to collaborate on a project, albeit with disastrous results.

Two other influential California poets, both of them contributors to the *Californian* and *Outcroppings,* also slipped into Harte's orbit in the 1860s. Harte met Charles Warren Stoddard, who wrote verse under the pseudonym "Pip Pepperpod," in 1863. Much as Frémont and King had been his patrons, Harte took Stoddard under his wing. He "exhibits indications of poetic excellence in my opinion, beyond any other writer on the coast," Harte declared in 1866. "He is full of poetic sensibility—a good deal like Keats in disposition as well as fancy." He edited Stoddard's *Poems* for publication by Roman the next year and plugged the book for good measure. Somehow, the young poet had escaped the "hardness, skepticism and Philistinism of life on this coast," Harte wrote, with more bombast than usual, and "preserved the serene repose of the true poet amid all this twitter, whirl and excitement." On his part, Stoddard considered Harte something more than a mentor. He was a genius with "penetration such as few possess, and exceptional fancy, imagination, and literary art."

The third of the so-called "Golden State Trinity" of poets, Ina Coolbrith, also held Harte in high esteem. He was "not as formidable as I imagined him; we get on very nicely," she wrote in January 1869, soon after she became an intimate member of Harte's coterie of writers. She observed forty-three years later that of "what he was or did after leaving California I can say nothing for he passed out of my life, but while here I bear witness that he was one of the most genial, unselfish, kind, unaffected and *non*-conceited of all the writers I have known." The three of them—Harte, Stoddard, and Coolbrith—met often in the parlor of Coolbrith's home on Russian Hill. "I took frequent 'notes,'" "*volumes* of them," as Coolbrith remarked shortly before her death; all of them were destroyed in the fire following the San Francisco earthquake of 1906. The regard in which Harte held the other two poets may be inferred from this startling fact: all but one of the seventeen lyrics in the first volume of the *Overland Monthly* were written by Stoddard, Coolbrith, or the editor himself.

Despite his sinecure in the Mint, Harte needed to supplement his income to support his growing family if not to pay for his own extravagancies. With the *Californian* foundering he became a part-time drama critic for the *Morning Call,* and he struck a deal with Warren Sawyer, managing editor of the *Christian Register,* a Unitarian weekly published in Boston, to become its California correspondent. He negotiated payment equal to what he received for articles in the *Californian:* "I could not write regularly for a less sum than $10 in gold," twice what the *Christian Register* normally paid for contributions. Clemens wrote his family in January 1866 that Harte had "quit the 'Californian' [actually, Harte's work would continue to appear in its pages through July] to write for a Boston paper hereafter." The paper halved its payment to its "special correspondent" after only five columns, however, prompting him to complain to Sawyer that "I think you will agree with me that I had some reason in expecting double the amount." He afterwards sent almost nothing to the *Register.*

Meanwhile, he negotiated a similar arrangement to write a series of California letters for the Springfield, Massachusetts, *Republican,* whose editor, Samuel Bowles, he had met in San Francisco in the summer of 1865. His connection with the *Republican*—one of the most influential newspapers in the country, which printed ten of Emily Dickinson's poems during her lifetime—was instrumental in his rise to national fame. As early as September 1866, Bowles reprinted the "quaint" satirical poem "To the Pliocene Skull" by "our special San Francisco correspondent, Mr. F. Bret Harte," and in January 1867 he favorably compared Harte with his erstwhile friends and rivals Webb and Clemens: Harte "is less demonstrative in his qualities than the others; his humor is more subjective, and his scholarship more thorough and conservative; but we have few newspaper and magazine writers in the East that have so charming and cultivated a fancy, so delicate and innocent a satire." Four months later, Bowles pronounced his benediction: Harte is the "best of the California humorists after all."

Though obviously not finished coin, the forty essays Harte sent the *Register* and *Republican* between January 1866 and March 1868 display an abundance of color. In manuscripts incongrously written in "a delicately, scrupulously finished hand" on "thin, dainty, highly finished French note-paper," he rehearsed the tone of polite condescension to things western that he would develop in some of his later writings. Though he had lived in California for a dozen years, Harte adopted an eastern point of view and assumed the pose in these letters of an expatriate or foreign correspondent. "When you meet" at "the Eastern borders of the continent," he urged his readers, think tenderly of the "unrelieved sentinels at the Western gate." Like a missionary in the field, he attempted to describe the curious habits and exotic customs normal to "California civilization." The people of the state are gamblers by nature, he asserted, famous for fast living and prodigal giving. Like the Arabian Prince, they "prefer their cream tarts with pepper." He complained that he had but rarely seen in the unruly West the sort of "neat farmhouses" and manicured estates he remembered in the East. Here "we have *ranchos* instead of farms and *vaqueros* for milk-maids." Still, he welcomed the chance to plug his friend Clemens's skills as a humorist immediately after he debuted his Sandwich Islands lecture at Maguire's Opera House in San Francisco on October 2, 1866. Clemens "took his audience by storm," Harte reported to the *Springfield Republican*.

In addition to their topical and biographical interest, Harte's essays for the *Register* and *Republican* detail the sources of some of his most characteristic works. The Radical Republican principles he had gleaned from Frémont and King and expressed in these essays (e.g., his expression of sympathy for the Chinese in San Francisco) foreshadow the satire of anti-Chinese prejudice in "Plain Language from Truthful James" (1870) and "Wan Lee, the Pagan" (1874). He referred to the fictional town of "Poker Flat" in his letter to the *Republican* dated February 28, 1867, his first allusion to the town he depicted more fully in "The Outcasts of Poker Flat" (1869). He would adapt in "Maruja" (1885) the controversy over Spanish land grants described in his letter to the *Republican* dated September 29, 1866, and in "Colonel Starbottle for the Plaintiff" (1901) he would burlesque a celebrated breach-of-promise suit described in his letter to the *Republican* dated April 10, 1867. One of these letters also betrays his willingness to shave an ethical point, however: his sketch of the Mission Dolores in the *Register* for May 19, 1866, was in fact a reprint of an essay he had first published in the *Golden Era* for March 22, 1863. That is, the *Register* paid him five dollars in gold for an article that he had sold to the *Era* three years earlier.

A week after he sent the next-to-last of these essays to the *Register* and *Republican*, Harte and his wife became parents for the third time. Their third son, probably born prematurely, lived only eight days, his health so fragile he was apparently not given a name before his death on October 27, 1867. Though Harte never mentioned this child in any of the hundreds of extant letters he wrote his family over the remaining thirty-five years of his life, he did express his grief a few months later in "The Luck of Roaring Camp," so often disparaged for its sentimentality. At the close of this story the "frail babe" Tommy Luck dies, and his soul, like a wisp of straw, "drifted away into the shadowy river that flows forever to the unknown sea."

His son's death may also figure in his chagrined response to the publication of his first book of fiction, entitled *Condensed Novels and Other Papers* and issued in October by the New York firm of G. W. Carleton. Harte described the book a year later as a "deformed brat." Clemens, whose "Jumping Frog" book had been rejected by Carleton in February 1867, worried that Harte "is publishing with a Son of a Bitch who will swindle him," and while Carleton was guilty of no crime, he certainly drove a hard bargain. The success of the volume, Harte recognized, would "depend entirely upon its sale in the East," but Carleton failed to promote it. Reportedly in press in February, it was still forthcoming in June but not actually published until October. More to the point, Harte was mortified by the "coarse" and "vulgar" illustrations Carleton commissioned for the volume. He was "incensed at its circus clowns dress and the painted grins that Mr Carleton had scattered through its pages." The book, he complained, was "malformed in its birth." Webb agreed it was "poorly printed, on wretched paper, with most *beastly* illustrations."

To be sure, it was reasonably well received by reviewers in the *Boston Transcript* ("among the raciest humorists in the country"), New York *Evening Mail* ("delicacy and good taste"), *Golden Era* ("genial yet caustic humor, fine and artistic taste and elegance of style"), San Francisco *Alta California* ("excels anything of the kind ever attempted"), San Francisco *Evening Bulletin* ("master of satire"), and *Atlantic Monthly* ("charming parodies"). Yet Harte's royalties on sales of the first edition totaled only about $180. His critical stock was so undervalued in 1867 that it was almost worthless. By December 1870, however, with his reputation climbing like a rocket, Carleton offered to sell the stereotype plates, woodcuts, and seventy-four remaining copies of *Condensed Novels* to Harte's new publisher, James R. Osgood. "The book is a real good book," he wrote Osgood, "& Bret Harte's popularity is so great just at this time, that either you or I could print from 3 to 5,000 at once, advertise it strongly . . . and sell the whole edition in less than a month, at a

profit of 1 to 2000 dollars—and with Harte's increasing reputation the plates would be a good paying property for a long
time." Though he thought the offer unseemly, Osgood capitulated and bought the plates, copies, and rights to the book for a
thousand dollars.

Harte's first collection of verse, *The Lost Galleon and Other
Tales,* which included some thirty lyrics and ballads, was issued
by a San Francisco publisher in time for the Christmas season of
1867. He had written the title poem in little more than a day for
commencement exercises at the College of California the previous June, when it was declaimed by Horatio Stebbins, King's
successor in the pulpit of the First Unitarian Church. The book,
which contained several of Harte's popular Civil War lyrics and
ballads adapted from Spanish legends, proved to be a solid
commercial success, with some five hundred copies sold within
its first three weeks in print. For the first time, however, he was
accused by critics of merely parroting more distinguished poets,
a charge that in one form or another would dog him for the rest
of his career. As the San Francisco *Dramatic Chronicle* alleged
in its review, Harte "borrows the thought and sentiment of
writers whom he admires," particularly Oliver Wendell Holmes,
John Greenleaf Whittier, and Robert Browning, "imbibes their
spirit, imitates their style, and reproduces them in his own language." *Putnam's* also noted that several of the verses were
"very much after the manner of Holmes," and in truth Harte
conceded that he had modeled "To the Pliocene Skull" on
Holmes's "De Sauty." Even Harte's friends at the *Golden Era*
averred that he only occasionally expressed "an original flavor"
in his verse. The *Nation* thought the most successful poems in
the collection were not the patriotic ones such as "How Are
You, Sanitary?" but the "purely comic" ones. Harte "would do
best for himself and his readers," this reviewer concluded, if he
would "make satire and fun his mainstay."

By the start of 1868, Harte had reached something of an impasse
in his literary career. He protested to a friend in February that
he hardly expected to "become the 'future great poet' you
kindly prophesy." He enjoyed a modest local reputation as a

writer, to be sure, but he had no formal connection to any eastern press or magazine, and his harshest critics considered him at best derivative, at worst dishonest. The only venues in which his work routinely appeared were in San Francisco, in such papers as the déclassé San Francisco *News-Letter and Commercial Advertiser*, edited by his friend Ambrose Bierce, or the Sunday feuilleton of the San Francisco *Evening Bulletin*. His story "The Right Eye of the Commander," in which he took an essentially benign view of Spanish colonialism, appeared there in December 1867.

He had also begun to chafe at his distance from the eastern centers of culture and to resent "these spoiled and pampered San Franciscans." He repeatedly lamented the subtle restraints on "intellectual life and activity" in the West. Even the local climate, with its fogs and gales, he publicly complained, "is fatal to abstract speculation." "The curse of California," he wrote privately in February 1868, "has been its degrading, materialistic influences." He began to consider (again) a move back to "the States"—reversing the gold rush of the '49ers—when in the spring of 1868 he became the beneficiary of another sudden stroke of luck. Anton Roman, the San Francisco publisher who had hired Harte to edit *Outcroppings*, decided to launch a high-toned monthly magazine modeled on the *Atlantic* in Boston, to be named the *Overland Monthly*. And he offered Harte the chance to edit it.

CHAPTER 2

The Overland Monthly

From "The Luck" to "The Prodigal"

FROM the start, Harte and Roman had very different ideas about what the magazine should be. The publisher wanted the *Overland Monthly* to promote "the material development of this Coast," and according to its subtitle the magazine was "devoted to the development of the country." He feared with good reason that Harte—who basked in the esteem of the San Francisco literary coterie—"would be likely to lean too much toward the purely literary articles." On his part, as Roman reminisced thirty years later, Harte "entertained serious doubts of the success of such an enterprise," much as he had questioned the commercial viability of the anthology of California verse Roman had commissioned two years earlier. "He didn't enthuse and threw cold water on the project. He said it couldn't be done," Roman remembered. Harte feared that there would be neither enough contributions "of a proper character to interest magazine readers" nor a subscriber base sufficient to support the magazine over the long term. "The *Overland* marches steadily along to meet its Fate," Harte wrote Charley Stoddard in March 1868 as he was planning the inaugural issue, "but what [it is] I know not." To his credit, Roman persuaded Harte to accept the editorship by selling advertising space to local businesses, upwards of nine hundred dollars of it a month on a guaranteed circulation of three thousand, which virtually insured its short-term success. Had the *Overland* failed to attract readers, however, those advertising revenues would have dried up and disappeared—all the more reason for the magazine to make an immediate "smash."

Roman needed the cachet Harte would bring as a contributor to its pages even more than as its editor, so for nearly three months prior to the issue of the first number of the magazine in July 1868 "we never dwelt apart." Together with their wives and children, Roman remembered, "we went, first to San Jose, then after a month or so to a pleasant retreat in the Santa Cruz mountains," to a cabin they built together, "and thence to Santa Cruz." The first issue of the *Overland* contained an unfunny sketch by Mark Twain, "By Rail Through France," based on his experience as one of the *Quaker City* pilgrims and reprinted with revisions in chapter twelve of *The Innocents Abroad;* poems by Harte and Coolbrith; several articles on western topics; unsigned book reviews by Harte and his assistant editor Noah Brooks; and a department of gossip and topical comment by the editor simply entitled "Etc." These articles were "excellent from a commercial and advertising view-point," Harte reminisced in 1899—that is, they satisfied the requirements of Roman's civic boosterism—but they contained none of the "wild and picturesque" frontier life he remembered from his years as a "youthful schoolmaster among the mining population."

The *Overland* predictably generated more heat than light in the local press, its future by no means secure. Despite his initial reservations, Harte "manifested the same fastidiousness" in managing the affairs of the *Overland* "that characterized his own work," according to Brooks. "I am trying to build up a literary taste on the Pacific slope," Harte wrote the New York Unitarian minister Henry W. Bellows, and "we may be short-lived. But I want to make a good fight while it lasts."

Still, the very survival of the *Overland* seemed unlikely when the August 1868 number, only its second issue, was put into production in mid-July. In his account of the genesis of the magazine, Roman claimed he had convinced Harte that "the early California gold diggers and their mining camps" were "comparatively new ground" for fiction, though Harte had been tapping this fertile vein of local color off and on since 1860. According to Harte, however, he called Roman's "attention to the lack of any distinctive Californian romance" in the first issue of the *Overland* "and averred that, should no other contribution come in, he himself would supply the omission." In any case, as Carl Van Doren declared in 1926, Harte's "discovery that California was full of fiction made almost as much a stir as Marshall's discovery that the State was full of gold."

For the second issue Harte wrote a subtle parody of the gospel accounts of the Nativity set in a mining camp, a nineteenth-century precursor of Monty Python's *Life of Bryan,* featuring a mixed-blood prostitute named Cherokee Sal, an ironic Virgin indeed, who gives birth to a transcendentally blessed child named Tommy Luck. While on the surface Roaring Camp seems to be regenerated through the agency of the child, the story ends when the camp is swept away and "the Luck" (a victim of blind chance) is drowned in a flood of biblical proportions. That is, the story resists any simple allegorical reading.

"The Luck of Roaring Camp" was set in type while Harte and Roman were at work in Santa Cruz; when they returned to San Francisco on July 22 they faced a crisis borne of the provincialism Harte disdained. The proofreader for the printer, Sarah B. Cooper, a religious enthusiast, was offended by the portrayal of Cherokee Sal and the elliptical cursing ("d----d little cuss") of the miners or ironic Magi of the piece. Cooper protested to the printer, who expressed his own reservations to Roman, who in turn feared a controversy over the morality of the story that would doom the nascent journal before it had begun to attract a regular audience. Roman later asserted that Harte "did not try to explain away" the printer's and proofreader's objections—in fact, agreed to substitute other matter for the story so there would be no delay in the issue. In his version of events, Roman gave the proof sheets to his wife, who wept as she read the tale. "That was enough" to change his mind, Roman remembered. "I rushed to the office, and, without explanation, ordered the article inserted" in the August issue. When the story was praised in the eastern press, Roman told his wife "that she was truly the sponsor of Bret Harte."

In 1879, after reading Roman's self-serving version of these events, Harte was appalled and "furious" at his "lies." He described in a private letter to Anna Harte how he had read her the story in July 1868 "and took heart and comfort from your tears over it"—a predictable response, given the death of their infant son ten months earlier—"and courage to go on and demand that it should be put into the magazine." "I was without a sympathizer or defender," he elsewhere remembered, and even Roman "felt that it might imperil the prospects of the magazine." Still, he made it a point of editorial prerogative that his manuscript be printed exactly as written. He

> informed the publisher that the question of the propriety of the story was no longer at issue: the only question was of his capacity to exercise the proper editorial judgment; and that unless he was permitted to test that capacity by the publication of the story, and abide squarely by the result, he must resign his editorial position. The publisher, possibly struck with the author's confidence, possibly from kindliness of disposition to a younger man, yielded, and "The Luck of Roaring Camp" was published . . . without emendation, omission, alteration, or apology.

Both Roman and Harte agreed that local reviews of the story in the secular press were cool and equivocal (the *Alta California* described it as "a pleasant little sketch"), while those in the religious press were more hostile. The advertisers "were gravely urged to condemn and frown upon this picture of Californian society that was not conducive to Eastern immigration," Harte recalled, and he "was held up to obloquy as a man who had abused a sacred trust." One of the religious papers even warned that it would discourage "investment of foreign capital" in the West.

The tide turned in Harte's favor only when news of the story's more favorable reception in the East reached San Francisco in October. Samuel Bowles praised "The Luck" without stint in the *Springfield Republican* ("a genuine California story," one "so true to nature and so deep-reaching in its humor, that it will move the hearts of men everywhere") and reprinted it in its entirety even before learning the identify of the author. Only at the end of September did Bowles discover that no one other than "our old friend Harte" had written "the best magazine story of the year." Similarly, the *Nation* applauded "The Luck" ("one of the best magazine articles that we have read in many months," with "pathos and humor" that "take it out of mere magazine writing and give it a place in literature"), and Clemens puffed it during his short stint as co-owner of the *Buffalo Express* as "the best prose magazine article that has seen the light for many months on either side of the ocean." (Clemens was just as complimentary in private. In the marginalia he scribbled in his copy of *The Luck of Roaring Camp and Other Sketches,* he noted that the title story was Harte's "most finished" work and "nearly blemishless.") In Boston, Susan Francis, a staffer for the *Atlantic Monthly,* was so delighted by the unsigned story that she passed it along to James Fields, who immediately sent a letter in care of the *Overland* editor to the anonymous author of "The Luck of Roaring Camp" offering to publish "anything he chose to write, upon his own terms."

Harte was elated—he opened the letter in Roman's presence—because he was vindicated by the very magazine that had spurned him five years earlier. As the San Francisco *Evening Bulletin* allowed in 1870, "The Luck" was "by general consent of Eastern critics regarded as the most original story of the year." "Since Boston endorsed the story," Harte explained in 1894, "San Francisco was properly proud of it." Suddenly a coveted literary name, Harte played the hand he was dealt like a poker-faced gambler in one of his stories. "I'll try to find time to send you something," he wrote Fields in reply. "The *Overland* is still an experiment," he admitted, and "should it fail . . . why I dare say I may be able to do more." In all, the favorable publicity the *Overland* enjoyed during Harte's tenure as editor paid off. At a subscription rate of four dollars per year, the magazine enjoyed a circulation of three thousand per issue—the minimum Roman had guaranteed his advertisers—within its first six months. By the end of its inaugural year, with the completion of the transcontinental railroad, the *Overland* sold as many copies in the eastern United States as in the states of California, Nevada, and Oregon.

The critical success of "The Luck" emboldened Harte, too, to resist Roman's brand of boosterism in conducting the affairs of the magazine. After an earthquake struck San Francisco on October 21, 1868, he ridiculed the local press in his next "Etc." column for downplaying the damage lest the news offend business interests in the city. "Much has been written about the lesson of this earthquake," Harte wrote in the November issue of the *Overland.*

> Judging from the daily journals, it seems to have been complimentary to San Francisco. In fact, it has been suggested that, with a little more care and preparation on our part, the earthquake would have been very badly damaged in the encounter.

According to Harte, the chamber of commerce worried that "one of the cheap photographs of the ruins in San Francisco" might circulate in the East and discourage investment in the city. "Local news was under an implied censorship which suppressed anything that might tend to discourage timid or cautious capital," he remembered in 1900. Harte treated the matter of the earthquake "with a levity which some of the dignified dons of the city found unbecoming," Noah Brooks later remarked. Clearly, as editor of the *Overland* Harte was not beholden to the local chamber of commerce, though he paid a price to beard the lions. He earned a reputation, deserved or not, as aloof, supercilious, and extravagant. In the summer of 1870 the state board of education received a petition to remove the *Overland* from school libraries "on the ground that it was impossible to forecast what might appear in its pages." Even more than the contretemps over publication of "The Luck," Harte's defiance of civic authority would prompt him in 1871 to resign his position with the *Overland* and to leave the West forever.

The success of "The Luck" in the eastern United States also enabled him, or so he claimed, "to follow it with other stories of a like character." The nine tales he wrote for the *Overland*—the stories that crystalized his reputation—were, in fact, pitched in every case to appeal to eastern readers who were intrigued by the romance of the gold rush. (Just as Harte understood in 1867 that the success of *Condensed Novels* depended upon its sale in the East, he early recognized that the success of the *Overland* and his own future prospects depended upon the reception of the magazine in the East.) Patrick Morrow has suggested that Harte "saw California in mythic and archetypal terms" and his tales "reinforced the values" of "the Eastern reading public" by showing how "picturesque Western scenes really were a part of universal experience." Or, as Harte explained at the time, he aspired simply to collect "the materials for the Iliad that is yet to be sung" in epic strains about gold-rush California. Predictably, Harte wrote his western stories not in the style of a realist but as a romancer, with an ensemble of such stock figures as the roguish gambler (e.g., John Oakhurst in "The Outcasts of Poker Flat," Jack Hamlin in "Brown of Calaveras"), the fallen woman (e.g., Mother Shipton and the Duchess in "Outcasts," Tommy's "dubious mother" in "The Idyl of Red Gulch," the title character in "Miggles"), the ingenue (Piney Woods in "Outcasts," Miss Mary in "Idyl"), the redshirt miner (Kentuck and Stumpy in "The Luck," the Partner in "Tennessee's Partner"), as well as the comic Chinese laundryman, the decayed Spanish aristocrat, the noble Indian, the profane stage driver, and so forth.

Harte's modern critical reputation rests almost entirely, of course, on the nine stories and half a dozen famous poems he wrote for the first five semiannual volumes of the *Overland*. What is less obvious is the extent to which Harte's humor resonated with readers and explains his contemporary popularity. J. C. Heywood noted as early as 1876 that it was "as a humorist" that Harte "was first introduced to people east of the Rocky Mountains," and Wallace Stegner asserted more recently that the comedy of his *Overland* stories is "pervasive, unprudish, often still fresh and natural." Harte's humor, derived from Dickens, was a trick of juxtaposition and paradox, "bundling together apparently incompatible qualities" in a single two-dimensional character. Harte's gamblers may be libertines, but they are also chivalrous; his miners may be coarse, but they share their grubstakes with the poor and friendless; and his fallen women may have "easy virtue," but in their breasts beat proverbial hearts of gold. (As Howells put it, in Harte's fiction "ladies with pasts were of a present behavior so self-devoted that they could often put their unerring sisters to the blush.") Whereas Clemens described the defeat of a dandy by a rustic westerner in such sketches as "The Celebrated Jumping Frog of Calaveras County" and the town dog versus the coyote episode of *Roughing It,* Harte's sophisticated narrator often mocks or patronizes such vernacular types. The author's moral dissolves in the satire, much as Harte, Howells thought, was so ironical in his person that "you could never be sure of" him.

Like "The Luck of Roaring Camp," several of Harte's other *Overland* stories parody biblical text or other moral fables. That is, Harte's best tales were often antiparables that not only defy conventional didactic readings but subvert the tenets of Christian or cultural orthodoxy. Though it may seem morbidly sentimental on the surface, for example, "The Outcasts of Poker Flat" (January 1869) both evokes the horror of the Donner Pass tragedy of 1846–47 and ridicules the myth of the hardy pioneers by burlesquing Hawthorne's "The Canterbury Pilgrims." The four exiles—the gambler Oakhurst, the two prostitutes, and the villain—meet the eloping innocents Tom Simson and Piney Woods on the mountain road to Sandy Bar. Trapped by an early-season blizzard, the outcasts suffer their deaths honorably, even virtuously—but there is no overt or even implied moral to the story. Still, it deserves its high rank among American short stories: Richard Harding Davis considered it one of the best tales ever written in English, and Howells included it in his 1920 edition of *The Great Modern American Stories.* In it, too, Harte created the type of romantic gambler apotheosized by Bret (sic) Maverick in the 1950s western television series *Maverick.*

Similarly, "Tennessee's Partner" (October 1869), Harte's personal favorite of all his stories, recounts how an ostensibly addled miner avenges his sexual humiliation by gulling an entire camp, much to the delight of the attentive reader who avoids the trap Harte set for the unwary. Although Cleanth Brooks and Robert Penn Warren in their influential textbook *Understanding Fiction* excoriated the tale for its rank sentimentality—"Harte is so thoroughly obsessed with the pathos of the partner's loyalty that he has devoted no thought to the precise nature of that loyalty"—they fall into Harte's trap and completely misread the story because they miss its humor. Hardly the moral or didactic fiction they consider it, "Tennessee's Partner" again explodes the myth of the faithful '49ers. The title character neither displays selfless friendship nor forgives Tennessee for stealing his wife; on the contrary, Partner exacts his revenge by insuring that Tennessee is lynched, then buries "the diseased" in the garden he tilled with his wife during their brief "matrimonial felicity" and sits triumphantly on the grave. The Partner victimizes Tennessee according to a code of the West: he not only defeats his enemy but he humiliates him as well. Much as "The Luck" parodies the gospel account of the Nativity, moreover, "Brown of Calaveras" (March 1870) travesties Christ's parable of the Good Samaritan and "Mr. Thompson's Prodigal" (July 1870) burlesques the parable of the Prodigal Son by representing the West as a "far country" that corrupts the young and innocent.

Another pair of Harte's *Overland* stories subtly contrasts the vulgar West with the more refined East. "Miggles" (June 1869) was loosely based on the life of the notorious actress and dancer Lola Montez after her retirement from the stage as Harte imagined it from the perspective of an effete eastern traveler. (Howells later remarked that this "Magdalene of the mining camp" may be Harte's "prime invention" in fiction, and the story was soon reprinted in the Boston suffragist weekly, the *Woman's Journal*.) "The Idyl of Red Gulch" (December 1869) juxtaposes a wanton westerner, the dissolute miner Sandy Morton, with a genteel easterner, the chaste schoolmarm Miss Mary, who is the lineal ancestor of such agents of civilization as Molly Stark Wood in Owen Wister's *The Virginian* and Amy Kane (played by Grace Kelly) in the movie western *High Noon*. Vladimir Nabokov also refers in *Lolita* to "the prim pretty schoolteacher arriving in Roaring Gulch"—a transparent allusion to Harte's story, even as he conflates "Roaring Camp" and "Red Gulch."

Harte's tale concludes, however, not with a reconciliation of West and East in a happy union but with Miss Mary's hasty departure for Boston on the Slumgullion stage when she learns of Sandy's adulteries. The plot resolution presages Harte's own departure for the East at the close of his tenure as editor of the *Overland Monthly.*

Still another story that Harte first published in the magazine, "The Iliad of Sandy Bar" (November 1870), in silhouetting his brief estrangement from Clemens in 1870–71, seems transparently autobiographical. Though Harte had privately helped Clemens edit *The Innocents Abroad* at his friend's request, he reviewed the book in the *Overland* for January 1870. Unfortunately, he had to buy the copy he reviewed, an oversight for which he apparently blamed Clemens, to whom he wrote (according to Clemens) "the most daintily contemptuous & insulting letter you ever read." By the time "The Iliad" appeared nearly a year later, the two men had been "off" for "many months." Significantly, then, Harte's story depicts the quarrel of two former partners in the "Amity Claim," Matthew Scott (Harte) and Henry York (Clemens). Even though their common claim (western humor) seems "worked out" and "worthless," it becomes a bone of contention. Scott wins a court battle, though "York instantly appealed" the verdict; that is, Harte seemed to blame their troubles on Clemens, who envied and resented Harte's greater popularity. The Scott-York feud escalates until York finally goes abroad, much as Clemens left for New York and the *Quaker City* excursion in late 1867, "and for the first time in many years, distance and a new atmosphere isolated the old antagonists." In the end, York returns to Sandy Bar and the two men are reconciled, much as Clemens returned to San Francisco after his trip to Europe and the Holy Land and enlisted Harte's help on his book. Read in this context, "The Iliad of Sandy Bar" seems a poignant and pointed reminder of their friendship and an open invitation to Clemens to bury the hatchet.

Though he depicted the West through a soft lens and in muted light, Harte fairly qualifies as a local colorist in these stories, too—the literary analogy is to the "genre" painters—for his attention to local setting and atmosphere and for the vernacular or regional character types depicted in an ironic if not sardonic tone. His ideal brand of tale, as he explained in his late essay "The Rise of the 'Short Story'" (1899), "was concise and condensed, yet suggestive. It was delightfully extravagant—or a miracle of understatement. It voiced not only the dialect, but the habits of a people or locality. It gave a new interest to slang," and it "was often irreverent" and "devoid of all moral responsibility." To the extent that his stories were distinctively western, Harte exploited in them a cultural moment or exotic milieu more fanciful than real. In effect, he wrote about the West to entertain readers unfamiliar with the region. "The gold discovery had drawn to the Pacific slope of the continent" a "heterogeneous and remarkable population," Harte explained, and he represented this idiosyncratic mix of cultures—the colonial Spanish, the immigrant Chinese, the mestizo, the Native, and the Anglo—with as much subtlety and nuance as he could muster. "Add to this Utopian simplicity of the people" the "magnificent scenery, a unique climate, and a vegetation that was marvellous in its proportions and spontaneity of growth," he averred, and he enjoyed as an author "a condition of romantic and dramatic possibilities" that was "unrivalled in history."

Harte's *Overland* stories were reprinted, in every case, within days of their first publication in such eastern papers as the *Springfield Republican, Albany Evening Journal,* New York *Evening Post, Providence Journal, Newport Mercury,* and *Hartford Courant.* In chapter twenty-five of Howells's novel *The Minister's Charge* (1887), the rustic hero Lemuel Barker reads one of Harte's stories aloud to the Boston Brahmin Bromfield Corey, a scene which should underscore, if nothing else, Harte's appeal among the eastern gentry and cultural elite.

Of course Harte's popularity soon extended to England. Such British magazines as *Fun* and the *Piccadilly Annual of Entertaining Literature* copied Harte's writings as soon as the *Overland* arrived by ship, and British publishers—particularly the infamous John Camden Hotten—soon issued pirated editions of his writings. The humorist Tom Hood routinely praised Harte's stories (e.g., "The Luck" was "worthy of Hawthorne"), and the Hotten editions were puffed in *Athenaeum, Public Opinion* ("a genuine poet"), and *Chambers' Journal* ("The Luck" was "one of the best short stories ever written"). The *Spectator* praised Harte's "novelty of subject" and "originality of style" even while regretting his occasional "attack of 'Dickens-on-the-brain.'" Ironically, shortly before his death Charles Dickens declared that Harte "can do the best things" and sent him an invitation to contribute to *All the Year Round*. After Harte learned of Dickens's death on June 9, 1870, he inserted a hastily composed tribute entitled "Dickens in Camp" into the July issue of the *Overland,* and it became one of his most popular lyrics. Around a campfire in the "dim Sierras" a miner takes from "his pack's scant treasure" a "hoarded volume," and "cards were dropped from hands of listless leisure / To hear the tale anew."

> And then, while round them shadows gathered faster,
> And as the firelight fell,
> He read aloud the book wherein the Master
> Had writ of "Little Nell."

In his autobiographical dictation nearly forty years later, Clemens scorned Harte's "Dickensian mode": "In the San Franciscan days Bret Harte was by no means ashamed when he was praised as being a successful imitator of Dickens; he was proud of it. I heard him say, myself, that he thought he was the best imitator of Dickens in America." Whether or not Clemens's memory is accurate, and if so whether or not Harte's boast is creditable, the fact remains that Harte was often compared favorably to "Boz" by his contemporaries. "Had Dickens lived in California," Warren Cheney once averred, for example, "his impressions would have given us stories of the same spirit as Mr. Harte."

Predictably, James Fields wanted to tie the rising star to the Boston firm of Fields, Osgood and Company and approached Harte as early as the spring of 1869 about publishing a volume of his tales. "In regard to your proposal to examine a collection of my California sketches with a view to republication," Harte replied in April to Fields's inquiry, "I fear that you have overestimated the number of my contributions to the *Overland,*" though he was "writing a little sketch similar in style" to "The Luck" and "have in view three or four more." He also suggested collecting "one or two California sketches" he had written earlier and asked what Fields "would pay for stories like these proposed." The two men soon agreed to terms, and Fields, Osgood and Company and its successor firms would remain Harte's U.S. publishers to the end of his life. *The Luck of Roaring Camp and Other Sketches,* issued in April 1870, contained the first five stories he had written for the *Overland,* "The Right Eye of the Commander" from the San Francisco *Evening Bulletin* for December 1867, and nine sketches that had originally appeared in the *Golden Era* between 1861 and 1863—one measure of the dearth of material Harte had ready to exploit his newfound popularity. He "eked out the book with some old and inferior things of his," as Howells confided to Henry James.

Still, the book sold reasonably well, mostly in the East—according to surviving financial records of the firm in the Houghton Library at Harvard, 9,850 copies were issued in seventeen separate printings before November 1872—and the notices were almost unanimous in their praise. The *New York Tribune* asserted, for example, that Harte's "peculiar merit" lay in his ability to catch "the gleam of poetic light which irradiates at moments common and vulgar." Thomas Wentworth Higginson commended the volume in the Boston *Woman's Journal,* Parke Godwin proclaimed him "a man of genius" in *Putnam's,* and Howells noted Harte's "very fine and genuine" appreciation of nature in his review for the *Atlantic.* Clemens likely penned the notice of the volume in the *Buffalo Express* ("Nothing so thoroughly picturesque or so thoroughly native in subject and spirit has appeared yet in American literature, nor has a finer genius displayed itself than that to which we owe these California sketches"), and similar reviews appeared in the *New York Times* ("sententious yet picturesque style"), the *Alta California* ("very correct photography of our local life"), the trusty *Springfield Republican* ("all that it contains is good"), and the *Saturday Review* ("a small but interesting volume"). Even the reclusive Emily Dickinson read the book.

Much as Harte had been liable to censure in the San Francisco press, to be sure, some religious periodicals objected to his religious skepticism and want of overt didacticism; e.g., *Zion's Herald* complained that "his heaven is free-love and good humor. Gamblers, harlots, thieves, murderers, men so vile as to have no trace of even good humor, sulky and villainous, entirely and completely, are sent by him to heaven." Harte tried to disarm such complaints in his preface by insisting that "as a humble writer of romance" he labored under no obligation to point "any positive moral." Predictably, however, given their challenge to mid-Victorian canons of taste, Harte's stories were sometimes denigrated in such prudish terms well into the next century.

Even though the *Overland* was critically acclaimed and modestly profitable, Roman sold it for $7,500 in June 1869, a year after launching it, ostensibly for health reasons. His differences with Harte over its tenor and target audience no doubt contributed to his decision. The new owner, John Carmany, publisher of the San Francisco *Commercial Advertiser,* immediately ran afoul of Harte, who pressed his advantage. Carmany in effect bought a literary property that was virtually worthless without Harte on board as editor and star contributor. On June 7, 1869, Harte submitted to Carmany a list of the conditions on which he would "continue in the editorial charge of the Overland Monthly," specifically that he have "exclusive control" of its contents, a private office, a salary of two hundred dollars a month plus one hundred dollars for each story and twenty-five dollars for each poem he contributed to its pages, and "acceptable editorial assistance" when the "income of the magazine shall justify the expenditure." These conditions were non-negotiable, or so he insisted the next day: "I will *not* modify nor alter any of the propositions in the terms I offered. They were made upon careful deliberation, and are, in my opinion, essential to the safety of the magazine and my reputation—in both of

which I have some little pride." Harte gave Carmany a dead-
line, 10 A.M. on June 9, "to employ me on the terms proposed
by me" or "I shall consider myself at liberty to enter into other
negotiations, elsewhere."

Carmany capitulated, though he soon had reason to regret his
decision. "As the publication of the third volume proceeded,"
he explained later, "I became fully aware of the controlling literary position Mr. Harte occupied towards the magazine,
which finally so strongly developed itself through his sudden
popularity that the importance of his remaining with the magazine was a constant subject of anxious thought on my part." He
later claimed, with some exaggeration, that he "spent thirty
thousand dollars to make Bret Harte famous," and he even
launched an *ad hominem* attack on Harte's character. Harte
was, he sniffed, "a dandy; a dainty man, too much of a woman
to rough it in the mines," who was habitually "dilatory" in his
editorial duties. Still, in August 1869, with the promise of both a
secure salary and editorial autonomy, Harte finally resigned his
position in the Mint to devote all his time to the magazine.

The next eighteen months, between mid-1869 and the end of
1870, can fairly be considered the heyday of the *Overland*. In
addition to managing its affairs, Harte contributed the last six
of his stories and a total of fifteen poems to its pages as well as
reviews of such books as James Russell Lowell's *Among My Books,*
Ralph Waldo Emerson's *Society and Solitude,* Nathaniel Hawthorne's *English Notebooks,* and Harriet Beecher Stowe's *Oldtown
Folks.* Stoddard testified to his rigor as an editor: "I am sure," he
insisted, "that the majority of the contributors" to the magazine
during Harte's tenure "profited, as I did, by his careful and judicious criticism." One measure of his temerity in the conduct of the
magazine: in April 1870 he rejected Walt Whitman's "Passage to
India" on the grounds it was "too long and too abstract."

The appearance in the September 1870 number of his own
poem "Plain Language from Truthful James" was perhaps his
greatest triumph. By any objective measure—the frequency
with which it was reprinted, the number of parodies it inspired,
the times it was cited or set to music—"The Heathen Chinee"

(as it was more commonly known) was one of the most popular American poems ever published. "No poem of its length in the language has furnished such a store of quotations to the newspapers," one reviewer remarked a year after its first publication. "It is not too much to say that it has sensibly modified the colloquial speech of the day." To be sure, Harte was quick to disparage the poem whenever he heard it mentioned in later years. His friend Pemberton remembered after Harte's death how "in quite recent years," while "reading his morning papers," he made "half humorous, half earnest protest" against the way the poem was cited in the press. Harte readily allowed that he had used it to fill out the issue of the *Overland* where it appeared. Clemens remembered that Harte wrote the poem "for his own amusement" and "threw it aside, but being one day suddenly called upon for copy he sent that very piece in." Ambrose Bierce also recalled that Harte had offered the poem to him for publication in the *San Francisco News-Letter*, but that he had convinced Harte it belonged in the more up-scale *Overland*— this before Bierce began to pillory the magazine as the "Warmed-Overland." Harte predicted in 1873, accurately enough, that the poem "will not live fifty years."

Nevertheless, the verse struck a nerve. It was as nearly an overnight sensation as was possible in the days when San Francisco was six or seven days distant from New York via transcontinental railroad. More than "The Luck of Roaring Camp" or "The Outcasts of Poker Flat," which had appeared without signature, "Plain Language from Truthful James" made Bret Harte a household name in the eastern United States. Clemens contended in March 1871 that Harte was "the most celebrated man in America to-day," "the man whose name is on every single tongue from one end of the continent to the other," and the poem "did it for him." Carmany later claimed that "the news agents in the East doubled their orders" for the *Overland* in the wake of its publication, with total circulation reaching about ten thousand per issue. One New York City bookseller reportedly had a standing order for twelve hundred copies per number. Within days the poem had been reprinted in dozens of newspapers and magazines across the country, including the New York *Evening Post* and *Tribune, Boston Transcript, Providence Journal, Hartford Courant,* and *Saturday Evening Post* (twice). Ironically, though the poem was undeniably popular, there was (and is) no consensus about exactly what it *meant*.

This question is not a vexed one of authorial intention. To judge from all available evidence, Harte clearly *intended* the poem to satirize anti-Chinese prejudices pervasive among Irish day laborers, with whom Chinese immigrants competed for jobs. As early as April 1863 Harte wrote in a sketch for the *Golden Era* that the Chinese were "generally honest, faithful, simple, and painstaking," and he blamed the campaign to restrict Chinese immigration on "the conscious hate and fear with which inferiority always regards the possibility of even-handed justice."

In a piece for the *Springfield Republican* in March 1867, Harte noted that the "quick-witted, patient, obedient and faithful" Chinese were "gradually deposing the Irish from their old, recognized positions in the ranks of labor." He predicted that "John Chinaman" would "eventually supplant Bridget and Patrick in menial occupations." Similarly, in his final article for the *Republican,* dated March 1, 1868, he bitterly alluded to the "hod-carriers and drunken Irish laborers" who assault Chinese workers "in the streets of San Francisco" and "blackguard" them privately. "Plain Language from Truthful James," which Harte formally modeled upon Swinburne's "Atalanta in Calydon," ridicules class resentment at precisely this point: the economic threat the Chinese posed to the Irish underclass. "For ways that are dark" and "tricks that are vain, / The heathen Chinee is peculiar," Truthful James insists. With his "pensive," "childlike," and "bland" smile, Ah Sin seems an easy mark to Bill Nye and the narrator, who stack a deck of cards against him. Ah Sin turns the tables on the Irishmen and beats them at their own game, however, by concealing cards in his sleeves and marking them with wax.

> But the hands that were played
> By that heathen Chinee,

> And the points that he made,
>   Were quite frightful to see,—
> Till at last he put down a right bower,
>   Which the same Nye had dealt unto me.

"We are ruined by Chinese cheap labor," Nye declares, before "he went for that Heathen Chinee," though the poem omits any description of overt violence. To the end of his life Harte insisted he wrote it "with a satirical political purpose," and Margaret Duckett has concluded that in the "context of Bret Harte's life and other writings, 'The Heathen Chinee' can have but one interpretation: It is a satiric attack on race prejudice."

Harte's intention, of course, has no necessary correlation with the cultural work the poem actually performed. In fact, "Plain Language from Truthful James" was read by many a xenophobic reader as satire not of the Irish cardsharps but of Ah Sin and the "yellow peril" he seemed to represent. Whether or not Truthful James spoke plainly, Harte's language was misconstrued. Much as Jonathan Swift's "Modest Proposal" seemed to endorse infanticide or Babo confounded the racist assumptions of Amasa Delano in Melville's "Benito Cereno," Ah Sin was liable to be misunderstood exactly to the extent that readers were as jaundiced as Bill Nye or as unwary as Truthful James. On the surface the poem seemed to epitomize what Edward W. Said has termed "the binary typology of advanced and backward (or subject) races" that emerged in the 1870s. On the surface, that is, the text constructs a racial Other in stereotypical terms; only when read ironically does it resist or subvert the stereotype. In the words of a hackneyed poem published later in the *Overland,*

> An able writer tells us
>   That all your ways are dark;
> He hit the case exactly
>   In that one trite remark.

Too often, rather than an ironic indictment of anti-Chinese sentiment, Harte's poem seemed to license that sentiment. The predominantly white, middle-class readers of the *Overland,* the

Saturday Evening Post, and the other papers that reprinted the poem identified not with the "heathen" Ah Sin but with his presumed racial superior, Bill Nye, the ostensible victim of his trickery. Foes of Chinese immigration recited it in public, and Senator Eugene Casserley of California, a vehement opponent of Chinese labor, reportedly wrote to thank Harte for rallying to his cause. While Harte may have meant to satirize prejudice, his poem had the opposite effect. More than any other writer of the period, according to Jeffrey D. Mason, Harte "shaped the popular conception of the Chinese."

This tendency to (mis)appropriate Harte's poem is painfully apparent in several illustrations that accompany reprintings of it. Before the end of 1870, for example, the Western News Company of Chicago issued a pirated edition illustrated by Joseph Hull that sold thousands of copies, to Harte's dismay. Though for the most part unremarkable, at least two of Hull's drawings pandered to racist sentiment by depicting violence against Ah Sin. Their reading of the poem is not only literal, without any sense of irony or ambiguity, but they revise Harte's text by picturing Nye's brutality and by imagining an adventitious scene of mob violence. Still, the *London Daily News* asserted that Hull's pictures perfectly convey Nye and the narrator's "patriotic indignation" at "the depravity of the heathen Chinee." The Hull chapbook also popularized the poem even as it (mis)interpreted it: while "strolling down Broadway" on New Year's Day 1871, the editor of the New York *Globe* "saw a crowd of men and boys, of high and low degree, swarming about a shop-window. . . . Elbowing our way through the crowd, we discovered an illustrated copy of Bret Harte's poem, 'The Heathen Chinee' displayed to the gaze of the public. . . . In all our knowledge of New York nothing like this has ever been seen on Broadway."

Put another way, "Plain Language from Truthful James" was transformed into a culture-text that was appropriated for a variety of purposes, few of them intended by the poet. Not only was it adapted to the campaign against Chinese immigration, it spawned a short-lived school of western dialect poets that

Joseph Hull illustration for *The Heathen Chinee.* (Chicago: Western News Co., 1870)

included Clemens, John Hay, and Washington Gladden. During its first months in print the poem was parodied at least fourteen times—e.g., to satirize flirtatious women ("Plain Language from Truthful Jane"), the presidential ambitions of Horace Greeley ("The Heathen Greelee"), cheating at British colleges ("The Heathen Passee"), the Treaty of Washington ("Plain Language from Truthful Bull"), and, ironically, anti-Irish prejudice ("The Game Hibernee"). News stories about murder and tax evasion were sometimes headlined with such phrases as "Ways That Are Dark" and "Tricks That Are Vain," and items on Chinese immigration were often entitled "The Heathen Chinee" or "Chinese Cheap Labor." In all, the poem worked to shape the debate over immigration policy in ways that Harte could neither have foreseen nor approved. It was quoted on the floor of Congress in January 1871, and each of the major political parties sought to outflank the other on the issue. The so-called "Heathen Chinee planks" in their platforms in 1876 were intended "not to secure justice for American citizens and certainly not to do justice to immigrants from China, but to make a bid for a majority of the votes of California, Nevada, and Oregon."

On the heels of the success of "Plain Language from Truthful James," moreover, Fields, Osgood and Company also issued a volume of Harte's *Poems* for sale during the 1870 Christmas season. Louise Chandler Moulton, the Boston correspondent for the *New York Tribune,* reported on November 5 that the publishers had received Harte's copy from San Francisco, "and the book will be issued immediately, before the current of popularity swelling up from the remarkable piece about the Heathen Chinee has time to ebb." It was, in fact, the most popular of all Harte's books—with six editions totaling some 2,200 copies sold within its first five days in print, some 20,000 copies sold by the end of 1872, and an additional 10,000 sold over the next five years—for which the poet was paid nearly four thousand dollars in royalties. It was also favorably reviewed in such papers as the *Boston Transcript, New York Tribune, Christian Register* ("genuine wit and pathos"), and the *North American Review* ("our Theocritus at last, and from California, whence we least expected him"). To be sure, there were a few dissenting voices: the London *Examiner* complained that Harte's poems were "neither humorous nor poetical," and the *Springfield Republican*, while commending his dialect verse, cautioned that "it is still too early to fix the rank of Mr Harte among the poets." Howells remarked in the *Atlantic*, similarly, on the "narrow" range of Harte's poems and predicted that "the man who has written them can do things vastly better, things universally valuable."

Still, by the close of 1870 and at the height of his popularity, Harte was one of the best-known writers (if not the best writer) in America. Editors from coast to coast wrote to solicit contributions from his pen, and "Bret Harte" became a type of literary brand name. Parke Godwin wrote him from New York in the spring of 1870 to offer him the editorship of the revived *Putnam's Magazine*, and Harte was sufficiently interested to offer terms. He had to exercise complete editorial control, "observing my own methods and after my own fashion as I do" the *Overland*, and he required "a salary of at least $5000 per annum, *guaranteed for one year*"—a proposal apparently vetoed by the publisher, George Palmer Putnam.

That summer, too, Whitelaw Reid, editor of the *New York Tribune*, offered him fifty dollars per letter for the sort of San Francisco correspondence he had sent the *Springfield Republican* and *Christian Register* three years earlier, though Harte declined because he thought California already "played out" as a subject:

> Literary and Art items w[oul]d not occupy a letter once in a year, while Society as it has gained in respectability, I fear has lost in picturesqueness, and differs now but little from that of most American second rate towns. The tourists have already exhausted superficial California and what is below is hard, dry and repulsive.

Francis P. Church wrote him from New York in September to invite his submissions to *The Galaxy*, though Harte sarcastically replied that his was "the lowest and least advantageous offer wh[ich] I have yet had the honor to receive from any one." In November the New York firm of Harper and Brothers promised to pay him at least one hundred dollars for every poem "illustrative of certain phases of Western life" published in their magazines. He also received proposals from Curtis Guild of the Boston *Commercial Bulletin* and J. G. Holland of *Scribner's*.

Meanwhile, Carmany put together a deal designed to keep Harte at the helm of the *Overland:* "When the wave of popularity was mounting higher and higher," Carmany remembered later, "I suggested to him that we take a trip East on a lecture tour, the financial management of it to be in my hands." In addition Carmany offered him "a salary of $5,000 per annum" and one hundred dollars for every story or poem he contributed, "together with a quarter interest in the magazine" to remain its editor.

Had he remained in San Francisco, moreover, Harte might have supplemented his income with yet another government job: Professor of Recent Literature and Curator of the Library and Museum at the new University of California in nearby Berkeley. Ambrose Bierce explained in the *San Francisco News-Letter* that Harte "could not afford to remain in California—where there is a conspicuous lack of the sense necessary to the appreciation of genius—unless he were bribed with a lucrative sinecure." The Berkeley offer was "a consummation devoutly to be hungered and thirsted after," and Bierce predicted on August 20 that "Harte will stay with us along with our Golden Gate, and our Yosemite, and our Big Trees, and our mammoth vegetables." "To stay here," Harte reported in September 1870, "I am offered a professorship in the University which will not interfere with my editorial work on the *O.M.* both of wh[ich] offices will make my income amount to ab[ou]t $6,000 (gold) per annum."

His appointment was opposed by one of the regents, "whose word was a power in the land," however, because he had twitted the San Francisco press for minimizing the severity of the October 1868 earthquake, and he no doubt anticipated some continued political meddling had he accepted the university appointment. Harte finally declined it on the grounds that "it would interfere with his profession" (that is, his writing) and a trip he planned to the East. Before he finalized those plans, he even considered buying the *Overland* from Carmany, who set the price of the magazine at thirteen thousand dollars. Nothing came of any of these offers, however, and Harte carped a few months later that Carmany had backed out, that "he hadn't confidence enough in me to risk the experiment for three mo[nth]s and the expenditure of $600. Why he might have made $15,000 the next year, or sold out his right to me for $20,000."

In the end, Harte was enticed to leave California by the promise of literary fame and fortune across the continent. As the *Cincinnati Commercial* joked in February 1871, while he was en route to the East, he had been hired to "write all the editorials, poetry and stories for all the daily newspapers of New York and all the weekly and monthly periodicals. He will also compose all the comedies and tragedies for the theaters" and "furnish sermons for the clergy of different denominations." In fact, he had received a pair of offers too lucrative to ignore, the first to edit the *Lakeside Monthly* in Chicago, the other to write exclusively for the family of magazines, especially the *Atlantic Monthly*, published in Boston by James R. Osgood and Company, successor to Fields, Osgood and Company.

The latter offer—sent him on June 21, 1870, and proposing an annual salary of five thousand dollars, the requisite sum "named by me as essential to my removing East"—piqued Harte's interest in particular. The conviction was "strong upon me that I should be somewhere near Boston at this date," he wrote Howells on November 5, 1870. "My coming being postponed, I send you two sun-flattered pictures of myself," one of them subsequently engraved for the cover of *Every Saturday*, another of the Osgood magazines. (That "remarkable picture," he later observed, was "so faint, so spiritual, so ghostly and apparition-like" that he was "afraid to stay in the room with it in the dark." "I expect still to see you this winter," he concluded his letter to Howells. He resigned from the *Overland* effective at the close of 1870 and laid plans to return to the East like a prodigal son to feast on the fatted calf. "I've just accepted an invitation from Mr. Fields to meet you and other distinguished folk at the Saturday Club" in Boston on February 25, he notified Howells early in the new year. "I would this had been put off until the tidal wave of my present cheap popularity had subsided, or until I had done something more worthy," but "my daemon wills otherwise and I go three thousand miles to be found out."

As assistant editor of the *Atlantic*, Howells had been instrumental in wooing Harte east. The two men first corresponded in the summer of 1869, when Harte only half-facetiously proposed that the editor of the *Overland* and the assistant editor of the *Atlantic* "exchange pulpits." At first, that is, Harte considered Howells his peer; he was delighted to learn later that they were virtually the same age. After Harte quit the *Overland*, the rumors soon swirled in Boston that he would be offered the editorship of either *Every Saturday* or the *Atlantic* upon Fields's retirement. Howells strenuously denied the rumor in a letter to his father in late January 1871:

> You needn't feel the least troubled about Bret Harte on my account. I have the most solemn and repeated pledges from Osgood as to my relations with the magazine when Mr. Fields retires. . . . I should never suffer myself to enter rivalry with any one; but at any rate Harte's and my own lives are so divergent that we should not come into competition. He will be engaged probably as a salaried contributor to the Atlantic, but I shall be editor.

If Harte considered Howells his peer or rival, Howells disdained such a comparison. Still, he invited Harte and his family to stay at his home in Cambridge immediately upon their arrival, and Harte accepted with alacrity. "I go East from here on Feby. 1st," he concluded his January 24 letter to Howells, "and will telegraph from Chicago or N.Y. when you can meet me at the Worcester depot." "There is a perfect furore in cultivated society now about Bret Harte," Elinor Howells confided to her sister-in-law on January 29. "All the young ladies are in love with him—but it is no use—he is married."

Cover of *Every Saturday,* January 14, 1871. Engraving by W. J. Linton.

A few days before he left San Francisco, Harte was feted at a farewell dinner at Louis Dingeon's restaurant, attended by about a dozen of his old friends and companions in literary work, including Noah Brooks and Samuel Bowles of the *Springfield Republican.* The party did not break up until 5 A.M. "Naturally Harte was the center of the little company," Brooks recalled, "and he never was more fascinating and companionable." Finally, on the morning of February 2, a day later than planned, he boarded the eastbound "Overland Express" with his wife and their two sons in tow and "burned his ships," as he put it a few days later, vowing never to return.

Most of the local papers lamented the loss to western letters. According to the *San Francisco Chronicle,* his departure left "a vacancy among the *literati* of the coast which it will be hard to fill. Whatever his enemies may say to the contrary, Mr. Harte is possessed of genius—not in large quantity, perhaps, nor of the most brilliant order—and to this he adds industry and a habit of study." On the very day he left, the *Alta California* reported that the "best-known and best-liked writer in light literature that we have" planned "to take up his residence permanently in the East." However, the *Call*—"that degraded 'Morning Call,' whose mission from hell & politics was to lick the boots of the Irish & throw brave mud at the Chinamen," as Clemens put it later—referred derisively to Harte's faults, "which were chiefly manifested in an overweening vanity," declared he had been "badly spoiled" by the "over-indulgence" of his friends, and concluded that his "head has been turned by too many allusions to the 'Heathen Chinee.' He has latterly given us nothing but sorry doggerel when asked for poetry." Not only would he not be missed, according to the *Call,* "his place here will be fully and capably filled."

However divided local opinion about Harte may have been when he left San Francisco, he traveled by rail across the continent in February 1871 a full-fledged literary celebrity. Howells later compared his trip to "the progress of a prince" in the "universal attention and interest" it attracted in the press. Similarly, Clemens remembered that Harte "crossed the continent through such a prodigious blaze of national interest and excitement that one might have supposed he was the Viceroy of India." Even the *London Daily News* heralded his movements in an editorial that began "America has a new star"—a copy of which Harte kept to the end of his life. In fact the Hartes arrived in Chicago, where they stayed a week with Anna Harte's sister on North La Salle Street, on February 7, traveling with such haste that "we saw nothing of [Omaha] from the cars." By all accounts they were hospitably received in the Windy City. The *Chicago Tribune* remarked on the author's presence there on February 9 and added that "movements are on foot by which, it is hoped, Mr. Harte may be persuaded to adopt Chicago as his future home."

The plan of several prominent local citizens, including the lawyer Wirt Dexter, was to install Harte as editor of the *Lakeside Monthly* at an annual salary of five thousand dollars and a stake in the magazine worth ten thousand dollars. Thirty Chicagoans had pledged five hundred dollars apiece to lure him to the city. On his part, Harte had assured the sponsors of this plan by telegraph before leaving San Francisco that he had not consummated an agreement with Osgood and Company "and that he would make no disposition of himself until after looking thoroughly into the Chicago project." "For many reasons," Harte wrote Josephine Clifford two weeks later, "I wanted the Chicago Magazine," though in his version of events "the childishness and provincial character of a few of the principal citizens of Chicago spoiled the project."

He and his wife were invited to a dinner party at Dexter's home to seal the contract but for whatever reason—because he expected a carriage to be sent for them though one never arrived, because his wife suddenly fell ill, or more plausibly because Anna Harte threw a tantrum when her sister was not invited to join them and she refused to accompany her husband—Harte failed to attend. He "promptly apologized, of course, as became a well-bred gentleman," according to the Chicago correspondent of the *Cincinnati Commercial,* "but the apology was voted unsatisfactory, and it was resolved to cut his accquaintance and destroy the subscription." The Chicago *Mail* reported on February 17 that the erstwhile publishers of the *Lakeside* had concluded "that a man who stands so much upon a point of California etiquette is not the one to run a *Monthly* in this go-ahead village." Kate Field, in Bloomington, Illinois, on a lecture tour, read about the dustup and thought that Harte "was guilty of a most outrageous breach of decorum" in Chicago and "has killed himself there." Another local wag burlesqued the occasion in a parody of "Plain Language from Truthful James":

> They sat down to their banquet, but their feelings were not festive,
> And the food lay on their stomachs in a way quite indigestive;
> And the things they wished the absent, in their anger, was a sin,
> And they swore that he should finger not a dollar of their tin.

On his part, Harte promised Bierce two weeks later that "some time I'll tell you my Chicago experience wh[ich] was very funny." Harte was dogged for years afterwards by the rumor that he lost ten thousand dollars by his "diffidence." In the wake of his faux pas, too, Harte was excoriated in the local press. While in the city, as the *Chicago Republican* reported a month later, Harte had visited the office of the Western News Company on State Street to investigate the sale of the edition of "The Heathen Chinee" illustrated by Hull: "He skulked around the corners, made inquiries of the cash-boys, and took notes of what he saw." Later, Osgood and Company attempted to interdict the further sale of the Hull chapbook, though the legal issue was mooted in October when the last copies of it were destroyed in the great Chicago fire.

In any event, the Hartes left Chicago on February 15, dallied briefly in Syracuse, arrived in New York on February 20, where they visited with his sister Eliza and her family at their Fifth Avenue home, and finally reached Boston on Friday, February 24. Howells remembered thirty years later that "when they met at the station" Harte had "pressed forward with his cordial handclasp" and winning laugh. Despite the embarrassing imbroglio in Chicago only the week before, Harte played the role of literary lion while in Boston as though to the manor born. The city "has had no such sensation since the demolition of the 'Coliseum' as the arrival of Bret Harte," the *Boston Commonwealth* declared. The local dailies were mosaicked with news of his movements that week. On February 25, his first full day in the Hub, he dined at the Parker House with the Saturday Club, where he met, among others, Lowell, Emerson, Holmes, Henry Wadsworth Longfellow, Richard Henry Dana, Jr., and the Harvard naturalist Louis Agassiz. Annie Fields confided to her diary her first impressions of Harte when "a part of the company adjourned to our tea-table" after dinner:

> Jamie thought him very satisfactory. His size is rather under than over the ordinary, his face deeply pitted with small pox which has left a redness about the eyes as it is so apt to do—otherwise he is fine looking and reminded us a little of what the young Dickens must have been. Less absorbing, but of kindred nature. Fine hazel eyes, full lips, large moustache, an honest smile—so much for his personal. His accent slightly western and his colloquial expression careless and inelegant often. His aplomb is good and not too great—He is honest and refined. Quite unconscious of himself as a prominent person during the evening, but talking and listening by turns altogether naturally.

During the week he stayed with Howells, he supped with Longfellow and Lowell and Agassiz and attended the theatre with Fields (Bronson Howard's "Saratoga" at the Globe). Howells recalled that "Harte was nearly always late for those luncheons and dinners" and "it needed the anxieties and energies of both families to get him into his clothes" and "into the carriage where a good deal of final buttoning must have been done." The highlight of the week was a dinner in Harte's honor at the Howells home on Berkeley Avenue in Cambridge on February 28 that was attended by the cream of Boston literary society, including the young Henry James and Henry Adams. "Why," Harte joked with his host, "you couldn't stand on your front porch and fire off your revolver without bringing down a two-volumer." "Till now, Elinor and I have met no young couple so congenial," Howells wrote his father at the time. Elinor Howells, while conceding the Hartes were "not quite au fait in everything," agreed they were "polished, cultivated people."

At least from his own perspective, Harte took Boston by storm. As he reported to Bierce, "I was so wined and dined by the literary folk whom I used to scalp in the *Overland* that between remorse and good liquor I hardly knew where I stood." Only Longfellow "escaped the corrosive touch of his subtle irreverence," Howells recalled years afterward. The poet was, Harte allowed, "the man I most revered," and he long remembered their stroll together late one night through the streets of Cambridge after dinner at Lowell's home. "Although I had met him several times before in a brief week of gayety," Harte recalled at Longfellow's death twelve years later, "until that evening I do not think I had clearly known him." At the gate of Craigie House, Harte said good night and made an abrupt departure. Had he stayed a moment longer, he told Annie Fields, "he should have put his arms around him and made a fool of himself then and there." If, in California, he had assumed an air of superiority, in New England he presumed he was in his proper sphere among the Brahmin poets.

Of course he was mistaken. Harte may have been the guest of honor at the Howells dinner, but William and Elinor Howells planned the party to repay scores of social debts they had accumulated over the months. "We've been here five years accepting civilities and never done much in return," Elinor Howells explained, "and this gave us a grand opportunity to really give our friends a treat." The Hartes' visit "went off splendidly," she added, "but *the party!* How shall I do justice to it?" The ostensible occasion for the dinner (to welcome Harte) masked its ulterior purpose (to fix Howells's rank among the custodians of culture). The same may be said of the lucrative contract Harte signed with Osgood and Company a few days later. If, on the surface, it seemed to signal his assimilation by the cultural elite, in fact he always remained an outsider, a "salaried contributor" and a "delightful guest." In 1910, Howells even entitled his memoir of Harte in the second edition of *Literary Friends and Acquaintance* "A Belated Guest."

Why, then, was he hired? Because the contract, whatever else may be said of it, was good business. Subscriptions to the *Atlantic* had plummeted by some fifteen thousand, to about thirty-five thousand, in the wake of the controversy over Harriet Beecher Stowe's "Lady Byron Vindicated" in the September

1869 issue. Harte was quite simply the beneficiary of fortuitous circumstances: he was the most popular writer in America at the very moment the publishers of the *Atlantic* needed a marquee name to shore up subscriptions and raise advertising revenue. By signing him to write for them exclusively for a year, whatever the substance or frequency of his contributions, the firm at least slowed the decline in sales of the magazine. Harte would earn his salary not by writing for the magazine per se but by becoming a literary property the firm could package for sale to subscribers and advertisers. As far west as Illinois, Kate Field got wind of the rumor that Osgood and Company "intend to make all sorts of offers and get down on their knees to him with *Atlantic Monthly* in one hand and half a dozen banks in the other." Harte admitted in a letter to Bierce from New York on March 5 that "of the commercial value of my own stuff I really had no conception whatever. . . . I have just accepted ten thousand dollars per year from J. R. Osgood, tho merely for the exclusive right to such of my poems & sketches as I may turn out in that space—and this does not include the 'half-profits' they offer me for republication." The agreement specified that Harte's contributions were not to number less than twelve—presumably one per month during the life of the contract.

The next day, he formalized the agreement in a letter to Osgood. "Of course I was sorely beset and tempted [by other proposals from publishers] here on my return, and I have made some pecuniary sacrifice for the sake of keeping my books in the one house"—Harte claimed he had been offered upwards of fifteen thousand dollars for a year's contributions—but "I am satisfied." (The rumor soon reached print, as in the Paris *American Register,* that Osgood and Company had engaged Harte "for the sum of fifteen thousand dollars.") In any event, Louise Chandler Moulton crowed that Boston "may still claim the proud distinction of being the literary metropolis" with the "capture of a literary quarry" so coveted as Harte: "He tarried in Chicago. He investigated New-York. He came to Boston, he saw, he was conquered."

For the record, the agreement did not cover any plays or dramatic adaptations he might write during the twelvemonth, even though before leaving California he had contracted to script a play for the actor Lawrence Barrett entitled "In the Sierras" based on his *Overland* stories. The title was registered with the copyright office, though the script was apparently never completed. The contract also permitted Harte to earn additional money by lecturing. The very day he wrote Osgood to accept the proposal, in fact, he claimed to have received an invitation to deliver four lectures for ten thousand dollars. The *Independent* also reported that spring that Harte had been offered five thousand dollars for a series of twelve lectures and "had the good sense to decline" rather than glut the market with more "Bret Harte." He would not begin to trade on his name by lecturing for nearly two more years, and his career by then would be in a fine mess.

CHAPTER 3

Mining the Slag Heap

The Commercialization of Local Color

CAME the reckoning. After reaching terms with Osgood, Harte suddenly faced the daunting prospect of earning the inflated salary he had negotiated and which he began to draw almost immediately. After visiting friends in Westchester County in early March, Harte and his family found temporary quarters at the Lenox House on Fifth Avenue in New York City. "I have just returned from Rye with a frightful cold, wh[ich] not only laid me up there, but has since bro[ugh]t on a damnable neuralgia wh[ich] has kept me from work by day and sleep by night," he complained to Osgood on March 14. It was merely the first in a series of excuses he would offer over the months for his blocked writing.

Moulton had predicted in her "Boston Letter" in the *New York Tribune* that Harte would "take his time about his work, as all authors must who would do their best and enhance their reputations." Similarly, F. W. Loring editorialized in the *Independent* that "the public will profit from the fact" that Harte would "write when he chooses, where he chooses, and upon what subjects he chooses" after escaping the "monthly drain" at the *Overland*, which "threatened to exhaust his power." Howells later extenuated Harte's literary failings by speculating that, though he was only thirty-four when he returned to the East, "he seemed to have arrived after the age of observation was past for him," that he was "in the midst of new and alien conditions," and that his "talent was not a facile gift." In any event, Harte had no sooner recovered from his cold than he and his sons succumbed to scarlet fever. "It is rather provoking to come three thousand miles to the home of one's boyhood to relapse into infantile diseases," he joked. He was also, at least initially, unsettled in the matter of lodgings. "If you hear of anything modest and quiet near Boston or in the suburbs, pray let me know," he entreated Osgood. "I shall, of course, get to the seaside in the summer but I want a home."

Meanwhile, Osgood planned to strike while the iron was hot, to exploit Harte's popularity and the favorable publicity his house had earned in signing him to the exclusive contract, by issuing an illustrated and authorized edition of "Plain Language from Truthful James." On March 6, in the very same letter in which he agreed to contract terms, Harte wrote Osgood that he had given the artist Sol Eytinge "several ideas about the 'Heathen Chinee' and his Pagan brother—the California miner." "I think that Eytinges designs would dispose of this tiresome 'Chinee' business at once," he wrote the publisher three weeks later, "by showing the inferiority of all the other illustrations." As Harte anticipated, Eytinge's eight drawings, first published with a reprinting of the poem in the Osgood weekly *Every Saturday* for April 29, proved so popular that the magazine soon sold out. Osgood soon issued a chapbook of the poem priced at a quarter, featuring Eytinge's sketches with a note that they had been approved by Harte, making it (unlike the pamphlet sold by the Western News Company of Chicago) "the only illustrated edition of the poem published with the author's sanction." However much Harte may have disparaged the poem in private, he willingly accommodated the demands of the literary marketplace in hopes of turning a profit. While Eytinge's drawings are aesthetically superior to Hull's, they interpret the poem in much the same way. Bill Nye and Truthful James are less caricatured figures, and the violence against Ah Sin is less blatant, but the sketches do not dispute the anti-Chinese reading the poem had been given in the press and elsewhere. Eytinge's illustrations "are as true to the spirit of the poem as the poem is true to the spirit of Western life," declared the *Portsmouth Journal of Literature and Politics.*

Harte was still living out of his trunks at the Lenox House in New York when, in late March, he was for the first (though by no

Sol Eytinge illustration for *The Heathen Chinee*. (Boston: Fields Osgood, 1871)

means the last) time compelled to respond to published reports of his ethical lapses. When he left San Francisco, so it was alleged in the *San Francisco News-Letter* for March 11, Harte had taken with him four manuscripts originally submitted to the *Overland*, which, while in Chicago and without Carmany's knowledge or consent, he had arranged to be published in the March number of the *Lakeside*. This was the issue of the magazine in which, "according to rumor," Harte was to debut as editor. The charge was telegraphed all over the West by the Associated Press agent in San Francisco, Albert S. Evans, "an infinitely small rascal," according to Harte, "whose *MS* I once rejected" and whose book *Our Sister Republic* he had criticized in the *Overland* for its "excessively opulent language." In fact, Harte insisted, he had been given the manuscripts by their authors after he quit the *Overland* for the purpose of placing them elsewhere. "All the *MSS* received by me for the *Overland*," he wrote Carmany, "except those returned by mail or to the authors personally, are or were left by me in the editorial rooms of the O.M. or in your publishing office." Harte was also accused in the New York *Globe* of "rejecting some fulsome female's *MS* and afterwards incorporating" part of it into one of his own essays. "I fear that if I begin to notice these things publicly," he admitted to Osgood, "I shall have my hands full as well as foul."

Two other controversies dogged Harte during his first weeks in the East, moreover. He was asked to write a few verses to be read at the reunion of the Grand Army of the Potomac in Boston and was appalled when he saw in the program that he was "set down for that dreadful thing—a 'Poem.'" He tried to sweat out "some exalted patriotic rhetoric," too late "recovered my good sense," and finally dashed off a short dramatic monologue in dialect entitled "The Old Major Explains." "I am painfully aware that my performance . . . lacks dignity and fitness" commensurate with the occasion, he allowed to the organizer of the event. Or as he conceded to James Fields, "That is why the verses were so bad." Worse yet, even though he was known in San Francisco as an indifferent reader, he was expected in Boston to declaim the poem publicly. "You could hardly find a worse reader than myself," he insisted in reply to the invitation. "This is one of several reasons why I do not come to deliver the verses in person." Instead, Harte recruited Fields to read the poem for him at the Globe Theater on May 12, and Fields was obliged both to defend his friend and to apologize to the veterans for replacing him in a few prefatory stanzas:

> If the poet whose absence to-day we deplore
>   Had struck but one note for his country's disgrace,
> If his lyre had betrayed you, ye heroes of war,
>   I could not and would not stand here in his place.
>
> But his soul was responsive to all that was grand,
>   And his loyal young spirit leaped up in a flame;
> And he fought with his pen for his dear struggling land,
>   As you with your swords, sons of glory and fame.
>
> And so, for my friend, I will take up his song,
>   And give it a voice, though, alas! not its own.
> To him the quaint verse and his genius belong;
>   To me but the accents of friendship alone.

Harte's reluctant muse was even more sorely tested in June, when he read the Phi Beta Kappa poem at the Harvard commencement. Lowell had invited him to the august occasion in March but, for whatever reason, Harte dallied at working on his verses. His defenders claimed later that Lowell was at fault for notifying the poet "he would have until Midsummer," forgetting "that the Commencement time had been changed" from mid-July to June 29. In the end Harte merely resurrected an old poem, "The Lost Beauty," first published in the *Golden Era* in December 1862, under a new title, "Aspiring Miss De Laine." As Howells remembered, it was "a jingle so trivial, so out of keeping, so inadequate that his enemies . . . must have suffered from it almost as much as his friends." Nor did Harte read the poem well. The *Boston Advertiser* carped that he "made so little effort to be heard that scarcely any one caught the meaning of all his lines, while people in the more distant parts of the church could not hear him at all." Lowell also wrote his daughter that Harte read his poem in so low a voice "that it did not hit as it would had he pitched his voice higher." Worse yet, Harte tried to strike a pose of genteel fashion by wearing a gaudy suit and foppish green gloves to the commencement; Lilian Aldrich, wife of Thomas Bailey Aldrich, thought his "poem was as inappropriate as his dress." Unfortunately, too, Harte imagined just such an embarrassing experience in his story "The Poet of Sierra Flat," in the *Atlantic* for July 1871, issued a week before the Harvard commencement. Nor was the story sufficiently well drawn to arrest the rumors; the New York *Evening Mail* thought it "not so good as his wont and in its *denouement* falling pointedly pointless." If, in reaching his lucrative agreement with Osgood, Harte had taken every trick, he misplayed every hand for months afterwards.

In retrospect he seemed almost destined to fail. Having left the West, he hoped to reshape the contours of his career, to reinvent himself as the type of man of letters who wore green gloves rather than buckskin breeches, to abandon the western local color with which he had built his reputation. Incredibly, he chose to change the course of his career in the resort town of Newport, Rhode Island, where he spent the summer of 1871 in a fashionable mansion with his family. Inevitably, given the exigencies of the literary market, the experiment ended in failure. More than any other comparable episode in his life, Harte's six-month residence in Newport exposed fault lines in his character and stress fractures in his work that would widen over the next few years.

His immediate problem that spring was to find a residence commensurate with his sudden success. He hated New York, "this noisy yet lonely city where they set such infinite values on finite and valueless things," and briefly considered moving to Springfield, Massachusetts, to be near his friend Samuel Bowles. He spent most of April searching for a house in New Jersey and Connecticut, and as late as May 15 he reported to Howells that he was "still house hunting. It is hard unsympathetic work. . . . And, dear me, what have become of all the farms I knew as a boy? Where are the farm yards—meadows, barns, orchards? There is nothing now between the shanty and the villa."

Given these stark alternatives, he chose the villa. On May 19 he visited Newport, probably boarding at Hannah Dame's inn on Broad Street. He crossed paths that day with the editor and author Thomas Wentworth Higginson, who noted in his diary that he liked Harte "very much"; he was "not striking in appearance or manner, but quite unspoiled; less shy than Howells and perhaps less refined; but manly and pleasing." Armed with a letter of introduction from his California friend Clarence King, a Yale-educated geologist and native of Newport who had contributed to the *Overland,* Harte received every courtesy from local residents while he searched for a house. Before the end of May he had agreed to rent Newbold Edgar's "pretty, picturesque" cottage on Harrison Avenue on the point by Brenton Cove through November for four thousand dollars, and he soon staffed the house with an Irish cook and a maid.

Local interest in Harte's arrival was so intense that it was reported in the *Newport Daily News.* According to a column in the paper on June 14, "Bret Harte is expected in Newport in a few days, and his admirers will be glad to see him." The next day, the paper announced that the writer "is in town and has taken possession of his cottage." Harte immediately invited Howells to visit the "very charming, roomy, comfortable house. . . . I think you and Mrs Howells might enjoy yourselves for a week or two." With its "good-sized library" and "large and blank expanse of barn," he bragged, the house and grounds were well suited for the entertainment of their children. There was also "a strip of beach near the house much frequented by the simple but hardworking clam, who amuses himself at twilight by expectorating on the legs of the sentimental tourist," where "we could walk at the sunset hour." However, Howells and his family did not visit the Hartes that summer. Harte wrote Osgood as late as September 24 to ask, "Where is Howells, and does he intend to come and see me in Newport?" Howells wrote his father on October 15 that there had been a misunderstanding about the dates and the trip had been canceled.

Such an explanation obscures the more likely reason Howells failed to vacation in Newport in 1871. Harte's submissions to the *Atlantic* had, quite simply, proved to be a bitter disappointment to the editors and publishers of the magazine. From all indications, Osgood lost faith in Harte during the months he lived in Newport, and the publisher complained with some justice that "never in his business career had he gotten so little out of a contributor, or with such pains." On his part, Howells claimed some thirty years later that Harte "saw nothing aright" in Newport, and the "net result in a literary return to his publishers" of the contract with him was "one story and two or three poems." In truth, Harte would fulfill the letter of the contract by writing more than the twelve articles specified as a minimum number while it was in force, though to be sure these poems and stories were decidedly dull. And while living in Newport he wrote only a pair of stories, pale self-parodies of his *Overland* tales ("The Romance of Madroño Hollow" and "Princess Bob and Her Friends," in the *Atlantic* for September and December 1871, respectively), and three hackneyed poems based on local legends, subjects with which he was simply unfamiliar.

While the reasons Harte was unable to honor the spirit of his contract with Osgood and Company are myriad and complex, they all relate at least indirectly to the circumstances of his life in Newport. He was, in the most charitable reconstruction of events, distracted by the privileged if not profligate social life he enjoyed there. By all accounts he wined and dined lavishly, exhausting his income and soon running into debt. He temporarily staved off his creditors until King arranged for the payment of Harte's bills for a month, and then King left him to shift for himself. It would become a familiar pattern. Though Harte's letters to Osgood at the time were punctuated by repeated requests to draw on his salary, he wondered toward the close of the season how much one New York creditor would "compromise for, cash down." At the close of the season, as Clemens reminisced thirty-six years later, Harte "left Newport in debt to the butcher, the baker, and the rest." Even among his friends, Harte was notorious for his failures to pay his bills. Noah Brooks allowed that he was "utterly destitute of what is sometimes called 'the money sense'" and as a result "was continually involved in troubles that he might have escaped with a little more financial shrewdness." Or as Annie Fields noted in her diary, "I find him always most lovely a[nd] interesting personally but he is not careful to say the least about having money to pay when the time comes." John Hay recalled on another occasion that he had been "complaining to Bret Harte of my lack of funds: 'Your own fault,' said the wise Argonaut. 'Why did you fool away your money paying your debts?'"

Though he had been hailed as the most promising literary genius of his generation, moreover, in polite Newport society Harte was liable to denigrate the very brand of western local-color writing he had popularized. On May 29 a dialect poem entitled "The Fate of a Fighting Dog," falsely attributed to him, appeared on the front page of the *Newport Daily News;* immediately upon his return to the village two weeks later, Harte contacted the newspaper—whose editors had printed it in his honor—to deny his authorship. As the Newport correspondent of the *Boston Transcript* then reported, Harte's "admirers will be glad to learn that this poem, which abounds in vulgarity and coarse wit, is not one of Mr. Harte's productions." Similarly, Harte disparaged "Plain Language from Truthful James" at the first dinner party he attended in Newport, at the home of the publisher Charles J. Peterson. As Mary E. W. Sherwood recalled later, the guests included the historian George Bancroft, the poet Julia Ward Howe, the dramatist George Boker, and the novelist Ann S. Stephens, all of them "summoned to do honor to the young man who leaped from obscurity to the very heights of Olympus." The "slender, rather handsome young man with very black hair" reminded Sherwood, as he had reminded Annie Fields, of a young Charles Dickens. He was also, she thought, exceptionally modest. "Just think of the degradation of going down to posterity as the author of such trash as *The Heathen Chinee,*" Harte said to her that evening, or so she later remembered.

Harte's presumption of literary respectability after moving to Newport is epitomized by his induction into the Town and

Country Club, which Howe founded that summer. Its select membership included Higginson and J. G. Holland, editor of *Scribner's;* William Watson Goodwin and George Martin Lane, professors of classics at Harvard; Charles T. Brooks, the local Unitarian minister; the engineer George E. Waring; and the writers Sara Payson Willis Parton ("Fanny Fern") and her husband James. Their plan, as the Newport correspondent of the *Providence Journal* reported, was "to meet once a week or so, as convenience, and other engagements permit, at some pleasant spot in wood, or on shore, or at some of the country residences. . . . Bret Harte comes up from his Point, and from other directions come other bright spirits." Or as Howe remarked, "My club-loving mind found sure material for many pleasant meetings, and a little band of us combined to improve the beautiful summer season by picnics, sailing parties, and household soirees, in all of which these brilliant literary lights took part." The mock-commencement meeting of the club at John W. Bigelow's Washington Street estate on August 24, for example, parodied the Latin program of the Harvard exercises and featured a poem (now lost) declaimed by "Franciscus Bret Harte" entitled "The Pacific Woman"—a burlesque of his performance at the actual Harvard graduation the previous June. A month later, Harte described to his friend John Hay a picnic-meeting of the club that he attended at which "the people were well-bred, respectable, refined folk, as society goes, and I was their guest." In all, while in Newport that summer Harte played to the hilt the part of the refined and genteel litterateur. Sixty-five years later, Ethel Parton, the daughter of James and Sara, remembered the striking figure Harte cut that season: "He wore drooping mustaches, a velvet waistcoat, a shiny looped watch chain, and looked very much like one of his own gamblers." He was, in effect, engaged in a high-stakes crap shoot. By aspiring, or pretending, to literary gentility, Harte effectively denied the type of writer he had been and the style of vernacular writing at which he had succeeded.

His literary productivity may have declined during the months he lived in Newport, too, in consequence of Anna's poor health. Less than six weeks after moving into Edgar Cottage, Harte went inland with his family because his wife could not tolerate the sea breezes. He again moved his family to Mount Vernon, New York, for a fortnight in early September when Anna, then in the early stages of her fourth pregnancy, suffered a relapse. "His wife has been very ill and has given him cause for terrible anxiety," Annie Fields noted in her diary. "This accounts for much left undone." "My wife's continued ill-health," Harte wrote Holland two weeks later, "has so preoccupied my heart and time that I have barely been able to furnish my quota of copy to my publishers." He even described the state of Anna's health during a visit with the Emersons in Concord in mid-October: by his account she was "a despairing invalid."

The Newport correspondent of the *Providence Journal* tried to cast Harte's delinquency in the most favorable light possible in his column: "Many brain workers complain of the lethargic state in which they find themselves here. 'I can't write here,' is the common expression one hears from the brain workers. Bret Harte finds this difficulty with many others." The next spring, when Clemens proposed that their families summer together near the coast, Harte demurred: "I fear," he explained, "that the sea-side is not 'indicated,' as the Doctors say, in Mrs Harte's case. She has hardly got over her last summer at Newport and longs for mountain air." As late as November 1888, Harte reminded his wife of "the effect of the Newport air upon your health" while they lived there: "it made you *sleepless* and *intensely nervous*."

Above all, Harte failed to honor the spirit of his contract with Osgood because he profoundly misjudged his audience. Like an actor who plays against type, Harte disappointed readers whenever he attempted to break with his western formula. As Whitman told John Burroughs in 1871, Harte "is a sharp, bright fellow, but entirely cut off from what he writes about by having cultivated foppishness and superiority." He tried without success in the poetry he wrote for the *Atlantic* in mid-1871 to exploit local legends of the Rhode Island shore, shunning the middlebrow piquancy of his California verse for a more inflated or ponderous style.

Nowhere was this failure more apparent than in his poem "A Newport Romance," published in the October 1871 number of the *Atlantic*. Harte began to plan the poem literally from the first day he lived in Edgar Cottage. As Moulton reported in the *New York Tribune* on June 14, Harte "has taken a house in Newport" with "a Blue Room" which

> has a ghost. A ghost of high degree, for she rustles in heavy, old-fashioned brocade, and her jewels glitter through the darkness. With her comes also the ghost of a perfume; for the legend is that she died of a broken heart, and the flowers which her faithless lover gave her are still upon her bosom, immortal as she. . . . If you would keep tryst with her you must make to the wee, small hours, and then, between 2 and 3 of the morning clock, if you have ears to hear and nose to smell, you shall hear a stately footfall and the rustle of silken robes, and smell the scent of mignonette which bloomed in the gardens of long ago. Bret Harte has been in strange company before now, and he may as well add a ghost to his visiting list.

Two weeks later, similarly, the Newport correspondent of the *Boston Transcript* remarked that "Bret Harte's cottage is said to be also the abiding place of a ghost, whose peculiar ways it is hoped the poet will give to the public in verse."

On September 5, during a visit to James and Annie Fields at their new home on the Massachusetts coast north of Boston, Harte again recounted the story. According to his hostess, Harte was "delighted with the fragrant lawns of Newport and has I believe put into verse a delightful ghost story," which he told them. This story "so fascinated my grandfather," Geoffrey Bret Harte wrote in his family memoir seventy years later, "that he decided upon a little hoax." Inviting "a housefull of guests" to Edgar Cottage, Harte told them the story "most impressively" after dinner one evening, "lingering particularly on the legend" of "the ghostly fragrance. As he was an exceedingly gifted storyteller, the guests were delighted, thrilled and but faintly skeptical." After they had retired, Harte opened the doors of a cupboard where he had secreted a large number of flowers. The next morning, the guests were to a person in "a very different frame of mind. They were not skeptical at all. Each and every one had a most exciting story to tell, fully believing at first to have been the only one to experience it. Every guest had distinctly smelled the perfume . . . in the air; could in fact still faintly do so, while more than one of them declared he had heard the sound of footsteps and the rustle of silk pass their doors."

However "exceedingly gifted" Harte may have been as a storyteller or "impressively" he told this story in company, the poem he based on the legend was banal at best. He simply did not possess the technical skill to evoke Newport as he had imagined the California gold fields. He identified too closely with the gentry to satirize them as he had satirized rustic miners. Put another way, Harte's craft suffered when he touched on any topic other than the California he resented and sometimes despised. "They say that she died of a broken heart," his poem begins, "But her spirit lives and her soul is part / Of this sad old house by the sea." By the third stanza the rhyme is forced and contrived: her fickle French suitor "Won the heart of this sentimental Quaker, / At what gold-laced speech of those modish days / She listened—the mischief take her!" Disappointed in love, she "kept the posies of mignonette / That he gave" her before he sailed away, and since her death

> . . . when the clock strikes two,
>   She walks unbidden from room to room,
> And the air is filled that she passes through
>   With a subtle, sad perfume.

After summarizing this thrice-told tale, the poet shifts to the present tense:

> I sit in the sad old house tonight,—
>   Myself a ghost from a farther sea;
> And I trust that this Quaker woman might,
>   In courtesy, visit me.

The next stanza, with its reference to a grand piano, suggests the luxury of Harte's rented villa but adds nothing to the poem and might easily have been omitted entirely:

> For the laugh is fled from porch and lawn,
>   And the bugle died from the fort on the hill,
> And the twitter of girls on the stairs is gone,
>   And the grand piano is still.

The next several quatrains not only fail to evoke the ghostly presence of the dead woman, they focus the reader's attention squarely on the self-indulgent poet. The final stanzas strain toward profundity in tortured scansion:

> And I hear no rustle of stiff brocade,
>   And I see no face at my library door;
> For now that the ghosts of my heart are laid,
>   She is viewless for evermore.

> But whether she came as a faint perfume
>   Or whether a spirit in stole of white,
> I feel as I pass from the darkened room
>   She has been with my soul to-night!

In all, "A Newport Romance" was not a successful literary performance. The topic was probably better suited to a prose sketch than to a verse ballad.

Still, because the poem was written by Harte before the bubble of his fame had burst, and because it appeared in the *Atlantic,* it earned at least a short-lived popularity. It was immediately reprinted in newspapers across the country, among them the *Boston Transcript, Providence Journal, Washington Evening Star, Chicago Tribune, Sacramento Union,* and the Boston *Woman's Journal.* Moulton thought it a "charming story of ghostly grace," and as late as 1879 Longfellow selected it for inclusion in his anthology, *Poems of Places: New England.* But its glaring flaws were also recognized from the first. The New York *Evening Post* complained, for example, that "Harte's poem is pleasing but not level with his fame, and has the blemish of a grammatical error" (no doubt the line "the air is filled that she passes through"). The *New York Times* also objected that the poem "is hardly up to the mark of his best work," and Tom

Hood allowed in *Fun* that it was "scarcely up to his standard."
Even Harte confessed privately that it was "poor stuff."

His failure was, in the end, one of conception rather than
execution. In this poem as in virtually all of the work he produced in the first months after his move east, as he struggled to
earn a living and reestablish his literary credentials, Harte pandered to the genteel New England tradition. Like a transplanted
piñon tree, he failed to take root and flourish in unfamiliar soil.
Though he remained in Newport until the expiration of the
lease on Edgar Cottage in mid-November, he soon became a
gypsy among the eastern literati. Much as he had abandoned
San Francisco for Newport, he soon abandoned the lavish enter-
tainments of Newport for the more comfortable society of New
York, the "noisy yet lonely city" he had scorned only six months
before.

While he moved his family into a modest town house on East
49th Street, however, he did not fundamentally change the
social circles in which he moved. Annie Fields noted in her diary
in January 1872 that Harte had "no sympathy" for "purely literary society," finding a circle of friends "among the Schuylers,
Sherwoods," and other New York blue bloods. When Noah
Brooks expressed his fear to Sam Bowles that Harte would run
into debt in New York and provoke a scandal, Bowles replied
"with his good-natured cynicism" that "there ought to be
enough rich men in New York to keep Harte a-going." Two or
three months after moving to the city, in fact, he had run into
debt "and his landlord was threatening to turn his little family
into the street," according to Clemens, who loaned him five
hundred dollars.

A hail-fellow-well-met, Harte in fact joined the upper-crust
Lotos, Acadian, Knickerbocker, Century, and Union League
Clubs; vacationed at Long Branch; toasted such celebrities as
James A. Froude, George MacDonald, Henry Stanley, Edmund
Yates, Lord Houghton, Horace Greeley, and the philanthropist
Peter Cooper at receptions at Delmonico's and elsewhere over
the months; and there rubbed shoulders with such distin-
guished guests as Emerson, Clemens, Howells, John Hay, William

Evarts, Robert Roosevelt, Edward Eggleston, T. B. Musgrave, Charles Watrous, Bayard Taylor, Whitelaw Reid, Clarence King, Henry Ward Beecher, William Cullen Bryant, Parke Godwin, John W. De Forest, Charles Dudley Warner, P. T. Barnum, George William Curtis, J. G. Holland, E. C. Stedman, and Richard Watson Gilder. Greeley for one observed that to "meet Brett Harte, John Hay, and Mark Twain under the same roof . . . should be reckoned an event in almost any one's life." Unfortunately, according to Clemens, during his residences in Newport and New York Harte "constantly went to dinners among the fashionables where he was the only male guest whose wife had not been invited." He once had "a row" with Anna after he escorted one "Mrs Soyia Saupich Clarke" to her home after such a dinner, as he confided to his sister Eliza, and on another occasion Anna "found a mare's nest in a note" he "began to write but never finished or sent" to Mrs. Clarke.

During this first winter of his discontent, Harte repeatedly ran afoul of his employers in Boston, too. The much ballyhooed agreement with Osgood and Company had served its purpose: advertising revenue and subscriptions to the *Atlantic* were increasing and there was no incentive to renew Harte's contract, given the infrequency with which he actually contributed to the magazine. When he failed to submit copy for the August 1871 issue, Osgood was at once desperate and frustrated. "I have forborne until now to press you, thinking that you must have cogent reasons for your silence," Osgood wrote him in Newport,

> But we kept the August Atlantic open at considerable inconvenience and no small loss, and we're compelled after all to go to press without you. . . . It is a serious damage to both of us that you should not appear in the August number. We have announced you, and now the 'swing' will be broken and the effect bad.

Elinor Howells reported in late November 1871 that Harte "has gone to New York to live" and that Osgood and Company "paid him $10000. this year—but I guess they will not pay him so much next year." Annie Fields was even more blunt in her assessment of Harte's fading star, noting in her diary for January 12, 1872, that he "has a queer absent-minded way of spending his time, letting the hours slip by as if he had not altogether learned their value yet. It is a miracle to us how he lives for he writes very little. Thus far I suppose he has had money from J. R. O[sgood] & Co. but I fancy they have done with giving out money save for a *quid pro quo*."

Harte spent a day with Emerson in Concord, where they sipped sherry and smoked cigars and walked around Walden Pond ("an easy, kindly, well-behaved man," the sage thought him), and in company with Bryant, Reid, and Taylor, Harte sailed from New York in late January for a brief holiday in Cuba and Nassau. Three of the four stories Harte published in the *Atlantic* in 1871–72 were in fact the last articles to appear in those issues, suggesting that they were set in type late in the production cycle. He was so dilatory in his work habits that the only exception to this pattern, Harte's Christmas story "How Santa Claus Came to Simpson's Bar," was published three months late in the March 1872 number—where it was the next-to-last article. Nor was this story particularly well received. The New York *Evening Post* pronounced it "disappointing in the extreme, as the catastrophe is far from being level with our expectations." Henry James thought the tale, with its false pathos, was "better than anything" in Harte's "'second manner'—though not quite so good as his first."

Nor had Harte yet discovered that, in the eastern literary market, writers were expendable, certainly ranked lower in the food chain than top-notch editors. He had been surprised in the spring of 1871 when Howells was named to succeed Fields as editor of the *Atlantic*. "I have not congratulated you, my dear fellow, on coming into your own," he jocularly wrote Howells, "for with your conscientiousness the position will be irksome and I do not know that you are to be congratulated." Whereas he had hitherto negotiated literary and other business with the avuncular Fields or Osgood, he was now obliged to answer to the more pragmatic Howells, and the strain on their friendship was soon evident. When he sent Howells the manuscript of the ballad "Concepcion de Arguellö" in March 1872, Harte was quick to resent the editorial suggestions about punctuating the Spanish phrases in it. "You see, my dear boy," he explained condescendingly, "for seventeen years my ear was as familiar with Spanish as my own tongue," and "I would trust my ear rather than any dictionary or the dicta of any set of Yankee Professors who give three syllables to 'Joaquin.'" (This was a dig at Longfellow.) Moreover, "I was for three years 'Keeper of the Archives' of the State of California in the Surveyor General's office," and "I consequently know something about the subject in question." (Three years later, in his review of Harte's *Echoes of the Foothills,* Howells averred that even if his "beautiful story of Concepcion de Arguello" was not strictly accurate, "Mr. Harte has made it true in telling it.") When Howells objected to the tone of Harte's letter, a contrite Harte quickly apologized: "There should have been no 'tone' to it at all; still less one unpleasant to you." He simply had not anticipated that his poem would be vetted by "a jury of Cambridge bigwigs."

Unfortunately, Harte learned nothing from this unpleasant experience. The following spring and summer, he struggled to submit manuscript he still owed Osgood and Company under the terms of his contract, including the poem "Dolly Varden," rejected by Howells and instead published in *Harper's Bazar;* the dull dialogue "Half an Hour Before Supper," in the *Atlantic* for September 1872 ("not quite all we want," Tom Hood remarked in *Fun*); and the two-part serial "Mrs. Skaggs's Husbands," which Howells declined to publish in the *Atlantic* though it eventually appeared as the title story of a collection issued by Osgood.

With the birth of his daughter Jessamy on May 31, moreover, Harte found yet another excuse to procrastinate: "the baby has occupied my attention as an author to the exclusion of all else," he wrote Howells on June 22. On July 3 Harte fled with his family to the boarding house his sister Eliza ran near Morristown, New Jersey, an hour and a half by train from New York, because Jessamy was dangerously sick from the summer heat. As he reported to friends, "The baby's critical condition has kept Mrs

Bret Harte in 1872. (Bret Harte Collection, Clifton Waller Barrett Library, Special Collections Department, University of Virginia Library)

Harte a close prisoner, and myself a walker of hospitals in quest of a wet-nurse—wh[ich] the Doctor says is all that will ensure the baby's recovery." Even two years later, when Harte congratulated Clemens on the birth of his daughter Clara, he remembered how he had "walked Bellevue Hospital at night through the female wards looking for the biped cow, with a telegram from my wife in my pocket that my poor little girls life hung upon that chance." Little wonder that Harte, who was easily distracted in any surroundings, published exactly one story and four poems between July 1872 and June 1873, when he should have been in the prime of his career. His circumstances in Morristown "inculcate laziness as a moral virtue," he wrote Clemens in late July 1872, and "work here is almost impossible." Harte lived with his family at various residences in Morristown (a "bigoted, self righteous hypocritical place") until 1876, supporting them by borrowing from friends, drawing advances on future work, and otherwise buying on credit.

Under more propitious circumstances, that is, the expiration of his contract with Osgood and Company might have proved a mixed blessing: while the firm remained the publisher of Harte's books, he was free to sell new periodical work to the highest bidder. Rather than risk any more departures from western local color, however, he reverted to formula. On June 12, 1872, only a few weeks after he was dropped from Osgood's payroll, he signed a contract with the theatrical impresario Augustin Daly "to write a play in five acts suitable for the Fifth Avenue Theatre," to be completed by September 1, for which he was to be paid a royalty of one hundred dollars per performance or six hundred dollars per week with a one-thousand-dollar advance upon delivery of the manuscript. Script writing was potentially much more lucrative than story writing in the literary market of the Gilded Age, which may explain why Harte, Howells, Clemens, and Henry James among them wrote over sixty plays, even though they are all known almost exclusively for their fiction.

Still, Harte never succeeded as a dramatist despite many attempts. He fiddled with the script commissioned by Daly, entitled "Kentuck" and featuring some of the characters from his

Overland stories, for several months—he complained to Osgood in September that "I am stuck here in N.Y. at my play"—before he finally asked Dion Boucicault to help him "reshape Acts 1 and 2" and "to construct and detail Acts 3 and 4," which Harte had not yet even "shadowed, much less written." News of their collaboration was leaked to the *New York Tribune*, which hailed it: "The skill and dexterity of Mr. Boucicault in dramatic construction, his mastery of all scenic resources, combined with that delicate insight and power of characterization which Mr. Harte possesses in such an extraordinary degree, offer a guarantee of a great success." In the end, however, their collaboration was not a happy one. Boucicault completed a cast raisonnée but vented his frustrations with his collaborator: "Harte is dilatory and erratic," he wrote Daly. "He is very anxious to get the work done—but thinks we can scurry over the ground more rapidly than is consistent with safety. For your sake—as well as for ours—the piece should be carefully done." Boucicault later told Stuart Robson that Harte was "a great man and a damned fool." Not surprisingly, Boucicault and Harte apparently failed to finish the script; certainly it was never produced.

On September 8—ironically, only a week after he was supposed to hand a finished play to Daly—Harte also signed a contract with Elisha Bliss to write a novel for the American Publishing Company of Hartford, the subscription house that had issued Clemens's *The Innocents Abroad* and *Roughing It.* (Clemens, a director of the company, had lobbied Bliss on Harte's behalf.) The novel, eventually entitled *Gabriel Conroy,* also featured some of Harte's *Overland* characters, including the gambler Jack Hamlin, the stage driver Yuba Bill, and Colonel Starbottle, whose inflated rhetoric and bombastic style of speech anticipates the vaudeville humor of W. C. Fields. The contract specified that Harte would receive a 7 $\frac{1}{2}$ percent royalty on American sales and 10 percent on British sales of the book.

Barely a year after his removal from the West at the height of his popularity, Harte also tried to salvage his fortunes by capitalizing on his celebrity. His name was still bankable, whatever the demand for his published work. He earned most of his income

for over two years after the expiration of his contract with
Osgood, in fact, by delivering his lecture "The Argonauts of
'49" by his own (exaggerated?) estimate as many as 150 times
around the country. The western humorist Sam W. Smith burlesqued Harte's recent career reversals about this time in his
poem "The Judge's Poetic Venture":

> But my friend, Mr. Harte,
> After making his start,
> Became a great poet contractor;
> Was to furnish the brain
> For an Atlantic train,
> That's run by a huge Boston factor.
>
> On his getting down east,
> His talent thar ceased,
> But he played out his hand on a bluff,
> Soon found in that climate,
> His muse wouldn't rhyme it,
> So, onrolling my bundle of stuff,
>
> He run that thro' the mill,
> The huge contract to fill,
> But the critics went after him lots,
> And 'twas in the end,
> That my talented friend
> Went to reading about Argonauts.

Harte's lecture was carefully crafted to exploit his reputation
as a western writer and popular historian of the gold rush,
which was "a crusade without a cross, an exodus without a
prophet," as he announced in the peroration. "It is not a pretty
story; I do not know that it is even instructive; I do not know
that it is strictly true." He then spent the next hour or so
regaling his audience with patronizing anecdotes about "the
lawless, irreligious band" who migrated to the mines from the
States. "In distant parts of the continent they had left families,
creditors, and in some instances even officers of justice, per-
plexed and lamenting. There were husbands who had deserted

their own wives,—and in some extreme cases even the wives of others,—for this haven of refuge." The fictional figures of Yuba Bill and John Oakhurst both reappeared in the lecture, and occasionally Harte recited "Plain Language from Truthful James" at its close. In all, "The Argonauts of '49" seems like a bricolage of his "legitimate" art. Harte wrote it, as the *Boston Advertiser* observed, "in the style of the sketches which first made him famous."

Harte contracted with the James Redpath agency of Boston in August 1872 to schedule his lectures, and by rights he should have prospered under Redpath's management. The agency specialized in booking popular authors on the lyceum circuit, and among the literary figures in Redpath's stable over the years were Emerson, Thoreau, Clemens, Whittier, Dickens, Howe, and Josh Billings. Redpath had wooed Harte after his arrival in the East with a short poetical tribute entitled "The New Evangel" ("St. Matthew's played out and St. Luke's no account, / It takes our St. Bret holy deeds to recount"). Much as Harte routinely quarreled with the middlemen of literary production throughout his career, however, he soon began to feud with Redpath over the conditions under which he would appear on the platform. On November 1, as he later complained, he received a list of engagements Redpath had scheduled for him that "were totally at variance" with the conditions he had laid down, specifically the distances he would need to travel and the fees he would receive. (Whatever amount he may have demanded from the agent, his regular fee soon became $150 per lecture, from which he paid his own expenses.) Harte forced a showdown with Redpath over these issues by insisting he cancel his first scheduled lectures, in Hartford on November 12 and at the Boston Music Hall on November 13.

Instead, like Ah Sin, Redpath turned the tables on Harte. Not only did he refuse to cancel these appearances, he booked Oliver Wendell Holmes to replace him in Boston and he publicly excoriated Harte for his failure to honor their agreement. "This is the third time that 'the Heathen Chinee' has insulted a Boston audience," Redpath declared from the Music Hall stage, alluding to Harte's earlier failure to appear at the reunion of the Grand Army of the Potomac and his disappointing performance at the Harvard commencement, "and I think it is time this man was taught his place." Harte claimed in a letter to the *Boston Advertiser* a few days later that Redpath was to blame for the fiasco because he had continued to publicize the lecture and permitted the audience "to gather to hear a man who he knew would be absent." On his part, Redpath replied that Harte's lecture in Boston was scheduled independently from his lyceum tour and that he had been so cavalier in honoring past engagements that he apparently regarded "managers and audiences as if they were a gang of plantation hands." Though Harte privately claimed Redpath had learned "that I am worth more than he thought," Redpath bested Harte in this exchange and would sue him for unpaid commissions at the close of the 1872–73 lyceum season, eventually settling out of court for $205.

Unfortunately, this was not the only embarrassment Harte suffered during his career on the boards. Like a theatrical company rehearsing a play out of town before opening on Broadway, he tested his lecture in Springfield, Massachusetts, on November 25, Baltimore on November 29, and Albany on December 3 before risking the slings and arrows of critics and audiences in Boston and New York. The early notices, or lack thereof, were not encouraging. His debut in Springfield was marred by his delivery of the lecture in an "inadequate voice" and the "destructive echoes of the city hall," according to the *Springfield Republican;* the brief notice of his Baltimore appearance was buried on the back page of the *Sun;* and his lecture in Albany was entirely ignored by the local press, save for the paid advertising.

When he arrived at Tremont Temple in Boston to lecture on the evening of December 13, moreover, a sheriff arrested him on behalf of "an impatient creditor," as Howells put it later. Osgood's partner John Clark, with whom the Hartes were staying, "gave his individual note on demand to liquidate the bill and release the prisoner." The sheriff was seated offstage during Harte's lecture and afterwards seized part of the box-

office receipts to satisfy the debt. (Is it possible that Harte canceled his Boston date the previous month to avoid the demands
of this creditor?) Ironically, Harte delivered his lecture "with
beautiful *aplomb* and untroubled charm. He was indeed the
only one privy to the law's presence who was not in the least
affected by it." Howells thought to spare Harte some embarrassment by making light of the incident: "Well, Harte, this is
the old literary tradition; this is the Fleet business over again."
He need not have been so sensitive, however. Harte "joyously
smote his thigh and crowed out, 'Yes, the Fleet!'" and "tasted
all the delicate humor of the situation." Annie Fields observed
in her diary, however, that "his wife was with him and it was a
bad scene." After the lecture, Anna Harte came to the Fields'
home on Charles Street "in much distress."

Against all odds, Harte's lecture in Boston was a critical if not
a commercial success. Normally a mediocre speaker, he apparently rose to the occasion, perhaps because he had refined his
delivery of the lecture during its out-of-town trials. As the *Boston
Post* noted the next day, Harte spoke "in a pleasant, graceful
and easy conversational tone," and to judge from "the lavish
expressions of delight" by the audience, "the lecture was a thorough success." The *Boston Transcript* also noted that Harte
"made a very favorable impression" with the lecture, "holding
the interest of his large audience to its close." Both the *Boston
Journal* ("much amusement") and the *Daily Globe* ("unusual
pleasure") puffed the lecture in their columns. James Fields, who
introduced Harte, assured him two days later that the audience
had included "artists, clergymen—chaps with brains" who
"applauded your wisdom and humour." According to Fields,
"they are all of one opinion—that you cannot be beaten! . . . In
short they swore so good a lecture, so delightful a speaker, had
not been produced on that platform for many a year!" Fields
urged the lecturer to "look sharp and see that your fee is as high
as that of any old and popular stager in the country," and Harte
assured Fields in reply that "my agent is quietly informing the
country lyceums, with a circular and notices, what they are
losing."

Harte repeated the lecture at Steinway Hall in New York on December 16 and at the Brooklyn Tabernacle the next evening, again to critical acclaim. By all accounts Harte genuinely entertained and instructed those who heard him speak in New York about "California's Golden Age," even while attired in evening dress and white tie, with gilt studs in his shirt and a watch chain across his vest. According to the *New York Tribune,* Harte handled his subject "as no other man living could have done it." The New York *World* reported that the "lecture was a good portrayal of California life in good old times," and the *Brooklyn Eagle* compared it to Harte's "best printed prose." The New York *Evening Post* praised the lecture without stint: "Harte constantly reminded us of the best passages of his prose, or recalled that masterly touch of his verse." He "has achieved a decided hit on the platform, and may choose between lecturing and literature hereafter with a certain confidence of success in either."

Unfortunately, Harte could never afterwards duplicate his stage successes in Boston and New York. Between December 23 and January 15 he lectured in Elmira, Hartford, Washington, Pittsburgh, and Newark to decidedly uneven reviews. The critic for the *Hartford Courant* was blunt: Harte's delivery "was not sympathetic and undemonstrative to a fault." The lecture itself "suffers somewhat from its construction. The thoughts and phrases that should connect its different parts are often wanting, at other times not ingeniously put in." The *Pittsburgh Daily Gazette* was even more outspoken: Harte "seldom looked up for any length of time from his manuscript," which he read in a monotone. Some "inconsiderate and ill-mannered auditors" even left the hall before Harte had finished. His lecture "could not be called a success. . . . Harte is more in his element as a writer than a platform speaker." Clemens, who heard Harte in Hartford, wrote that he "has an excellent lecture this season, & reads it execrably." Unlike the westerners, including Clemens, who perfected a brand of deadpan humor in their performances, as William Rideing remembered, Harte "often spoiled his stories as he told them in his lectures . . . by laughing himself, before his audiences had time to."

Part of the problem with Harte's delivery may have been that, while traveling alone on his lecture tours, he was prone to drink heavily. His letters to his family during this period are filled with laments: "I felt dreadfully lonely on my Washington trip," he wrote Anna from the Monongahela House in Pittsburgh on January 9, 1873. "I am usually tired out when I arrive in any town," "depressed in spirits," "very blue and low toned," he elsewhere complained. He often retired to the hotel bar under such circumstances. He also used liquor for medicinal purposes on the road, or so he purported: he lived, he said, "on beef-tea and champagne while lecturing. An hour or two before I speak I find great relief and strength in bathing my chest and arms with bay rum." Before falling to sleep, as he wrote his sister Eliza, "I breathe a silent blessing on Leibig and that dear old monk, Dom Perignon." The publisher Henry Harper once remembered that he had seen Harte "shaking up cocktails" before a lecture, and Howells later allowed that he had been "notorious for drinking" during these months. Annie Fields saw Harte, "cigar in mouth," in Dutton's bookstore in New York in mid-March 1873 and observed in her diary that "his face shows the wrinkles of too much smoking if not ruder dissipations." A newspaper correspondent who crossed his path in Washington in mid-November 1874 described him as an "old-young man" with "heavy" eyes and "reddened" lids.

Part of the problem, too, may have been that Harte simply did not dress the part of a rustic westerner in his public appearances. Unlike Joaquin Miller, who paraded in sombrero and pantaloons, and unlike Clemens, who was adept at many types and styles of performance, Harte simply failed to play to type. His auditors expected a droll humorist in a boiled shirt, and instead they got a soft-spoken dandy. As the Pittsburgh critic remarked, "Those who had expected to see a physical illustration of an 'Argonaut' were most grievously disappointed," for Harte wore "a suit of black broadcloth" and "a waistcoat, cut low, to expose an amplitude of linen, set off with a glittering diamond pin and jewelry, of the most pronounced character; altogether the appearance of the poet was that of one who has paid some attention to the demands of fashion." Jeanette Gilder recalled that, during his visit to Newark, Harte was outfitted in a "long ulster and peaked astrachan fur cap set jauntily on the side of his head, as was the fashion of the day." Years later, Harte admitted he had utterly confounded audience expectations:

> What the people expected in me I do not know, possibly a six-foot mountaineer, with a voice and lecture in proportion. They always seemed to have mentally confused me with one of my own characters. I am not six feet high, and I do not wear a beard. Whenever I walked out before a strange audience there was a general sense of disappointment, a gasp of astonishment that I could feel, and it always took at least fifteen minutes before they recovered from their surprise sufficiently to listen to what I had to say. I think, even now, that if I had been more herculean in proportions, with a red shirt and top boots, many of the audience would have felt a deeper thrill from my utterances and a deeper conviction that they had obtained the worth of their money.

As in Newport, Harte preferred genteel fashion and respectability to vulgar dress and vernacular style. The problem was exacerbated when, after exhausting the market for his lecture in the major eastern cities, he began to carry it to such midwestern and southern towns as Atchison, Evansville, and Selma. In these venues, among more rural audiences, he was extremely overdressed, in stark contrast to the miners whose adventures he chronicled and with whom he was invariably identified.

Like many other writers of the period, Harte was also compelled, in the absence of strong copyright laws, to fend off literary pirates who tried to capitalize on his fame. The false attribution to him of such works as "The Fate of a Fighting Dog" was a minor irritation compared to more blatant violations of his literary rights. In September 1872 Harte consulted Stephen Walker, Osgood's Boston attorney, about the sale of cheap reprints of *Condensed Novels* and *That Heathen Chinee and Other Poems (Mostly Humorous)* published in London by John Camden Hotten and imported into the United States through

Canada. In February Hotten assured Harte that he was "anxious to give you a financial interest in the sale of your books here in England, & if you will re-edit them for me I am prepared to pay you whatever is equitable." Nothing came of this proposal save Hotten's unauthorized sale in England of a new volume entitled *Stories of the Sierras* that contained Harte's *Overland* tales with an appended story by Joaquin Miller. Harte tried to block Hotten's piracies by contracting with a Toronto bookseller, Adam, Stevenson and Company, to issue "the only authorized and complete edition of my works in Great Britain and Canada." This maneuver failed, however, so Harte and Osgood successfully sued in federal court in May 1872 to restrain the sale of Hotten's reprints in the United States. As early as 1873, moreover, Harte's stories were available in multiple German translations, and his books far outsold those of any other American writer, including Clemens, in Germany. Not surprisingly, Harte became an outspoken advocate of international copyright; in 1885 he would sign a memorial sent to Congress: "I am in favor of any and all legislation that recognizes the equal rights of any and all authors to their own property in any and all countries."

Harte was even more dismayed in the spring of 1873 by another swindle perpetrated in his name by his old friend and editor Joe Lawrence of the *Golden Era*. Lawrence began to reprint Harte's 1863 version of "M'liss" in his paper in March 1873—and to increase subscriptions he promised that "the story, which never got beyond the sixteenth chapter [in Harte's version], will be continued to the end." Lawrence had hired the local writer Gilbert S. Densmore, best known today for his unauthorized dramatization of Clemens's *The Gilded Age,* to "finish" in sixty-two chapters what he implied Harte had left undone in the first sixteen. Whereas Harte's original story about M'liss, "The Work on Red Mountain," serialized in four parts in the *Golden Era* in 1860, ran to about 10,000 words and his revised 1863 "M'liss" to about 25,000 words, Densmore's "completion" ran to about 160,000 words. Harte wrote a card protesting this forgery to the San Francisco *Bulletin,* whose editors not only failed to print it but defended the *Golden Era* in their columns.

"While the obvious plan of the original fragment [sic] is adhered to," the *Bulletin* noted, Densmore "strikes out into new paths of invention, creates several new characters, and to all intents and purposes makes a new story." Harte asked Osgood to "frighten them by copyright," to no avail. Worse yet, the Densmore "completion," listing Harte as the author, was published as a 148-page book in the fall of 1873 by Robert M. DeWitt of New York. On page 34, where Harte's story ends, DeWitt inserted a note to the reader: "The remainder of this story was written by another hand than Bret Harte, but it will be found equally interesting and able."

Harte was infuriated by "this most patent fraud." As he wrote R. R. Bowker, literary editor of the New York *Evening Mail*, "I shall push the matter to an end, as I am somewhat oppressed by the monotony of the various outrages to which my literary good name and property have been subjected." Clemens had recently fought literary pirates by contending that "Mark Twain" was not simply a pseudonym but a brand name. Similarly, Harte sued DeWitt in late December to enjoin the further sale of Densmore's *M'liss* on the grounds that this use of his name, which he regarded as a trademark, infringed on his "rights in such trademark" and injured his "reputation as an author." Harte did not raise the copyright issue, conceding that he had forfeited all copyright to the original chapters he had published in the *Golden Era*. The New York Supreme Court justice who heard the case agreed with the argument made by Harte's lawyer: "The case seems to me to be analogous to that of a trade-mark." The New York press, no less than the law, also sided with the plaintiff. The *New York Times* agreed that "a great wrong" had been inflicted on Harte, who "is advertised as the author" of a "vile" book. Bowker editorialized that "Harte seems to have been selected by the piratical craft from all quarters as a favorite prize."

Even as he was protecting his name, Harte was fighting a rear-guard action to defend his reputation. Whereas his literary standing went up like a rocket in 1870–71, it fell like a stick in 1872–73. On December 15, 1872, only two days after the backstage debacle following his lecture in Boston, the poet W. A. Kendall published on page one, column one, of the San Francisco *Chronicle* one of the most damning articles about Harte to appear during his lifetime. A former contributor to both the *Californian* and the *Overland,* Kendall claimed that while still living in California Harte had been "a loose and not infrequent borrower of considerable sums" of money, despite his generous income, "and then a cool ignorer of the gracious loaners." In addition, he accused Harte of swindling contributors to the *Overland* by skimming their payment. "If the eminent editor of an eminent magazine may indulge in such nefarious pilfering of contributors with impunity," Kendall wondered, "who is deserving of public reprobation, and for what are the whips of justice braided?" Since Harte had left California, according to Kendall, he had disappointed the public, mortified his friends, and humiliated himself.

Predictably, Harte was outraged when he read this article a few days after it appeared. "I have been lately pretty well abused from unexpected sources," he wrote Clemens, but Kendall's fusillade "caps the climax. . . . I don't mind his slander; that I can refute— but how am I to make this dog know he is a dog and not a man?" Ironically, Clemens cited this article as proof of Harte's perfidy almost six years later in an ill-tempered letter to Howells when his own relations with Harte were at their lowest ebb.

Between late February and mid-April 1873, Harte was touring with "The Argonauts of '49" almost incessantly, from Toronto, Detroit, East Saginaw, and Cleveland, to Brooklyn, New York, Ottawa, Montreal, then to Louisville, Wheeling, and Harrisonburg, Virginia. He briefly considered the idea of taking the lecture to London and the principal cities of Great Britain, but his engagements in the Midwest were simply not as profitable as they might have been. The winter was particularly severe, which both depressed attendance and complicated Harte's travel plans. He was forced to hire a special train to carry him from Hamilton to Toronto, dressing "in the cars at the rate of 60 miles an hour—the most rapid and extraordinary toilette I ever made," arriving at the hall an hour and a half after he was scheduled to speak. Two nights later, his train to Detroit also broke down, "and although I had given myself 3 hours lee-way" he was again late for his lecture. In Ottawa he spoke twice "but the whole thing was a pecuniary failure," as he wrote Anna. "There was scarcely enough money to pay expenses and of course nothing to pay me with." In March he "unavoidably postponed" a lecture in New York for ten days and canceled another date in Buffalo. Railing west in early April, he missed an engagement in Hudson, Ohio, because his train took "forty nine hours coming from New York to Cleveland. . . . From Syracuse to Rochester we literally felt our way along—the track being hidden below two feet of water and floating ice and railroad ties, and the engine fires narrowly escaping being put out." Though he telegraphed the lyceum committee in Hudson to explain his cancellation, the *Cleveland Plain Dealer* reported the next day that "Bret is famous as an engagement breaker." His petulant cancellation of the Redpath dates early in the season would not soon be forgotten.

The notices of his lectures in these cities were typically polite but restrained, moreover. According to the *Toronto Mail*, "Bret Harte can scarcely be called a lecturer, nor is he even a reader." His voice "betokened excessive fatigue," and his speech "fell from him as though he deprecated the doing of it." The audience greeted the close of a pathetic anecdote "with laughter. Applause would not have been out of place, but it was entirely the fault of the lecturer that in a great crowd many mistook the sublime for the ridiculous." Harte even delivered the lecture, to the dismay of this critic, in a down-east accent, betraying "peculiarities of diction that he did not pick up between Poker Flat and Lone Mountain." The *Wheeling Daily Intelligencer* also remarked on the "somewhat languid manner" of his delivery. The *Montreal Gazette* lambasted the lecture in no uncertain terms:

> To be perfectly candid . . . it is hardly up to the standard of the author's other writings. It lacks that individualization which constitutes the charm of Mr. Harte's more popular compositions. Certainly, if the author were judged of by this lecture, he would hardly occupy the rank among satirists which he now enjoys.

Little wonder that, as his friend Pemberton later reported, Harte "always hated the platform."

That summer and fall he returned to his writing desk, dashing off a trio of dialect poems and three personal essays for the *New York Tribune* and a pair of stories and a poem for *Scribner's*. In late December 1872, at the invitation of his friend Whitelaw Reid, who had assumed control of the *Tribune* after Horace Greeley's death, he vowed that "I really want to connect myself in ever so humble a fashion with The Tribune." (Of course he had also indicated to Elisha Bliss only four days before that "I am, by the terms of my contract, bound to you, exclusive of any other purely literary work.") The short essays he sent the *Tribune* are unremarkable save for the undeniable fact they were written barely a year after the expiration of his contract with Osgood. Only one of the three essays, "Bret Harte's Discovery," about a 107-year-old woman in Basking Ridge, New Jersey, who remembered George Washington, was collected in his complete writings. The other two pieces, one about a visit to the house in Morristown where Washington was headquartered during the Jersey campaign of 1777, the other the report of a college boat race in Springfield, Massachusetts, in mid-July, were utterly forgettable journalistic fluff.

In Springfield he stayed with his old friend Sam Bowles, and after the race he went to the offices of the *Springfield Republican* to file his story. He worked until after midnight on the dispatch. "He did not enjoy his commission, and frankly said so," one of the *Republican* staffers remembered. "Those who saw him labor obtained the settled conviction that daily newspaper work was quite too sudden" for him. "Bret Harte isn't used to the newspaper pace," Reid privately conceded a day or two later. Even such modest production was sufficiently newsworthy to be mentioned among the "literary notes" in the New York *Evening Mail* in October: "Bret Harte is at work again." His story "An Episode of Fiddletown" was serialized in *Scribner's* between August and October; part of the manuscript of his Christmas story for the magazine, "A Monte Flat Pastoral," was "already in the printer's hands"; and he had completed a long dialect poem entitled "Luke," which was "said to be very characteristic, delicate and tender." Though his reputation was tarnished, Harte still commanded reasonably high prices: he sold poems to the *Tribune* for one hundred dollars each, and *Scribner's* paid him one thousand dollars for the "Fiddletown" serial (over over fifty dollars per printed page) and five hundred dollars for "A Monte Flat Pastoral" (over seventy dollars per page).

Still, he was unable to support his family in the style to which he had become accustomed with the sale of a few stories and poems. So in October he set out for the West for three weeks, the longest lecture tour he ever made, opening in Chicago, where he spoke at the Kingsbury Music Hall on the 14th. He had not been to Chicago since his ill-fated pass through the city in February 1871, but fortunately this second trip was not so controversial as the first. The *Chicago Inter-Ocean* rehearsed the old grounds for civic complaint against Harte, and while its review of his lecture was generally favorable, it also emphasized that he was no orator: "his voice is not strong enough to give his utterances the effect they might make." The *Chicago Times* also remarked on his "low tone and inaudible expression." Rather than deliver a new lecture entitled "Some Bad People" that he had announced, Harte merely read his lecture from the season before, a fact noted by many papers along Harte's route ("we had the pleasure of reading that lecture, *verbatim ad literatim,* in the New York *Tribune* lecture series, nearly a year ago"). Still, Harte genuinely enjoyed his stop in Chicago. "I have no words to describe the lordly and magnificent conceit of rebuilt Chicago" after the Great Fire, he reported to Anna.

Moreover, the local publishers Carpenter and Sheldon, under whose auspices Harte lectured in Chicago, inquired a few weeks later whether he might be enticed to settle there and edit a new magazine they were planning—that is, they offered him the same opportunity he had fumbled away two years before. Harte was interested—under the right circumstances. "I have always believed that the West offered an excellent field for an original, first-rate magazine that should be purely and distinctively American," he replied, and "I have always been ready and am now to take the literary charge of such a venture." However, he insisted, it could not be merely a local magazine "patronized by Chicago interests." To survive, a magazine edited and published in Chicago would need to be supported by "subscriptions outside of Chicago, by St. Louis, by Cincinnati, by Omaha, by San Francisco." Would "Chicago Capitalists" subscribe at least one hundred thousand dollars to start such a magazine? Harte doubted it, though if his sponsors could arrange financing,

> I will be ready to take the helm at any moment. As I should have to give myself up to it completely, and remove to Chicago, I could not do this [for] under $10,000 a year—irrespective of my contributions in the way of a serial novel or sketches for which I should expect my usual price, guaranteeing only that no article of mine should appear elsewhere. I would be willing to take a part of the $10,000 in an interest or share in the magazine. But I have no money to invest in it otherwise.

Predictably, given Harte's conditions and reservations, nothing came of this proposal.

Four days after speaking in Chicago, Harte inaugurated the fall lyceum course in St. Louis to the same refrain of criticism. The *St. Louis Globe* reported that Harte was "no orator," with a voice "hardly strong enough" to fill Mercantile Hall, and the *Missouri Republican* similarly remarked that Harte, "in full dress costume with spotless linen and diamond studs," delivered his lecture with such "gentle and elegant languor" that "fully one-half of the people failed to catch the discourse." Overall, the lecture by "the Spanish looking exquisite" was "an extremely dull affair." In his room at the Southern Hotel, Harte privately fumed to Anna at the

> style of criticism which my lecture—or rather myself as lecturer has received. . . . I certainly never expected to be mainly criticised for being what *I am not,* a handsome fop—but this assertion is at the bottom of all the criticism. They may be right—I dare say they are—in asserting that I am no orator, have no special faculty for speaking—no fire, dramatic earnestness or expression, but when

they intimate that I am running on my good looks, save the mark! I confess I get hopelessly furious. You will be amused to hear that my gold "studs" have again become "diamonds," my worn out shirts "faultless linen," my haggard face that of a "Spanish-looking exquisite," my habitual quiet and "used up" way, "gentle and elegant languor."

Given his mounting debts, however, Harte could not simply suspend the "hard, wearisome trip" in disgust.

Instead, he lectured thirteen times over the next two weeks in Topeka, Atchison, Lawrence, Kansas City, St. Joseph, Omaha, Des Moines, Davenport, Bloomington, South Bend, Ann Arbor, Delaware, and Cadiz, Ohio. "A sensible man lectures," as Clemens once avowed, "when butter & bread are scarce." Harte wrote about a hundred pages of his Christmas story for *Scribner's* while on the trains during the day, but, as he explained to his sister Eliza, "I am almost exhausted with traveling all day and lecturing each night." He later vented some of his frustrations in his little sketch "A Sleeping-Car Experience," in which he wondered "why it would not be as well to sit up all night half asleep in an ordinary passenger-car as to lie awake all night in a Pullman" sleeping car.

When he was stranded fifteen miles from Atchison four hours before his lecture was scheduled to begin because his train broke down en route from Topeka, he hired a horse, strapped his lecture to his back, "and so tore off" across the prairie. "You can imagine the savage, half-sick utterly disgusted man who glared at that audience over his desk that night, and d----d them inwardly in his heart," he wrote Anna. His train to Ann Arbor was also delayed by a blizzard, and so he arrived three hours late. He worried constantly about missing a train, which might in turn cause him to "lose a 1/2 dozen engagements." To reach Cadiz from Delaware, Ohio, he "was obliged to ride 24 miles at midnight in a buggy to Columbus," which he did not reach until 5 A.M., "and then without rest or food I took the cars," arriving in Cadiz only "an hour before the lecture. It was the last straw that almost broke the camel's back for I had been without sleep for the previous 48 hours. But I won. I have not broken or lost a single engagement in my 3000 miles of travel."

Five years later, he remembered that he had "travelled in the dead of winter from New York to Omaha 2000 miles, with the thermometer varying from 10° to 25° below zero." Nor did he earn as much money as he had hoped—his expenses were "very great—the West is another California for high prices even in railroad fares"—and his lecture was no better received toward the end of the tour than at its start. The Lawrence *Republican Daily Journal* initially declared that it "realized the highest anticipations" of Harte's "most sanguine admirers," only to retract the compliment the next day: "We find that a large portion of the public" was "disappointed," that the lecture was too much "pose and polish and prettiness." The *Kansas City Times* also complained the lecture was "wanting in novelty and interest"; the *St. Joseph Daily Gazette* urged him "to drop his attempt at polished rhetoric and be more of an Argonaut"; the *Iowa State Register* concluded that "Harte as a lecturer is a dead failure" and that "the hundreds of dollars Mr. Harte's lecture cost Des Moines would have procured many better lectures from our home talent"; the *Daily Davenport Democrat* reported that a "great many" in Harte's audience in that city "were disappointed"; and the *South Bend Tribune* allowed that "he can lay little claim to eloquence." He was fast exhausting his store of accumulated good will and literary capital.

Back in Morristown, Harte spent the winter of 1873–74—in the only house in the town, as he once said, where Washington never slept—plotting his next moves. He wrote a new lecture on "American Humor," which he tried out at the Methodist church in Morristown and in Hornellsville before taking it to New York City in January 1874. Harte took a less anecdotal, more scholarly tack in this new lecture. He rejected the idea that there was a distinctly national humor, insisting "that our later American humorists are not so much purely American as they are modern." He praised the breed of western humorists, especially Orpheus C. Kerr, Petroleum V. Nasby, Artemus Ward, and his friend Clemens, who "stands alone as the most original humorist that America has yet produced." Harte is known to have delivered this lecture only five times, however, probably because it was not well received. The lecture "wasn't worth listening to," one critic suggested. "The impression which it left was that it was a careless piece of hack-work, gotten up simply to be advertised on the bills." Harte eventually misplaced the only script of the lecture—he wrote Anna frantically in July 1879 to ask whether it was "among the papers you discovered. I cannot find it among my things *here,* and it is of great importance to me." Unfortunately, no copy of it survives, though after Harte's death Charles Meeker Kozlay partially reconstructed it from news reports. Not surprisingly, during a quick tour of upstate New York in early March 1874 Harte merely reprised his old "Argonauts" lecture.

Throughout 1874 he was scrambling for cash, peddling stories and poems like feet in an overworked mine to the Sunday feuilleton of the *New York Times* and other papers. He experimented with juvenile stories, publishing a Disneyesque tale about a lovable grizzly cub entitled "Baby Sylvester" in Mabel Mapes Dodge's magazine *St. Nicholas.* In April he sold his story "The Rose of Tuolumne" to the *Times* for $600 and regretted only that he had failed to ask $750 for it. He conceded to Anna that "my great needs I think frightened me" into settling for less. The *Newark Advertiser* called this sentimental tale of young, unrequited, sacrificial love Harte's "best production" since "his advent in the East" and expressed the hope that "he may overcome the *dolce far niente* enough to continue at work." In June Harte sold "A Passage in the Life of Mr. John Oakhurst" to the *Times* for $500 and confessed to Clemens that he again "might have asked and got more I dare say." He claimed later that he wrote the story in a single night, outlining it while sitting on a bench one afternoon in Washington Square, beginning to trick it out after dinner, and finishing it before breakfast the next morning.

Under the press of mounting debts, that is, his methods of composition had changed dramatically since his days with the *Overland,* when he had spent hours rewriting a single sentence.

He also tried to make amends with Osgood by selling him a dramatic monologue, "For the King," at a bargain price. Though Harte assessed its value at $400 "were I to offer it for sale," he was willing for it to appear in the *Atlantic* in order "to adjust the little differences which exist between us in regard to my performance, and a recognition of and atonement for my delay in execution" under the terms of their earlier contract. Of course he also drew $340 on his account with Osgood even before sending the manuscript to him; in effect, that is, he offered the poem to Osgood after he had been paid for it.

Unfortunately, much as he had objected to Howells's editing of "Concepcion de Arguellö" in March 1872, Harte took umbrage at Howells's changes to the poem he was selling cheap to the *Atlantic:*

> I'm sorry you should have all this trouble, my dear fellow, but it is not really of my making. So little do I value that kind of criticism wh[ich] you have, I know in perfect goodness, indicated I might receive for these irregularities, that I would have been perfectly satisfied had you printed the poem as I sent it. . . . I know, my dear Howells, that your suggestions are kindly, but it vexes me sorely that even in kindness, you should voice the 'blameless prigism' of a certain kind of criticism. If you find any more errors leave them,— dear boy,—to give a flavor of originality to the poem.

Ironically, after the press reported that Harte received $400 from the *Atlantic* for the poem, "a poet cut me dead in the street, and afterwards wrote a savage *critique* in wh[ich] he endeavored to show how much a line I asked and that it wasn't worth the money." Even at such extravagant prices, Harte lamented to Clemens, "I make barely a decent living by my work in the magazines. Please God, with my novel—if I ever get it done—I'll be able to pay my debts and lay something by." The *Springfield Republican,* once his staunch ally, also savaged the poem, alleging it was little more than a pale imitation of Robert Browning's "The Statue and the Bust," that "in the exhaustion of his own vineyard" Harte had begun to steal "purple clusters" from others' vines. Even Louise Chandler

Moulton, who regarded Harte as "a man of true and independent genius," conceded that he erred by donning "the singing-robes of Mr. Robert Browning."

In July 1874 he finally began to write the novel he had contracted to write for Bliss two years before. He mailed the first forty-nine pages of manuscript—"the hardest work I have done"—to Hartford in midsummer. "I have written about 350 pp. to make this beggarly 49," he complained, and he hoped "with the Prologue done and the story fairly launched I shall get on faster. Otherwise it wont pay. Meanwhile how am I to live?—I've been a month at 50 pp." The answer, simply put, was that Harte relied on Bliss to bankroll him. He periodically touched the publisher for advances over the next year as he finished the novel. As Clemens remembered, "About once a month Harte would get into desperate straits; then he would dash off enough manuscript to set him temporarily free and carry it to Bliss and get a royalty advance." On at least one occasion, Clemens interceded on behalf of his friend. Bliss subsequently sent Clemens a chapter of the novel in manuscript as security, noting on the back that the money was charged to him. By the end of 1874 Harte had, by his own estimate, finished about two-thirds of the novel. His advances on royalties would eventually total about $3,600.

Harte's anxiety, desperation even, during these months may be inferred from his bizarre negotiations to sell a new comic love story, "The Fool of Five Forks." In early September he carried the manuscript to New York and spent two days trying to dispose of it. "The best offer I had was $350 from *Scribner*," and Harte thought "I ought to get more," so he "telegraphed to Howells to know if he could give $500." Despite their vexed relations, Howells had again invited Harte to become an exclusive contributor to the *Atlantic*, albeit at a much lower salary than the one he was paid when he first arrived in the East, and Harte had just sold his poem "Ramon" to the magazine for the below-bargain price of $125. Howells replied in good faith that "any story by you or any other writer would not be worth $500" sight unseen, "but a particular story might be worth that sum," and he asked Harte to forward the manuscript to him for examination "before asking the publishers"—Hurd and Houghton had recently acquired the magazine from Osgood—"to buy it at an extraordinary price." Furious at the delay, Harte forwarded Howells's letter to Anna in Morristown. "I must *wait now until I see what they write*," he groused. "I shall have to take any price I can get." In the end Howells was apparently so unimpressed with the story that Henry Houghton made only a token offer of $150 for it, precipitating Harte's final break with the *Atlantic*. His pride wounded, he wrote Howells in a tone of bitter scorn:

> When I tell you that, since my arrival East, I have never received so small an offer for any story as that made to me by Mr Houghton; that the lowest offer from any magazine or newspaper was $150 *more* than his, and that before sending it to you I had already refused $450 [sic] for the *MS* that I might make it the basis of terms with the *Atlantic*, you can readily imagine that I was considerably exasperated, and I think justly so, to have waited a week for such a reply.

Harte sold the story to the *New York Times* for $400, he reported, "which was all I asked for it from them. . . . I had no time to spend nor inclination to hawk my wares further, so I contented myself with losing $50 and a weeks time for the pleasure of knowing Mr Houghton's valuation of my services in the *Atlantic*." "I dont blame you, my dear Howells, and I believe you acted conscientiously and for my best," he added, "but I do wish you lived out of a literary atmosphere which seems to exclude any vision of a broader literary world beyond,—its methods, profits and emoluments."

As if in oblique reply, Howells soon suggested in his review of *Echoes of the Foothills* in the *Atlantic* that since he had become famous Harte's craftmanship had deteriorated: His "verse is more slovenly and seems more wantonly careless." Harte never sent another manuscript to the *Atlantic* and, though he had helped save the magazine from financial failure in 1871, he was conspicuously absent from the famous Whittier birthday dinner in Boston sponsored by the *Atlantic* in December 1877. By then, living on credit and very nearly on the street, Harte was crossed off many a guest list. On his part, Howells turned to Clemens when his "Bret Harte negotiations" collapsed and offered him twenty dollars per page for a series of articles published in the magazine in 1875 under the title "Old Times on the Mississippi." When "The Fool of Five Forks" was announced as forthcoming in the *Times*, Bliss complained to Harte that he should be devoting all of his time to the novel. Harte offered a characteristic defense: "Dont blame me, if, when I can get $400 for *retouching* an old story of 40 pages, I do it to eke out my expenses, which go on while I am with difficulty grinding out an elaborate and entirely new work on which my reputation is to be based—for $250 per 100 pp."

To his credit, Harte wrote one story during these months for reasons not entirely crass: "Wan Lee, the Pagan" in *Scribner's* for September 1874. He drew his premise from personal experience; indeed, this tale was the first one he had written set in San Francisco since moving east. In his "California Letters" to the *Springfield Republican* in February 1867 and March 1868, Harte had deplored the "late riots and outrages on the Chinese," and how "the youth" of San Francisco "throw stones" at the Chinese "in the streets," and he returned to the race issue in the story. The Chinese boy Wan Lee, who is apprenticed to the narrator, befriends a young white girl, and Harte hints at the racial toleration of children. In its final paragraphs, however, the story veers away from a sentimental denouement. "There were two days," the narrator abruptly observes, "which will be long remembered in San Francisco,—two days when a mob of her citizens set upon and killed unarmed, defenceless foreigners because they were foreigners, and another race, religion, and color, and worked for what wages they could get." The innocent Wan Lee was "stoned to death in the streets of San Francisco" by "a mob of half-grown boys and Christian school-children." Unlike Harte's poem "Plain Language from Truthful James," which was liable, when misread, to reinforce anti-Chinese prejudice, "Wan Lee, the Pagan" was unambiguous in its condemnation of race hatred. Tom Hood in *Fun* thought it was written in

Harte's "best form." Of course such a story hardly endeared him to California. Not that it mattered—he had long since burned his bridges.

Nevertheless, by 1874 he seemed trapped in a cycle of self-parody by the demands of the literary market. The San Francisco *Alta California,* in a retrospective of his career since leaving the West, concluded that he "has shown no disposition for exertion; he contents himself with working over old material into new shape, without important variation; or he writes little squibs that indicate no power." When the rumor surfaced in the New York and Boston press that, through influential friends, he had been offered a position in the New York Custom House (where he would have become Herman Melville's coworker) at an annual salary of three thousand dollars "as a relief from pecuniary embarrassments," Harte felt obliged to deny it publicly: "I have always found my profession sufficiently lucrative and, but for the gossip suggested as the origin of such a statement, quite as honorable and manly as any." To be sure, he would seek such a government job as an escape from insolvency and grinding debt soon enough, but for the moment he was still able to hold his creditors at bay by trading on his name and literary reputation.

CHAPTER 4

Popularizing the West

Lecture, Novel, Play, Pulp Fiction

BETWEEN late October and mid-November 1874 Harte was on the hustings again across the South. He opened in Louisville on October 26 and traveled east and south for the next three weeks, going to Evansville, Nashville, Atlanta, Augusta, Milledgeville, Macon, Montgomery, Selma, Knoxville, and Washington. "I have had occasion to change my views of the South very materially," he reported to Anna, "and from what I have seen am quite satisfied that the North is profoundly ignorant of the real sentiments and condition of the people." Though he had been a rabidly pro-Union poet under the tutelege of Jessie Frémont and Starr King a decade earlier, he sympathized with the plight of Southerners under Reconstruction: "They are so shiftless, so helpless—so like spoiled and petted children—who have been suddenly punished and brought face to face with duty that I cant think of them seriously as men and women." The freed slaves he thought an "innocent, miserable wretched degraded" lot. Even a decade after Appomattox, he was struck by "the spectacle of the utter devastation and ruin brought by the war."

Ironically, though his audiences in the South were smaller than expected, his lectures were critically well received, perhaps because he spoke in smaller halls. To be sure, the reviews contained the usual complaints about his delivery and diction, but they also praised the substance of his "Argonauts" talk; e.g., it was "a finished production" (*Nashville Union*) with "many beautiful pictures and word paintings" (*Atlanta Constitution*). Despite his failings as a speaker, "one cannot listen to him without falling under the charm of his genius" (*Augusta Chronicle and Sentinel*). The "unique and charming lecture" (*Knoxville Press*) was "equal to the best of his inimitable prose sketches" (*Montgomery Advertiser*).

With both his tailor and the family butcher pressing him for payment and Anna in Morristown pregnant with their fifth child, Harte headed west again. He lectured six times in the space of a week in early December 1874, from Saratoga Springs to Gloversville, Buffalo, Jamestown, Chicago, and Madison, Wisconsin, to modestly favorable notices in the *Buffalo Express,* the *Buffalo Courier,* and the *Jamestown Daily Journal.* His lecture on "American Humor" in Chicago was a bust, however. He lectured five times in the space of a week in late January 1875, from Rock Island to Jacksonville, Illinois, then Iowa City, Fort Wayne, and Toledo, once more to modestly favorable notices in the Rock Island *Daily Union* and the *Jacksonville Journal.* After he spoke in Rock Island a Davenport paper reported, much to his disgust, that Harte "was dressed in plain black and his fingers and shirt bosom sparkled with several diamond rings and studs." As he explained to Anna, he had worn "absolutely lustreless, dead white, porcelain buttons" on an open shirtfront, "lest some Western reporters bleared eyes and whisky exalted brain should again deceive him!" So much for precaution. "This kind of work grows more and more laborious to me each time," he allowed, and he "gave up two-thirds" of his western engagements just to appear in Jacksonville and so "save my reputation from Chicago pens." After lecturing in Philadelphia on February 18, he would not speak in public again for nearly four years, though he continued to receive invitations to appear. He was scheduled to speak in Providence as late as November 10, 1875, for example, but he canceled at the last moment, ostensibly on account of illness.

He returned to the manuscript of *Gabriel Conroy* like a thief to the scene of the crime. "I am working exclusively on the novel," he wrote Bliss on February 23, and he depended upon prompt remittances from Hartford as he submitted copy, especially after the birth of his daughter Ethel on March 9, 1875. "I have no draft yet from Bliss," he complained to Anna from New

York on March 16, as he was trying to complete an installment even though

> I am so nervous I can hardly hold a pen. . . . It is hard for me—Nan—but it is worse for you, poor dear girl, alone and sick there [in Morristown]! I would have returned each night, but for the expense and the certainty that my presence there without money would only provoke my creditors. God knows how you are getting on—I dare not think! I am almost beside myself with apprehension.

On April 4, in the midst of this financial crisis, Harte's mother died at his home in Morristown.

Meanwhile, his financial problems literally mounted by the week. He had been sued for $230 by the New York tailors Teets and Throckmorton in July 1874, though he would not satisfy the judgment until, a decade later, the plaintiff petitioned the State Department to intervene. He was also sued in the New York City superior court late in 1874 by the New York haberdashers Lord and Taylor, and the plaintiffs had been awarded about $1,150 on their claim. Harte tried to evade payment on jurisdictional grounds. He lived in New Jersey and earned royalties from a publisher in Massachusetts, he argued, so how could a business in New York garnish his income? Lord and Taylor refiled their suit in Massachusetts, and the dispute dragged on for months. "If it is decided that they can, without separate process, seize all profits that are to accrue on my copyrights present or to come, I shall not trouble myself to provide pabulum for these cormorants," he declared to Osgood on April 18. "I will give up all further publishing in the state of Massachusetts rather than submit to this Yankee gouging." In a miracle of rationalization, Harte accused Lord and Taylor of "hoggishness" because they were not as "patient and obliging" as his other creditors. Finally, on September 4, the Massachusetts supreme court found in favor of Lord and Taylor and ordered Osgood to pay them from "such sums of money as may now be due or hereafter fall due to Harte." Predictably, Harte was outraged, though he would not make good on his threat to stop publishing in Massachusetts. "I have done all a poor man, with a large family, can do toward settling a debt that he cannot pay outright," he whined.

His slow spiral into destitution during these years was arrested briefly during the spring of 1875 by the remittances he received for the fragments of *Gabriel Conroy* that he sent Bliss. He finally finished the last pages of the manuscript on June 9, 1875, almost a year after he began writing it. Incredibly, Roswell Smith, one of the founders of *Scribner's* and the business manager for Scribner and Company, had offered in May to pay six thousand dollars, to be divided equally between Bliss and Harte, for serialization rights to the sight-unseen novel-in-progress. That is, Bliss would receive from Scribner virtually the entire amount he had advanced Harte on the manuscript before he finished it in early June. Harte in turn would stave off insolvency for at least the remainder of the year, and he publicly claimed he had "never done better work."

Still, the arrangement proved a mixed blessing. Because the novel appeared serially in *Scribner's* between November 1875 and August 1876, Bliss delayed its publication in book form until September 1876, some four years after Harte contracted to write it. Its serialization effectively killed its sales as a subscription book, moreover, and invited hostile reviews like a magnet attracts iron filings. Although the story began promisingly, with another thinly fictionalized account of the ill-fated Donner Pass tragedy, it was written so hastily, so episodically, that it soon collapsed into incoherence, a maze of false starts and digressions. Only by "a judicious distribution of earthquakes" was Harte able to develop the story, opined the *Boston Daily Globe*. It was "told in so desultory a manner and with such a superabundance of characters" that readers lost interest "long before the final chapter," according to the *Illustrated London News*. "In point of construction" the novel "is indeed from beginning to end hopelessly and irredeemably bad," asserted the *Saturday Review*, and Thérèse Bentzon declared in the *Revue des Deux Mondes* that the "fears of [Harte's] friends are in a great measure realized by this book." In fact his friends abandoned him on every side: the *Springfield Republican* dismissed the novel as "a moral and literary failure of uncommon magnitude," and Horace Scudder remarked in the *Atlantic Monthly* that "all the dark passages" through which the reader must wander lead finally "not into the light, but into the vegetable cellar." Howells admitted privately to Charles Dudley Warner that he thought it "very cheap in passages" and that it "drew too wildly upon the last reasons of the novelist—starvation, cannibalism, etc.," though he added that "you know this isn't the quarter in which Harte is most admired."

In any event, only 3,354 copies of *Gabriel Conroy* were sold during its first year in print, and when Harte left the United States in 1878 he still owed (according to Bliss's account books, which were not always to be trusted) about $2,500 in advances and interest, a debt he would never erase. "The book has never had a fair show in America—through its infelicitous birth in Hartford," he complained to Osgood in 1880. "It was a wretched mistake of publication." Predictably, too, he was outraged in 1884 when he learned that Bliss, in an apparent attempt to turn a bad debt to account, sold dramatic rights to the story, which he did not own contractually, without so much as consulting the author, much less sharing the proceeds with him. Still, no less a luminary than James Joyce seems to have been influenced by the novel. He gave the protagonist of his story "The Dead" the name Gabriel Conroy—and Joyce may even have borrowed his title from the caption below the illustration of "the dead" Jack Hamlin opposite page 460 of the first edition of Harte's novel.

The race to escape his creditors, if not to pay his debts, left Harte little breathing space. The success of such frontier melodramas as Augustin Daly's *Horizon* (1871) and Clemens's *The Gilded Age* (1874) emboldened him to try his hand at another play, so on March 18, 1875, nearly three months before he completed his novel, he signed a contract at the urging of his friend Lawrence Barrett to script a comedy that summer for the comic actor Stuart Robson. Barrett even witnessed the signing of the contract—it specified that the playwright would receive a total of three thousand dollars in advances and an additional three thousand dollars in performance fees so long as the play kept the boards—and he found and furnished a house for the Hartes near the seaside villas in Cohasset, Massachusetts, where he and Robson lived during the summer. Harte settled his family in the house in Cohasset, which they nicknamed Skunkmill Heights, in mid-July and began work on the script under the supervision of his actor-friends. As Robson later remembered, Barrett soon concluded that Harte was a "snob," and in any event his "play progressed very slowly. Harte would write a scene and bring it over, and he would get mad when we tried to explain to him how impossible it was." Robson had expected "to find that he knew something of stage mechanics," but no: "He brought over one act with seven scenes in it; another time he had a quick change of scenes, both of which were full stage interiors," which would have required resetting the entire stage "in less than a minute."

Harte finally finished a draft of *Two Men of Sandy Bar,* a Frankenstein's monster of a script that grafted the trunk of "Mr. Thompson's Prodigal" to the head of "The Idyl of Red Gulch," on September 17. By his own estimate, the play in its original version would have required over four hours to perform. Robson thought it would take six. Still, Harte was delighted by what he had written. He carried copies of both his novel and the unabridged play to the Fields' home near Manchester for them to read, and Annie Fields remarked in her diary that Harte "has evidently enjoyed the play, and he enjoys the fame and the money they both bring him." When John Carmany wrote him that month from California to invite him to resume editorial charge of the foundering magazine, Harte haughtily declined, explaining with some exaggeration that he could "make here, by my pen, with less drudgery, with more security, honor and respect thrice as much as I could make in California at the head of the Overland." For the record, Harte's rent was overdue and his furniture bills in arrears when he moved at the end of September from Cohasset to a hotel in Lenox. Much as Clarence King had covered Harte's debts in Newport in 1871, Barrett paid these bills from his own pocket to avoid embarrassment.

However careless he may have been about expenses, Harte was fussy and exacting in matters of income, and he soon regretted disposing of his script as he did. On January 2, 1876, he complained to Clemens that "Stuart Robson has it in his pocket while he is quietly drawing a good salary" for performing in the cast of *Rose Michel* at the Union Square Theatre in New York. In fact, Robson had given a copy of Harte's play to Barrett, "who made the changes he thought necessary to get it into working order," including the entire omission of one of the four acts Harte had written. The problems with the play, as well as with his marriage, were taking their toll. When the popular lecturer Anna Dickinson saw Harte in New York in early March, she thought he looked in poor health. "Poor fellow," she wrote her mother, "he ought to have lived in the day when rich men were the patrons of genius. If he could be put into a great library & be fed & clothed, & have all his worldly wants supplied, & be allowed to write & work unrestricted & unhampered he would do what is in him to do but will never now come out of him." In fact, he and Anna had been quarreling. He left New York on March 10 to visit friends in Cleveland and, as he wrote Eliza the next day, "I am very lonely and low spirited, my dear Sister.—I have just been shown a dispatch from Anna" inquiring "if I had arrived," and so he had "written a few cold lines to her by this mail. I could have wished the anxiety and the dispatch had come, through you, from *somebody else*. It was so hard that the first line from home was *hers*." He did not return to New York for three weeks.

In retrospect, it is clear that *Two Men of Sandy Bar* was doomed from the start, with a production history that is more of a screwball comedy than the play itself. Once again, Harte failed to gauge his audience; he exhibited no technical skill as a dramatist; his script contained some of his most mannered writing; and he provoked a silly scandal in theatrical circles merely to publicize and prolong the life of a play that should have been allowed a natural death. The first production of the melodrama at Hooley's Theatre in Chicago in mid-July was eagerly anticipated: the *Boston Globe* reported in late May that

Harte's script "reads like some delightful story"; the *Chicago Tribune* declared on July 2 that the two-week run of the play would be "the most important event" of the local theatrical season; and its convoluted plot was summarized at length in the *New York Times, New York Tribune,* and *Chicago Tribune.* "The conditions under which it was written were not entirely favorable," the latter paper conceded, "yet it contains the hopes of many excellent and judicious actors who have seen it and passed judgment upon its merits. No man can tell whether it will succeed or not. It reads marvellously well." In fact the script is a pastiche of anecdotes so convoluted—Dion Boucicault thought it "contained material for half-a-dozen plays"—that it defies brief synopsis. Suffice it to say that through a series of mistaken identities and a tangle of sexual deceits, the gambler John Oakhurst and the miner Sandy Morton are reformed and become partners in a banking house.

The play opened in Chicago to packed houses, though the initial reviews after the premiere on July 17 were equivocal. The *Chicago Tribune* suggested it "won a complete popular, and a partial artistic, success." With the overhaul of "the obnoxious last act" and the compression of some of the speeches, "we believe the play will enjoy in New York a higher artistic success than it gained here." The *Chicago Inter-Ocean* was more ruthless: "This is the work of a clever amateur, indicating fine literary skill, but defective in dramatic tact, if not of dramatic instinct." Like a baggy suit to the tailor, the script "must be returned, after a week's wear," to the playwright "or some more experienced artificer" for alterations. Inexplicably, Harte had changed John Oakhurst from the daring gambler of his *Overland* stories into "a mere sentimental sneak and milksop" in the play. In all, *Two Men of Sandy Bar* is a "succession of episodes, in some miraculous manner strung together—without a string."

Privately, the manager of the Adelphi Theatre in Chicago, Leonard Glover, tried to doctor the script but was finally "forced to the conclusion that little could be done to mend it. . . . [T]o give S[andy] B[ar] any considerable dramatic importance would require three or four of the characters to be wholly rewritten,

which might make a very bad play of what, at present, the
public seem to consider very good nonsense." Unfortunately,
too, the first performance of the play in Chicago was panned
the next day on the front page of the New York *World:* "Abandoned to his fate, bound by the fetters of a golden contract to
furnish a play at all hazards, the faint Harte spunked up and
devised the melodramtic mystery in three acts, as demanded by
Robson." Back in New York, as Harte explained, "I could do
nothing" about the "Chicago business." He had hoped to
attend rehearsals so "that I might make what changes struck me
then as advisable" in the play. He was angered by "the critique
that appeared in the New York *World* the morning after its
Chicago production, evidently written before the play ever saw
the footlights and prepared with care from a careful perusal" of
the script. Harte and Robson were amply forewarned, long
before the play opened in New York, that the script needed to
be overhauled and rewritten.

Predictably, the production sailed directly into a squall when
it premiered on Broadway in late August. Yet either Robson or
Harte, or more likely both, were more interested in turning the
free publicity about the play to account as soon as possible and
cashing in on the popularity they believed the play would enjoy.
Harte attended a rehearsal at the Union Square Theatre and
insisted that the melodrama be performed "just as I wrote it,
with a few stage changes" and the restoration of the act omitted
in Chicago. Robson claimed later that he recognized the flaws
in the script. It had "some ugly defects," he told an interviewer
in October 1876, but he thought "with some amendations" it
would succeed. Many years later, however, Robson confessed
that he had grossly misjudged the play: it was "bad" and "very
properly roasted. I see that now, but I didn't see quite so clearly
then. The savings of six years was at stake." The play "failed
because its gifted author violated every law of successful dramatic construction."

Simply put, *Two Men of Sandy Bar* inspired some of the most
hostile opening-night reviews in the history of American theatre. The *New York Times* condemned the play in no uncertain

terms: it was "the worst failure witnessed on the boards of our theatres for years" and "the most dismal mass of trash that was ever put into dramatic shape before a New-York audience." Harte had not written a script but a "nondescript," and Robson "probably for the first time in his career" was "an object of public pity." The *New York Herald* declared that Harte had "lived upon his reputation" ever since leaving California and that "we have never known so celebrated a writer to produce such a worthless work." The critic pronounced the play "an absolute outrage upon the intellectual reputation of the country" and concluded that the story resembled "one of Beadle's dime novels struck by lightning." William Winter, the drama critic for the *New York Tribune* and one of Harte's early champions, compared the play to a "garbage barrel," and the New York *Evening Post* averred that one of the two men of the title, the dissipated Sandy Morton, "excites disgust rather than pity or sympathy."

The reviews were so adverse that Boucicault publicly denied the rumor he had helped rewrite the script. Harte awoke the next morning, as he later remarked, "to find myself infamous. I awoke to find the morality of my writings questioned, the old issue I had thought dead and buried in my successes, to find myself criticised as if I were a mere tyro in literature." He was worried that Robson, who had invested his entire fortune in the play, would be despondent, but "when I met him I found him cheerful to hilarity over what he regarded as the success of the piece." Robson soon explained in a note to Harte the reason he believed the play had been attacked mercilessly by the New York drama critics: he had refused to submit to blackmail in exchange for favorable opening-night reviews. The play "answers my fullest expectations as an actor" and "its success with the public is unmistakable," Robson insisted at the time, and he had fully anticipated the "abuse of the critics" who extorted bribes. "In the bitterness of my disappointment," he recalled later, "I remembered the man who had offered to buy me a favorable notice for a paltry hundred" dollars, so "I fought the newspapers" and "got Harte to fight them," too.

More likely, Robson and Harte simply schemed to publicize their play over the objections of the critics, much as Harte had turned to advantage the critical fire storm over *Outcroppings* a dozen years before by stirring up a scandal. Four days after the New York premiere of *Two Men of Sandy Bar,* Harte published a letter to the editor of the *New York Herald* in which he quoted Robson's letter to him and accused the local drama critics of corruption. (Harte claimed later that he had specifically asked the actor "if he was willing to let me use the letter as it was," and he "assented at once." On his part, Robson protested later that his "note to Mr. Harte" was "not intended for publication," though after Harte published it "I certainly stood by it.") In any event Harte and Robson doubtless welcomed the controversy that erupted over their allegations. The *Hartford Courant* reported three days after Harte's letter appeared that the "play, or the criticisms on it, fill the Union square theatre nightly." The *New York Clipper,* a theatrical paper, noted that the allegation "secured a good deal of cheap advertising" for the play, and Robson conceded later that "the row we had with the critics helped us" sell tickets. At any rate, the play completed its entire five-week engagement on Broadway as originally scheduled, though at a terrible price: Harte's reputation, already tainted by rumors of debt and dissipation, was irreparably damaged.

When the editors of such papers as the *Evening Post, Sun, Commercial Advertiser,* and *World* publicly demanded proof of the charges he had brought, Harte hedged and equivocated and evaded the issue. If his allegation were false, he replied, then the papers could sue him for libel. The editors of the *World* had already been given the name of an employee who had been "promptly dismissed" for soliciting a bribe, he insisted. Ironically, the *World* was virtually the only New York paper that did *not* revile the play in its opening-night review. Was the most favorable notice of the play written by the one critic Robson and Harte accused of corruption? The very question betrays the flimsiness of their allegations. They were soon, and properly, held up to public ridicule. The editors of the *Sun* accused him at the least of "bad judgment," and the *Evening Post* thought him "cowardly" and "foolish." Howells thought he had "acted crazily." The *Nation* joked that "no candid person" who had seen the play would dream of a "self-respecting critic speaking well" of it "without a large bonus of ready money paid in advance." When Harte "recovers his mental equilibrium," the editors of the *World* warned, "he will bitterly regret the injustice which he has done, not only to persons who have never wished him any harm, but to himself and his own good name."

Robson took the play on the road, to Washington, Baltimore, Newark, New Haven, Hartford, Springfield, Providence, and Boston over the next six weeks. The initial profits evaporated on tour as a result of heavy expenses. The *Chicago Tribune* claimed Harte never attended a performance of *Two Men* before it was staged in Baltimore and never "told the waiting world" what he really thought of it. "If he was bored as badly as some other people he might be frank enough to own up that the critics were right." Robson's company performed *Two Men* as late as September 1878 in San Francisco, where it was panned by the *Argonaut* ("about as miserable [a play] as ever was put on the stage") and the *Alta California* ("overweighted with a ballast of rubbish and inconsistencies"). Robson later estimated that he lost a total of about ten thousand dollars on his investment. Still, the script was translated into German by Otto Randolf and later made into an early silent western movie.

One of the few people on whom the play made a lasting, favorable impression was Sam Clemens, who saw it performed during the second week of its New York run. He wrote Harte a note the next day to the effect that he "did not laugh once," given the cruel bargain Robson had made for the script. Thirty years later, Clemens reminisced that Harte had once penned "a play which would have succeeded if anyone else had written it." He particularly enjoyed the Chinese laundryman Hop Sing, a role acted by Charles T. Parsloe, even though he appeared in the melodrama for little more than five minutes and delivered a total of only nine lines in tortured pidgin English. In truth, Parsloe's Hop Sing, another incarnation of Ah Sin, the first "stage Chinaman" to appear on Broadway, was virtually the only character in the play whom audiences applauded. Though he is "brought on the stage for no discernable cause" and "has nothing whatever to do" with the plot, he "makes the audience laugh," as the *Commercial Advertiser* noted. On the whole, reviewers thought "there was too much of the two men and too little" of Hop Sing. When he was urged to build an entire play around the character, however, Harte protested that Hop Sing "would become tiresome and monotonous as the central figure in a three-act play." Nevertheless, when he proposed to Clemens in the fall of 1876 that they script a comedy together "& divide the swag," Clemens persuaded him they ought to build the play around the Chinese laundryman and offer Parsloe a one-third interest to star in it.

The result was the most disastrous collaboration in the history of American letters. At first, to be sure, they worked well together, to the extent that they worked together at all. Clemens later remembered that Harte "came down to Hartford and we talked [the play] over and then Bret wrote it while I played billiards, but of course I had to go over it to get the dialect right. Bret never did know anything about dialect." After outlining the scenario, they backfilled the script:

> Harte set down the dialogue swiftly and I had nothing to do except when one of my characters was to say something; then Harte told me the nature of the remark that was required. I furnished the language and he jotted it down. After this fashion we worked two or three or four hours every day for a couple of weeks. . . .

Harte was drinking heavily at the time, too: Clemens's Hartford neighbor Isabella Beecher Hooker looked in on the two men in the billiard room of Clemens's home the day after Thanksgiving and noted in her diary that "there were bottles of spirits near." Clemens recalled, too, how Harte drank two entire bottles of whiskey alone one night in early December 1876 while working on his Centennial potboiler "Thankful Blossom." The "ancient gray suit" he wore during these weeks was "so out of repair," Clemens added, "that the bottoms of his trousers were

C. T. Parsloe
as Ah Sin,
1876.
(Hampden-
Booth
Theatre
Library, New
York)

frazzled to a fringe" and "his shoes were similarly out of repair and were sodden with snow-slush and mud."

Unfortunately, Harte and Clemens quarreled in February 1877, shortly after completing a draft of the script, and fell out entirely before the play went into rehearsals that summer. The nub of their disagreement, as usual in such cases, was money. After running through his advances on *Gabriel Conroy*, Harte was broke. He tried to borrow a few hundred dollars from Clemens, who refused the loan but offered Harte a salary of twenty-five dollars a week and board to write a second play with him—an offer Harte promptly spurned. In his oft-quoted letter to Clemens on March 1, 1877, written from New York, Harte detailed the issues at stake in their dispute from his perspective. He accused Clemens of conspiring with Bliss to cheat him out of royalties he was owed on his novel; of offering Parsloe "the very sum you refused to advance your *collaborateur*" to travel to San Francisco and "study Chinese character"; and of insulting him with an offer of a meagre salary to write another play with him. "I think that if I accepted it, even *you* would despise me for it," Harte remonstrated. "I can make about $100 per week for a few weeks here at my desk." He charged Clemens with attempting to exploit "my poverty, but as a shrewd man, a careful man, a provident man, I think you will admit that in my circumstances the writing of plays with you is not profitable. . . . I think I'll struggle on here on $100 per week—and not write any more plays with you." As for the script of *Ah Sin*, as they had named it, Harte asked Clemens not to mar it "any more by alterations until it is rehearsed" and asked him "to allow me some understanding of the characters I have created."

Clemens ignored the last request. He may not even have read that far. He scribbled a note on the back of Harte's letter that he had only "read two pages of this ineffable idiotcy." At any rate, the finished script of *Ah Sin* was mostly Clemens's. Though the cast of characters derive largely from Harte's 1874 story "A Monte Flat Pastoral," Clemens wrote Howells on August 3 that he had "left hardly a foot-print of Harte in it," and the extant fragments of dialogue in Harte's handwriting do not appear in the prompt copy of the play that survives. Never mind that Ah Sin himself exists mostly in the margins of another story that defies brief summary. Clemens's version of "the heathen Chinee" is mere caricature, mocked in the first scene as a "moral cancer" and an "unsolvable political problem." As Duckett observes, "almost every character in the play at some time speaks scornfully" of him, "much of the humor is at his expense," and "his frequent beatings and cuffings" are but "clumsy antecedents of the jokes" on Jim in *Huck Finn*.

Meanwhile, Clemens and Parsloe joined forces against Harte. One day early in March 1877, Parsloe passed Harte on Broadway and ducked his questions about rehearsals of the play. Parsloe told him he already knew everything he ought to know—whereupon Harte blushed and stalked away. "To have the annoyance with Harte that I have," Parsloe complained to Clemens, "is too much for a beginner." Though he had first proposed the play to Clemens, Harte was entirely cut out of all plans for its production. Even the complimentary passes Harte gave his friends were refused at the theatre. Harte telegraphed the producer John T. Ford after the debut of the play in Washington on May 7 to "thank your people for their honest endeavor and clever interpretation of the varied characters in 'Ah Sin,'" and he telegraphed Clemens on May 16 to request his share of the box receipts "if any." There were and would be none, because the play would never show a profit. In any event, Harte's telegram was the last direct contact between the two men. They were scheduled to share the stage of the Fifth Avenue Theatre on September 1, the night the play closed in New York, but neither of them appeared. "In the early days I liked Bret Harte," Clemens reminisced in 1907, "but by and by I got over it." Would but the story of their spat ended here.

The initial reviews of *Ah Sin* after its performances in Washington on May 7–12, in Baltimore on May 14–19, and in New York after its Broadway debut on July 31 were mixed at best. On the one hand, such papers as the Washington *National Republican* ("many passages which are unexcelled by anything in the other works of the two authors as specimens of literary skill"), the *Baltimore Bee* ("one of the most amusing and successful productions in the country's dramatic annals"), and the *New York Tribune* ("the dialogue is almost invariably good, sparkling with wit, and richly flavored with delicious absurdities") praised the play. On the other hand, the New York *Sun* ("weak, commonplace, and not at all original") and the *Spirit of the Times* ("few plays of the American stamp can be mentioned whose literary execution is so bad, whose construction is so ramshackly, and whose texture is so barren of true wit") panned it. Clemens wrote Howells in early August that the play was "a-booming at the Fifth Avenue" theatre, and if only Harte "had suppressed his name (it didn't occur to me to suggest it) the play would have received as great applause in the papers as it did in the Theatre."

Again Harte struggled to get news of the play after it opened in New York. He contacted Augustin Daly, who had doctored the script before its premiere, for information: "I don't want any accounts from you or Parsloe, only a simple expression of your opinion as to whether the play was or was not successful, and as one of its authors, this does not seem to me to be an inconsistent request or calculated to wound anybody's—say Parsloe's—sensitive nature." In August Parsloe offered to buy Harte's one-third interest in the production, and as usual Harte made a stupid business decision by refusing to sell. In mid-October, after Parsloe took *Ah Sin* on tour to St. Louis and a string of cities in upstate New York, Clemens finally admitted to Howells that the play was "a most abject & incurable failure." He was "sorry for poor Parsloe, but for nobody else concerned." In the end, ironically, poor Parsloe fared much better than Harte: the next year he commissioned Bartley Campbell to write a gold-rush melodrama that would again feature him in the role of a Chinese laundryman, and this play, *My Partner,* made him a fortune. *Ah Sin* closed not with a bang but a whimper in Pittsburgh on November 10.

Though he had lost almost every hand he had been dealt since he arrived in Boston in 1871, Harte still had a few tricks up his sleeve. While he was in Washington to attend the premiere of *Ah Sin* in May, he agreed to contribute a serial novel to the *Capital,* a local mugwump weekly edited by Donn Piatt, for which he would be paid $2,000, half of it secured in an escrow account, in installments of $125. "It is a chance to get money quickly—which I must have or I shall go mad," he wrote Anna on June 24. He moved into the Georgetown home of his cousin, Georgianna Cooper, and her husband David, an engraver for the Treasury Department, and set to work on "The Story of a Mine," a thinly disguised defense of the directors of the New Idria Mining Company, who had been charged with fraud and bribery in developing a quicksilver mine on an old Spanish land grant in California. He originally hoped "to finish the work in a month, for I have nothing to invent—only romantically and dramatically cast a really wonderful *true* story." By mid-July he was "writing hard day and night to get far enough along in my story so as to draw $400 or 500 at once from Bank." On July 22 he gleefully sent promising news to Anna: Piatt had offered him an annual salary of $5000 "if I will share with him" the job of editing the *Capital*—Harte had not worked as a magazine editor since resigning from the *Overland* seven years earlier—"or he will give me a smaller salary (secured) and a 1/2 interest in the paper. Both offers are good; perhaps the $5000 in hand is worth the 1/2 interest in the bush." He was convinced that "Washington is the place for a literary man to make money," and he thought "the tide is turning. At least I begin to feel my way ahead, slowly."

The only problem: he would need to reside permanently in Washington, and the city was "very unhealthy in summer for children." (Such a complication anticipates the myriad excuses Harte offered in later years to forestall his reunion with his family.) In mid-August he agreed to become coeditor of the *Capital* for $3,000 a year and a half-interest in the paper, and his lawyers drew up a contract "to protect myself from any indebtedness of the Company over and above my share in it." To be sure, Charles Dana of the New York *Sun* and several other newspaper men had discouraged him from taking this step. They did not think "any Washington paper can succeed—but I am satisfied to try."

His high hopes were slowly dashed. In early September the serialization of "The Story of a Mine" was briefly interrupted, and the New York *World* alleged that Harte had been "bought off or frightened by a decision of the Attorney General" in favor of the plaintiffs in the New Idria case. A week later, Piatt refused to sign the contract Harte's lawyers had drafted because "some old debts against the paper had lately come up." Harte was devastated. He still hoped to finish the serial and "get a couple of hundred dollars out of it from Osgood. . . . It isn't a bad story—even if it has been written in the sorest trouble I have ever had." George Stewart observes that the nouvelle is "biographically one of the most illuminating of Harte's writings. Despair lies over it like a dingy fog." Harte had no money and would have none "until the story is finished," he wrote Anna on September 21. Worse yet was the realization "that you are left alone, penniless, at that strange hotel" at Sea Cliff, Long Island.

A month later, Harte finally admitted to Anna that his fond hopes for an editorial position and half-ownership of the *Capital* "amount to nothing." The paper was bankrupt and even the money he expected for his story was "seized by its creditors." He was told to "expect nothing" for the political satire he had written to order, "that wretched story" for which "I've been vilified and abused in the papers." He remained in Washington three more weeks, trying to salvage a few dollars from his deal with Piatt, knocking off a lame parody of a dime-novel western for *Godey's Lady's Book* entitled "The Hoodlum Band," and then he joined his family on Long Island. The Philadelphia *Evening Bulletin* reported that Harte "has left Washington, severing his reported literary engagement there." Harte wrote the poet Mary E. W. Sherwood that "I was three months last autumn at work in Washington—but are not all these things written in the papers—in the column called 'Personal'?" He put the best face possible on his disappointment in a private note to Osgood: "An all ruling Providence prevented me from becoming a publisher in Washington."

In a word, his literary career was in ruins. His name appeal among readers had so dwindled that his review of *Our National*

Jubilee, a collection of Centennial poems, appeared without signature in the New York *Sun* in July 1877 and the editors of the
Independent rejected outright a poem he submitted to the magazine in April 1878. He sold a parody of Longfellow's "Excelsior," to be used in a Sapolio soap ad, to Enoch Morgan Sons
for fifty dollars. As the *Boston Traveller* remarked at the time, he
was "floating on the raft made of the shipwreck of his former
reputation." The New York *World* observed that "it is an open
question as to what improvement in Mr. Harte's style would be
wrought by his reduction to a state of abject penury; but the
experiment of ruining him is worth trying." In December 1877
he learned that, instead of receiving from Osgood a check for
royalties on his book sales, his account was "balancing the wrong
way. But why didn't you tell me this before?" He had drawn
advances that had outstripped his earnings. In a fit of despair, he
wondered whether "I had not better learn an honest trade" and
retire from writing.

He was very sick with a hacking cough during these months,
"much overworked" and "quite run over in flesh and spirit."
With the wolf at his door, Harte begged William Waldorf Astor,
great-grandson of John Jacob Astor, for a job, any job, that
would help him feed his family through the winter. As he wrote
Astor on January 5, 1878:

> You'll think me importunate, but even at that risk, I feel I must
> recall to you our conversation in your office, and ask you if you
> have any news for me yet. Is there anything I, myself, can do
> towards forwarding the matter? Have you heard of any position
> that you think I could fill, and is get-at-able? And if so, how?
>
> I hate to bother you, knowing how much your time must be
> preoccupied with larger and just now more pleasurable things, but
> the fact is that I [am] becoming really very much distressed. . . .

He was appalled, too, to read in the New York newspapers on
February 9 that Osgood had merged his firm with Hurd and
Houghton—and that his name did not appear among "the bril-
liant list of authors" in the stable of the new publisher, Houghton,
Osgood and Company.

He angrily lashed out at Osgood the next month, in fact, for failing to rush into print *Drift from Two Shores,* his most recent volume of sketches, the very title of which evokes their ephemeral quality. "Do you think you are treating me exactly right?" he plaintively asked. "It is now some three weeks since I wrote you" about his proposed new book and he had received no reply. "I am anxious to know if this lengthy consideration of my proposition is to be taken as a form of declining, and if I am to have the privilege of trying my luck with another publisher." In April he briefly considered an invitation from a Brazilian steamer company to travel to Rio de Janeiro. "If all else fails," he grumbled to Anna, "here is a trip and a rest for two months, sure." To the end of his life he remembered the hardscrabble winter of 1877–78, that "awful, terrible last winter" in America, "our old, shiftless, hand-to-mouth life in N.Y." and "that nervousness that daily bent me." "I could not, and *would not under any circumstances,* again go through what I did in New York the last two years and particularly the last winter I passed there," he wrote Anna later. "I don't know—looking back—what ever kept me from going down, in *every way,* during that awful December and January."

He had literally run up more debts than he could remember. He was later hounded by such creditors as the Leland brothers, proprietors of the Sturtevant House in New York, and the New York grocers Park and Tilford. "I hope to live to pay these bills, for they *ought to be paid,*" he insisted in 1883, though he added with characteristic illogic that "it would only plunge me in debt again to attempt to pay them now." Among Harte's other disgruntled creditors: the Wall Street banker Thomas Bateson Musgrave, who aspired to be considered a patron of the arts and literature, according to Noah Brooks, and to whom Harte had dedicated *Gabriel Conroy.* By sheer chance seated next to Clemens at a farewell dinner for Bayard Taylor in New York in early April 1878, Musgrave told this story (or some version of it). He had lent Harte money "gladly" over the years, and "Harte always gave his note" until the debt totaled about three thousand dollars. Musgrave said that Harte's notes were a distress to him, because he supposed that they were a distress to Harte. Then he had what he thought was a happy idea: he compacted the notes into a bale and sent them to Harte on the 24th of December '77 as a Christmas present; and with them he sent a note begging Harte to allow him this privilege because of the warm and kind and brotherly feeling which prompted it.

As Clemens recounted the anecdote, however, "Harte fired the bale back" the next day "with a letter which was all afire with insulted dignity" but "nothing in it about paying the notes sometime or other." Whether or not Clemens embellished the story, this much is known: two years later, Musgrave refused to guarantee Harte's bond when he was appointed U.S. consul to Glasgow.

At the absolute nadir of his career, Harte enjoyed yet another stroke of good fortune as significant under the circumstances as his chance encounter with Jessie Frémont in 1860, his initial success with the *Overland* in 1868, and his original contract with Osgood in 1871. He was appointed to a minor diplomatic post in Germany that permitted him to lay aside his pen yet support his family and reschedule his debts if not escape his creditors. The tangle of events that led to the appointment has never been chronicled in detail, however. Harte had plans to solicit a patronage job—like the one in Liverpool that Nathaniel Hawthorne had been given in 1853 by his friend Franklin Pierce—as early as November 1876, when he told Clemens as they were writing the script of *Ah Sin* that he would not vote for either Hayes or Tilden for president because he had been promised a consulate by friends of each candidate. "I told him," Clemens claimed, "that nobody would appoint him to an office, or ought to." Nevertheless, in June 1877, after Hayes's inauguration, he was nearly appointed to the China Mission.

Behind the scenes, Clemens was by then making trouble for his former friend. "Three or four times lately I have read items to the effect that Bret Harte is trying to get a Consulship," Clemens wrote Howells on June 21. He urged Howells to intercede with Hayes, his wife Elinor's cousin, to prevent the disgrace of literature & the country which would be the infallible result of the appointment of Bret Harte to any responsible post. Wherever he goes his wake is tumultuous with swindled grocers, & with defrauded innocents who have loaned him money. He *never* pays a debt but by the squeezing of the law. He borrows from all new acquaintances, & repays none. His oath is worth little, his promise nothing at all. He can lie faster than he can drivel false pathos. He is always steeped in whisky & brandy; he gets up in the night to drink it cold. No man who has ever known him respects him. . . . You know that I have befriended this creature for seven years. I am even capable of doing it still—while he stays at home. But I don't want to see him sent to foreign parts to carry on his depredations.

Either Howells or his wife passed this letter through members of the family to Hayes, who passed the word back before the end of June that "there is no danger" of Harte's appointment, news which Howells in turn relayed to Clemens: "I think *now* there is no danger of the national calamity you feared, and I don't believe there ever was much."

On his part, Harte was mystified. "As regards Appointments, I know nothing," he reported to Anna on July 8. "Whatever is done now, must come to me without solicitation." Not surprisingly, the job with the China Mission evaporated into thin air, and Harte burlesqued the intrigue of political patronage in a bitter tongue-in-cheek bagatelle he wrote the next week for the New York *Sun*. In "The Office Seeker," a rustic westerner named Expectant Dobbs settles in Washington with hopes of a job in the Bureau for the Dissemination of Useless Information or the Envelope Flap Moistening Bureau of the Department of Tape. Over the months, while waiting for the bureaucratic wheels to turn, he becomes "quite seedy" in appearance. After he is finally given a job filling water pitchers, he loses it as the result of Civil Service Reform.

Harte obviously blamed Secretary of State William Evarts, who had interviewed him in June, for his initial failure to land a diplomatic appointment. He said as much to Piatt, who as Washington correspondent for the *Cincinnati Enquirer* reported that Evarts "should have ignored the commercial and looked only at the literary" side of the issue and "provided for a man whose genius has given more respect to our name abroad than all the diplomats we ever possessed." Ironically, Piatt also conceded the argument *against* the appointment:

> Harte has been carrying a heavy load in a wife and four children, to say nothing of some rather luxurious tastes and habits, upon the wit of his pen. In consequence he has had hungry creditors and financial complications. To add to his trouble he writes slowly and with no little labor, and when held by affairs he could not manage or control he found it impossible to write at all. From this came sundry allegations and stories not creditable to Bret in the ears of a commercial community.

This paragraph was widely copied in papers across the country under such banners as "Why Bret Harte Doesn't Get an Offer." Or as Harte complained to Piatt, "Every gutter snipe of the press, who hates me, rolls it as a sweet morsel over his tongue, and praises Evarts for his wisdom."

Nor did Clemens cease to make trouble behind the scenes, even though his wife Olivia had cautioned him not to "say harsh things about Mr. Harte" or "talk against Mr. Harte to people." At virtually the same moment Harte was begging Astor for a job, Clemens arranged for a slanderous story about him to appear in the *Cincinnati Commercial,* an influential Republican journal and the president's hometown newspaper. The New York correspondent of the *Commercial* quoted Clemens, though not by name, in early January 1878 to the effect that Harte "was absolutely devoid of a conscience. If his washerwoman had saved $500 by long years of careful industry, he would borrow it without the slightest intention of repaying it." The correspondent dredged up "the old story about his lecturing in Boston, with a Sheriff's officer at each side of the platform," waiting for Harte to pay "for the dress suit in which he was lecturing," and concluded "it is a melancholy thing to witness the rapid decline of one who stood so high and had such brilliant promise. But his friends [e.g., Clemens] have ceased to defend him." Vulnerable to such innuendo whether or not he deserved it, Harte was acutely aware that his "enemies were trying to poison Mr. Evarts ears"—the allusion here is to the usurper Claudius's murder of Hamlet's father—"with reports of my debts, extravagances, &c."

Fortunately for Harte, Clemens was so embarrassed by the fallout from his speech at the Whittier dinner in Boston in mid-December, in which he seemed to insult Emerson, Longfellow, and Oliver Wendell Holmes to their faces, that he fled the country with his family in March, settling in Heidelberg in May 1878. Meanwhile, Harte began to campaign in earnest for a diplomatic appointment, not by counting on the influence of western congressmen as he had the previous summer but by calling on the stalwarts of the Republican Party in New York and Ohio. He enlisted the support of such men as Stanley Matthews, U.S. senator from Ohio; James Dix, former governor of New York; Charles Watrous, an old friend from California and now a wealthy New York businessman; and Dana, the editor of the *Sun*.

Unbeknownst to Harte (or to Clemens, for that matter) his application was also endorsed by Howells, who was not only related to the president by marriage but had also written his official campaign biography during the 1876 canvass and whose judgment Hayes trusted implicitly. The president wrote Howells on April 5, 1878, to ask his private opinion, allowing that he had "heard sinister things" about Harte from Clemens. Two years later, Howells would model the character of the scoundrel Bartley Hubbard in his novel *A Modern Instance* upon Harte, but in his reply to Hayes on April 9 he offered equivocal support for his appointment. He explained that he had seen Harte "arrested for debt in Boston," a reference to his lecture at Tremont Temple in December 1872. "He is notorious for borrowing and *was* notorious for drinking," Howells added, though he "never borrowed of *me*, nor drank more than I (in my presence)." The appointment "would be a godsend to him," Howells conceded, for "he is poor, and he writes with difficulty and very little." In all, "he has had the worst reputation as regards punctuality, solvency and sobriety, but he has had a terrible lesson in falling from the highest prosperity to the lowest adversity in literature" and "I hear he is really making an effort to reform." Should he be appointed, he could always be recalled if he fouled up. Howells ended this letter by asking Hayes to show it to no one and "kindly return it to me at Cambridge." As Henry Nash Smith and William Gibson observe, Howells "would help Harte if he could, but he would not risk his friendship with Clemens for Harte's sake."

On April 18, nine days after Howells recommended him for a job, Harte was promised an appointment in the diplomatic corps by Frederick W. Seward, the assistant secretary of state. John Jay Knox, the comptroller of currency in the Treasury Department, rallied to his defense, refuting the allegations that he was unfit for a position of fiduciary trust. Knox had audited the books of the San Francisco Mint during Harte's tenure as secretary there and wrote Evarts that he "had held a most responsible position" and that in Swain's absence he was "virtually Superintendent of the Mint and had been in the confidence of one of the best business men in California. So that, in one blow, all the stories of my extravagance, debts, &c. &c." were "demolished!" The site of his posting was still undecided—Hayes had mentioned Nice, and Matthews told Harte he could have for the asking "the position of First Secretary of Legation to St Petersburg, salary $2,600," though he realized "I could barely keep up appearances on the salary." Evarts and Carl Schurz, the secretary of the interior and a Republican power broker, proposed "sending me to the Netherlands, Switzerland, or perhaps a little higher up in the diplomatic scale."

Seward suggested Crefeld, Germany, on the Rhine near Düsseldorf, famous for its exported silks and velvets. The salary was $2,500 a year plus a percentage of the export duties on invoices certified by the consulate, and the office was vacant so Harte "could take it at once." As he wrote Anna, "you can imagine that, with all my disappointments, this seemed like a glimpse of Paradise." When he learned that he had indeed been assigned to Crefeld, he was reconciled to the post. "I am beginning to think that perhaps it is, as Mr Seward says, the best thing for a beginning," as he wrote Anna. Despite all the maneuvering on his behalf, Harte's capacity for self-deception was undiminished. He pretended his good luck was justly deserved: "Whatever I receive from the Department of State," he insisted on April 23, "I have won by my own individual efforts; I have not had to wet the sole of my shoe in the political mire." He posted his bond with the department on May 11 and formally accepted his appointment as U.S. commercial agent at Crefeld. After a free fall of many months, he had finally landed on his feet.

To finance the trip, he began to write again—a long poem entitled "Cadet Grey" commissioned by the artist Homer Lee for the giftbook *West Point Tic Tacs* and two more of his popular "Miss Edith" poems for *Scribner's*. (Not that the critics were mollified: "Miss Edith Makes It Pleasant for Brother Jack," published in September, was "incalculably the worst" poem in the issue, according to the *Boston Transcript*.) On June 4 he transferred to Houghton, Osgood and Company his copyright to fourteen books and granted the publisher the right of first refusal to all of his future books in exchange for $1,500 cash and the removal of all "pecuniary indebtedness" he had incurred from its ledgers. He borrowed additional money from Dana, to be repaid with copy for the *Sun* sent from Germany. The plan was to leave Anna and the children on Long Island until he could get far enough ahead financially to bring them over. On June 27, across the Atlantic and some two hundred kilometers southeast of Crefeld, in his rooms at the Schloss Hotel in Heidelberg, Clemens fumed that "after the letter I wrote last summer" the president had "ignored my testimony." As he ranted to Howells, "Harte is a liar, a thief, a swindler, a snob, a sot, a sponge, a coward, a Jeremy Diddler, he is brim full of treachery. . . . To send this nasty creature to puke upon the American name in a foreign land is too much." He had just gotten wind of the appointment, and he was determined that "Harte shan't swindle the Germans." He demanded to know "what German town he is to filthify with his presence" so that he could warn the authorities.

The same day, Harte sailed from Hoboken pier with Osgood in tow aboard the *Suevia*. "The boys will tell you how they left me," he hastily scribbled in a penciled note to Anna that afternoon as the ship lay off Staten Island. "God bless you, Nan, keep up a brave heart, and be patient." Neither of them could have surmised at the time that his exile would be permanent. Harte would never return to the United States and, while she would receive regular letters and monthly drafts from him, Anna Harte would not see her husband again for over twenty years.

CHAPTER 5

Crefeld, Glasgow, and the Literary Recuperation of the West

CLEMENS once compared Edward Everett Hale's "man without a country" to Harte, whom he thought "an invertebrate without a country." Like so many of his hyperbolic remarks about Harte, the phrase contains no more than an inkling of truth. Harte in fact was in his country's employ for the first seven years he lived abroad, and while he never returned to his native shore, he was a patriotic American for the rest of his life—albeit one who near the very end played such sports as golf and tennis and affected a clipped British accent.

En route to England he "made one or two notes of certain little experiences" aboard the ship "which were new to me, and which I shall use hereafter," he wrote Anna—and he soon sent Dana a sketch, "A Tourist from Injianny," obviously a satirical takeoff on the international theme of Henry James's "Daisy Miller," to satisfy part of his debt to the *Sun*. (He would, in fact, pay it off with "copy" within the year.) On July 8, after a passage of eleven days, he and Osgood landed at Plymouth and quickly railed to London. Harte was so impressed by the "vivid color and verdure" of "woodland England" that "it half atoned for the voyage." He spent several hours the next day touring London in a hansom cab. Joaquin Miller, who met him that day at Westminster Abbey, recalled later how Harte tarried over the grave of Dickens. Harte also accompanied Osgood to the home in St. John's Wood of the publisher Nikolaus Trübner and his wife Cornélie. The historian J. A. Froude, who was summering at his estate in Devonshire, wrote to invite him to the country.

Otherwise, Harte was underwhelmed by the reception he received from the English literati. The novelist Charles Reade, to whom Boucicault had written Harte a letter of introduction, "was barely civil," and Richard Monckton Milnes, Lord Houghton, failed even to reply to the card Harte sent him. After three frustrating days in London, Harte left for Paris, where he visited his sister-in-law Dora Griswold, wife of Anna's brother Charles, and his niece Gertrude, a voice student at the Conservatoire. To his dismay, as he wrote Anna, "Gertie told me the French and English papers copied all the ugly things that were said about me. That may account for the incivility" he suffered in London. He spent most of three days in Paris with Dora and Gertie "in style too decorous for you to understand much less imitate," as he joked with Osgood, and "saw so little of that highly glazed metropolis while I was there that I couldnt identify it under oath." He assured Anna that London had "seemed to me a sluggish nightmare" and Paris "a confused sort of hysterical experience." Privately, however, he was eager to sample the charms of rural England and Paris as soon as the consulate was up and running.

He finally arrived in Crefeld ("a cramped Philadelphia without its neatness") on July 17 and registered at the Hotel Wildenmann until he could rent a flat. "I have audaciously travelled alone nearly 400 miles through an utterly foreign country on one or two little French and German phrases, and a very small stock of assurance," he allowed. "Its been uphill work ever since I left N.Y. but I shall try to see it through, please God! I don't allow myself to think over it at all, or I should go crazy." As late as 1884 he reminisced about "the unutterable loneliness of 'Der Wildmann,' the first week I came to Crefeld." With the help of the U.S. consul in nearby Barmen, he soon hired Rudolf Schneider, a local clerk fluent in English, French, and German, as his vice-consul. Schneider would perform the work of the consulate out of his home on Linnerstrasse for all the fees above $2,500 per year—that is, for the commissions above the $2,500 Harte would receive. That salary Harte had earmarked for his family in the United States, while he planned to live on the money he earned from writing and lecturing. He also rigidly observed a new rule in the conduct of his personal financial affairs: "*I will not make a single debt.*" With the secure salary of his government job, he was "better off than I was during the two or three years previous to my leaving" the United States, "but not as well as when I first returned to New York from California."

He soon formed close friendships with Schneider and his family. Schneider's brother-in-law Wilhelm Jenges, one of the wealthiest men in town, even invited him to move into his palatial home until he could find an apartment. "It is a gorgeous picnic all the time," he wrote his son Frankie, "and not like home one bit." More to the point, Harte never felt at home in Crefeld. He wrote Bayard Taylor, the new U.S. ambassador in Berlin, within the week to solicit his help in meeting local officials: "Do you remember you once offered, if we chanced to be in Germany together, to make me known to some ducal friend of yours? Now, my dear fellow, I should be content to know even a Burgomaster or Police Inspector, if he lived in this District. For here I find myself quite unknown." Taylor had fallen ill, however—he would die in December—and he never replied to this request, much to Harte's dismay and consternation. (He complained to Anna three weeks after Taylor's death that "I did not feel very kindly toward him, nor had he troubled himself much about me when I came here alone and friendless.")

As he was angling for a transfer later, Harte griped to John Hay that "during my eighteen months residence here I have not received the *first* official civility or even recognition from Mayor or Burgomaster. My cards have been unacknowledged." He told Pemberton years later that he sometimes walked the streets of Crefeld "listlessly" hoping to recognize "a face that would greet [me] with a smile." In truth, too, Harte, who was always a bit of a snob among those he considered his social inferiors, made little effort to adapt to German manners and customs. "Heaven forbid," he wrote Anna, "that I do not become like these lethargic, fat-witted Germans about me, who live altogether below their waists and whose hips and stomachs are the largest part of them." "Miserable dyspeptic that I am, God help me from ever becoming one of these fat-witted rosy satyrs."

Or as he wrote Hay, "I dont like sausages, nor the conditions of life that permit or accept them."

On July 29—that is, after less than two weeks on duty in Crefeld—Harte hurried back to Paris without so much as requesting a leave from the State Department. "I shall at once apologize (when I return to my post) averring my ignorance as a novice," he pertly explained to the consul at Sonneberg. In truth, he would not return to Crefeld for over six weeks. He was "thoroughly steeped in iniquity and dissipation" for a week in Paris, or so he joked to Anna, visiting the Exposition, Notre Dame, and Napoleon's tomb; then he crossed the Channel and spent another week in London before railing to Froude's summer home in Devonshire on August 15. "It is, without exception, one of the most *perfect* country houses I ever beheld," he reported, and Froude was "in some respects" the "most interesting man I ever met."

On August 23 he returned to London, and Joaquin Miller soon decoyed him to Newstead Abbey in Nottingham, an old Norman abbey and the former home of Lord Byron. His hosts, William and Geraldine Webb, urged him "to come here whenever I want, do as I like. . . . I thought Froude's place was beautiful, but here is so much beauty, with history, with a certain grandeur, and, above all, with all the melancholy of Byron's genius." He wrote a humorous poem of twenty-three quatrains about Byron for "Miss Geraldine" that has never been published, though it survives among the papers in the Harte Collection at the University of Virginia. The first stanza suggests its comic tone:

> There once was a gent., as was quite free from chaff—
> He was a Lord Byron—the sixth and a half—
> But the stock it was blighted and bloated, and he
> Was the only green leaf on the family tree.

A master of ingratiation, Harte also met the Duchess of St. Albans ("a sweet, bright, sympathetic, graceful lady to whom I took a great fancy") and dined with the duke and duchess at nearby Bestwood Lodge during his first visit to Nottingham. He finally left Newstead—"in the week that I was there I felt more at ease than I have felt anywhere since I left America"—and returned via Queenboro and Flushing to Crefeld on September 10. That day he promised Gertrude Griswold, who was vacationing in the south of France, to "break my heart" in learning German "and attend strictly to the Consulate and literature."

During his six-week trip to France and England, Harte composed a story, "The Heiress of Red Dog," that is chiefly noteworthy today for its veiled attempt to make peace with Sam Clemens. The title character, Peggy Moffat of Calaveras County, seems to represent Clemens, whose married sister Pamela was surnamed Moffett. The heir of a "deceased humorist," Harte's heroine "suddenly sprang into opulence and celebrity." She loses some of her money in "prolonging the miserable existence" of a local newspaper much as Clemens in 1871 had sold his interest in the *Buffalo Express* for ten thousand dollars less than he had paid for it. At length she is befriended by a "handsome, graceless vagabond" like Harte, "a cyclone of dissipation" named Jack Folinsbee. "I was as soft on that freckle-faced, red-eyed, tallow-haired gal," Folinsbee declares, "as if she'd been—a—a—an actress." Or perhaps a playwright. When he proposes marriage, Peggy Moffat offers him twenty-five dollars a week allowance, exactly the same deal Clemens had offered Harte to write another play with him; and Folinsbee tells her "to go to ---- with her money," much as Harte had spurned Clemens's offer. In the end, however, Folinsbee concedes Peggy Moffat's right to spend her money as she wishes—in effect, that is, Harte acknowledges Clemens's identical right. He recognized that Clemens's offer was not intended as an insult. Unfortunately, the veiled apology failed to repair the rift between them. Though Harte's British publisher sent Clemens a copy of *The Heiress of Red Dog and Other Tales* in the spring of 1879, presumably at Harte's request, and though Clemens read the volume at least twice, he either failed to recognize the apology coded in the story or refused to accept it.

After his return to Crefeld, Harte covered his long absence by catching up on his consular work. He filed his quarterly reports

with the Department of State, though Secretary Evarts reportedly complained that Harte failed to supply necessary information "with such definiteness and precision as might have been
desired." He settled into an apartment in nearby Düsseldorf
and took a train to Crefeld every workday, but he admonished
Anna not to expect an early reunion of the family. "I know of
no happiness, comfort, pleasure—mental or bodily, that can be
had by a residence in Germany," he warned her in early October,
"that cannot be had in America with less trouble and expense."
The comment foreshadows what would become a familiar
refrain. "I shall not think of sending for you until I see clearly
that I can stay *myself*," he wrote her. Under the worst circumstances, "I shall try to stand it for a year, and save enough to
come home and begin anew *there*."

Relieved of immediate financial distress by his posting to
Crefeld, Harte gradually put his literary career back on track. "I
think I've got back my old strength and pleasure in my pen
again," he reported to Anna. "Its a great relief not to have to
work against *time,* and to work for my own pleasure at my own
leisure." Unfortunately, he had lost most of his American audience over the years. "They are not paying me well for my articles in America—nor do they seem to care much for them," he
griped in March 1879. "The *Atlantic* don't want anything, and
Scribner has only taken one. Even Dana grumbles at my prices."
He suspected that his American publishers Houghton Mifflin,
the successor firm to Houghton, Osgood and Company, "are
swindling me," his royalty checks from them were so small—
"less than I can get for the *translation*" rights in Germany.
American reviewers were also critical of his writing when they
noticed it at all. The San Francisco *Argonaut* complained, for
example, that Harte named a horse thief lynched for his crime
in "The Great Deadwood Mystery" after Josh Silsbee, a come-
dian in San Francisco in the early 1860s: "We question the taste
if not the motive of Mr. Harte in fastening upon this blameless
gentleman's memory an immortality of shame." His old nemesis
the New York *World* dismissed him as "a hack" whose career
had "petered out." Harriet Preston carped in the *Atlantic* that

Harte "planted himself long ago on his inalienable literary right to give his readers just as little as they will take for their money."

As was his wont, Harte gauged the precise demand for his stories and adapted to the exigencies of the popular British and foreign markets. "I shall have no difficulty in disposing of my work here, at good prices," he assured his wife. "I think I can make from my pen nearly twice as much as before." He began to offer original stories and poems to such London journals as *Belgravia* and to authorize German translations of them to appear in such periodicals as *Deutsche Rundschau, Frankfurter Zeitung,* and the Vienna *Neue Freie Presse* before sending them to Dana for reprinting in the New York *Sun.* Hailed by such eminent German poets as Theodor Fontane and Ferdinand Freiligrath, Harte (not his rival Clemens) was by all accounts the most popular American writer in Germany in the 1870s and 1880s. "It is quite wonderful," as he bragged to Anna in 1882, "what a large and growing audience I have all over the continent; anything I write is instantly translated."

However hackneyed his plots, Harte adjusted to his new literary markets by pandering to European readers' ideas about "the Wild West" and by writing increasingly sensational stories punctuated by violence and sexual trangression or illicit romance. As Henry Adams noted in his *Education,* Harte insisted on the power of sex in his stories "as far as the magazines would let him venture." Still, such western tales as "The Great Deadwood Mystery" and "The Heiress of Red Dog" were cut from the same bolt of bright calico. "I grind out the old tunes on the old organ and gather up the coppers," he explained, "but I never know whether my audience behind the window blinds are wishing me to 'move on' or not." Having invented the formula western, as Howells reminisced later, he "wrote Bret Harte over and over again as long as he lived." It "was the best thing he could do" because the "cockney-syntaxed, Dickens-colored California" of his imagination seemed to satisfy "the insatiable English fancy for the wild America no longer to be found on our map." In 1884 the British publisher Andrew Chatto ranked Harte fourth, after Ouida, Charles Reade, and Clemens, among the writers in his stable, and the next year Lewis Rosenthal reiterated in the *Critic* that Harte "is of all living Americans the best known and most read" in Germany.

To be sure, early in his European exile, much as in 1871 when he settled in the East, he experimented with other literary forms, albeit with little success. He was no more an astute or reliable observer of German life than he had been of Newport society. Each day his "ideas and judgement of what I see" seemed to change "so that I do not dare to draw upon the capital I am collecting," he explained to Dana in September 1878. "I've tried my hand at one or two descriptions of how things 'struck me'—but before the article was half done I found I was either wrong or prejudiced." In December Harte was asked to write a tribute to Bayard Taylor for the *Berliner Tageblatt,* whose editors then commissioned him to write "a series of frank, honest observations on my impressions of German Life and Character." Though he planned a series of short essays for biweekly publication in the newspaper, in the end he published only one: "Der Spion" or "Views from a German Spion," a sardonic mood piece that touches on "the unreality of German art," the simplemindedness of German servants, and the extreme gravity of German children. The original manuscript version of the essay was apparently even more candid. He asked the editors of the *Tageblatt* to "point out any passages that might be open to misunderstanding," and "they did—very frankly and kindly—condemning the ridiculous sensitiveness of their countrymen, offering to print as I wished—but pointing out three or four of my best passages." He omitted those paragraphs lest he compromise "my half-diplomatic position here. That position so ties my hands in criticism" that he decided to "defer any further observations on German character for the present."

As usual when he strayed from his western formula, Harte not only misjudged his readers but blamed them for his failure: "The people here are very sensitive, and very stupid." He wrote his sister Eliza in September 1879 that if he were to satirize German "incidents and episodes" with "American freshness," he would "only become a Mark Twain. I could write descriptions

like the 'Innocents Abroad'—for much is here that is a sham—
but I wont." Not surprisingly, whereas his western fiction was
normally hailed by reviewers in England, "Views from a German
Spion" was dismissed in *Athenaeum* as "a somewhat commonplace magazine article." Harte failed to entertain "when he travels
away from California. The stories that deal with life in other
regions, whether humorous or pathetic, are commonplace."

To exploit his celebrity in Europe as a California writer, Harte
also dusted off his old lecture on "The Argonauts of '49." He
delivered it before some four hundred Americans and Brits in
Wiesbaden on December 2, for which he was paid one hundred
dollars, and he contracted with the agent D'Oyly Carte, best
known today as the producer of Gilbert and Sullivan operettas,
for a lecture tour of England in late January and early February
1879, for which he expected to be very well paid. "If I can only
get a couple of thousand dollars in this way *ahead* I'll go
through the agony and misery of the lecture work," he promised Anna. He worried, however, that Carte was "too sanguine"
and "too anxious for me to speculate with him." He was granted
a seven-week leave of absence by the State Department "to lecture before various societies in Great Britain, on purely literary
topics," so despite his forebodings he hustled to London, staying
at the Trübners' home on Upper Hamilton Terrace, before
debuting in the Crystal Palace in Sydenham on January 28. The
"large, bleak hall was moderately well-filled," according to the
London Daily News, but Harte's elocution had not improved
with the years. Only a few minutes into the lecture "the inevitable storm burst from the back benches" and Harte was rudely
interrupted by demands from the audience that he speak up.

While the lecture was otherwise reviewed favorably in *Athenaeum* ("choice language excellently spoken" by "a true artist")
and the *London Morning Post* ("graphic descriptions of scenery,
clever sketches of men and manners, romantic adventures, and
copious anecdotes"), Harte was convinced Carte had blun-
dered by booking him to open in Sydenham, "which would
have been about equal to an *entree* in New York at Yonkers." Or
as George W. Smalley, the London correspondent of the *New*

York Tribune, remarked, Harte's agent "badly managed" his first lecture. "The eight miles of miserable journey by rail discouraged crowds who would have flocked to St. James's Hall to hear him." Harte wrote Schneider that the tour was "frightfully mismanaged," a "wretched blunder all through. Nothing has gone right, except the *Press,* and the *people.*" Indeed, Edmund Yates wrote in the London *World* that Harte was "not merely the most original, but without question the most popular" American author in England.

While he appeared as scheduled in Hull on February 4, Southport on the 11th, Hastings on the 13th, and Nottingham on the 14th, Harte postponed his other dates and returned to Germany. Yates abandoned plans to host a public dinner, chaired by the Earl of Rosebery, in Harte's honor on March 15. "The tour was a miserable failure financially—just as I feared," he reported to Anna from Crefeld on February 21. His half-share of the Crystal Palace box receipts amounted to only about seventy-five dollars, and in the end he cleared only about two hundred dollars over expenses for the five lectures. "I was bound in honor to perform them or I should have returned when I found how I was *swindled.* Only a fear of repeating the 'Redpath' experience kept me from doing it." Of course he also wrote off the cost of a new wardrobe ("I had to spend some money in laying in a stock of clothes, shirts, &c, for I can not find anything decent in Germany"). That summer he packed "a whole tailor's shop of new clothes" to take on vacation.

When Harte returned to England to resume his lectures in late March, he was accompanied by Callie Thacher Cooper, the daughter of his cousin Georgianna Cooper, in whose Georgetown home he had stayed during his abortive tenure with the *Capital* the year before. "A mature, yet youthful woman, of health, beauty and goodness," according to a friend, Callie Cooper had arrived in Düsseldorf in October to study painting, and she probably shared Harte's flat during the year she resided in Germany. (Harte explained to a friend in December 1878 that he took rooms on Drüsbergerstrasse in Düsseldorf when she "came from America to visit me.") While there is no evidence of any impropriety in their relations, Harte never so much as mentioned his young second cousin in any letter he wrote Anna during this year, while he freely mentioned her in letters to his friends in Germany and England. That is, he was remarkably discreet for someone who had nothing to hide. In fact, he conspired with his sister Eliza to conceal from Anna the fact that Callie was living in Düsseldorf. "I have not mentioned [Callie's] name to Anna, nor said anything of her being in Germany," he explained, "knowing how Anna felt about it." He added that Eliza might tell Anna if she wished, "but I have thought as she [Callie] was going to return so soon," it would only "make Anna feel—if she still feels—uneasy." Only once, in 1893, when Anna wanted to send their daughter Jessamy to Paris to study art, did Harte allude to his cousin in a letter to his wife: "Callie Cooper at Düsseldorf spent her money hopelessly with the Professors." Certainly Harte was careful to arrange chaperons for his cousin whenever they traveled together. As he wrote Callie's mother in mid-March, "I am trying to persuade her to go with me to London when I go there to lecture, as I am satisfied she needs some change from the monotony of her life here. She has lately been working too hard. Mrs Trübner . . . would be very glad to have her pay her a visit."

With Callie in tow, Harte returned to England at the end of March. He had been offered $450 to speak in Manchester and he was determined, as he wrote Anna, to "get the money." The lecture in Free Trade Hall on the 27th attracted an audience Harte estimated at about a thousand, and he made, he thought, "a most decided *hit.* . . . They received me with the greatest enthusiasm" and even cheered "*when I stopped to drink a glass of water!*" According to the notice in the *Manchester Guardian,* the lecture was repeatedly interrupted by laughter and Harte was enthusiastically applauded at the close. Unfortunately, he collected only about half the fee he had been promised. While he also spoke in Halifax on April 1, Brighton on the 3rd, and Birmingham on the 7th, his income from the tour, deducting expenses and Carte's commission, "amounted to very little." The Brits, he groused, "with all their kindness and compliment to me, do not understand that Americans lecture for *money* alone."

He was, in fact, generously received and feted while on tour. After speaking in Halifax, for example, he made a driving trip to the abbeys of eastern Yorkshire, to the battlefield of Marston Moor, and to Haworth church and parsonage, sites made famous by the Brontës, in company with Sir George Wombwell; Wemyss Reid, editor of the *Leeds Mercury;* and Charles O. Shepard, the American consul at Bradford. The party dined at the Yorkshire Club in York, where they were joined by the novelist William Black. "I remember few more lively evenings," Reid remembered. Harte and Black, fast friends, "vied with each other" in the stories they told "and the repartees they exchanged." In Brighton he lunched with the mayor, met the local aldermen, and "a deputation waited upon me, and presented me with an *illuminated scroll!*—a very elegantly and eloquently prepared piece of parchment, like a patent of Nobility." In Birmingham he met T. Edgar Pemberton, an industrialist and later drama editor of the *Birmingham Post*. He was forced to decline an invitation to dine the same evening with Arthur Sullivan and the Prince of Wales. On April 10, in London near the close of his trip, he breakfasted with Lord Houghton, whom he had last seen in New York in 1875, and who notified Harte of his election to honorary membership in the Beefsteak Club. He was also elected an honorary member of the Reform Club in London. On April 13 he and Callie were escorted around the city by the painter Frank Miles. They left for Germany two days later, though Harte was invited to return in a few weeks to attend the Literary Fund Dinner and the Dinner of St. John's College at Cambridge.

He was also invited by Sir Frederic Leighton, the painter and president of the Royal Academy of Arts, to reply to the "Toast to Literature" at the Royal Academy dinner on May 3, the first non-British writer to be so honored. However, the prospect of making a speech "terrifies me," as he wrote Anna. Considered "purely as *business,*" the occasion would be "a good *advertisement,* and make some people I know of in New York and Boston

Bret Harte caricature by "Spy" in *Vanity Fair*, January 4, 1879.

ashamed." But he would need to pay his own travel expenses, and he worried about "a fuss in the papers" should he leave his station again so soon to make a public appearance in England. He finally begged off on the grounds that Schneider's ill health required his presence in Crefeld. Froude spoke in his stead and "complimented me handsomely." When Reid invited him to the Edinburgh University Dinner three weeks later, Harte declined again, protesting only half-facetiously "that same lofty and self-sacrificing devotion to the interests of my Government, which kept me here at the Consulate certifying to invoices, when I might have been dining with Princes of the Blood at Royal Academy and Literary Fund banquets."

Besides, Harte planned to vacation that summer in Switzerland and needed to work at least a few weeks before leaving Crefeld again. He had complained privately about the "inclement and sickly" weather in Crefeld since his arrival, and his doctor ordered him "to the mountains for my neuralgia and dyspepsia," or so he claimed. (He first wrote Anna that "I shall try to go somewhere in Switzerland or Italy, if I can get away," then that his doctor urged him to "go to Switzerland or the sea shore this summer.") He asked S. H. M. Byers, the American consul at Zürich, about "the prices and quality of accommodations" near the Zürichsee. Byers and his wife soon persuaded Harte to come with his cousin to Switzerland, to the old chateau at Bocken ten miles from Zürich where they summered. To finance the trip Harte hastily wrote a pulp novella, "The Twins of Table Mountain," a story of sexual intrigue in the mining camps, for a cheap newspaper in Berlin. "It keeps the pot boiling," he told Byers, though on his part Byers thought it beneath his character and fame and he detected few signs that Harte "wasted any enthusiasm on the tale."

Harte and Callie Cooper left Crefeld on July 27, traveled by train through the Rhine valley to Koblenz, Mainz, and Strasburg, then to Zürich, and arrived in Bocken on July 30. "It lies above the lake, looking over it, and towards the snow-peaks in the distance," he reported to Schneider. He went to Obstalden and to the Rigi for the air over the next few days but disliked both: the former "smelt and looked as dirty as if it had been in a cellar," and the latter "gave me no stimulation whatever." He could not afford the usual tourist haunts "for the prices and the altitude are equally *high*." On the whole, moreover, he was unimpressed by Alpine scenery. "As the Rhein is inferior to the Hudson so is Switzerland to California, and even to the Cattskills in New York," he wrote. "The snow peaks visible from my window are fine but I have seen finer views from a wayside hotel in Calaveras county."

Byers's account of Harte's month-long holiday in Switzerland also reveals the likely cause of his ill health: he was again (or still) drinking heavily. The two men shared a room in the chateau, and Byers noted the decanter beside Harte's bed "from which he frequently refreshed his memory during the night." Byers accompanied Harte and his cousin to Laufen Castle at the Falls of the Rhine on August 25, Harte's forty-third birthday, where they toasted his health with a bottle of Mumm's extra dry. Harte and Callie Cooper left the next morning by train, traveling through the Black Forest to Freiberg and Heidelberg ("we could have stayed there two or three days and enjoyed ourselves") before arriving back in Crefeld on August 26. After Callie returned to the United States in October, Harte considered traveling with Byers and his wife to Italy, perhaps Bellagio on Lake Como, but the proposed trip fell through. Years later, Byers by chance again crossed paths with Harte at the Langham Hotel in London, but "there had been a change" in Harte's manner, Byers thought. His "hair was long now," he noted, "and even grayer than before. Some way, somehow, he seemed another man."

Harte had already concluded that "Germany is no place for me—I feel it more and more every day." While the prospect of a posting to Crefeld had seemed like "a glimpse of Paradise" only a year before, he now believed he deserved better. Shepard, the American consul in the small English town of Bradford, claimed that he earned eight thousand dollars a year from his office. As Harte adjured Anna, "Think how a place like that would have answered all our wants, and saved me breaking my heart over this horrid German language and ruining my already weak digestion with their filthy fat and vinegar!" His repeated complaints about Crefeld to friends eventually surfaced in the American press. The *New York Times,* for example, reported on August 29 that Harte "is said to have experienced such ill-effects from the climate" that "he is doubtful if he can remain at his post."

He first requested a two-month leave of absence and a transfer from the State Department on October 7 on "advice of my physician." As he wrote Anna,

> I can get any number of certificates from the best German physicians here that this part of the country is injurious to my temperament and condition. You will perhaps smile and remember how you used to accuse me of making the like charges against every place where I ever lived. I only know that certain symptoms disappear when I leave Germany, if only for a week or two, and invariably return when I am here.

As if to prove the point, he left for Paris on October 11, four days after filing his request for a transfer, in the faint hope of getting some recognition from European newspapers that published unauthorized translations of his stories "of my rights to my literary property." To his surprise the editors of Paris *Figaro* agreed to his demands: they would pay him whenever they printed translations of his work—"a small sum it is true, but better than nothing."

With the permission of the State Department, Harte also escaped to England towards the close of 1879, leaving his station in mid-December for another holiday. To finance the trip, he cranked out another potboiler, "Jeff Briggs's Love Story," a "pure California idyll with a dramatic snap at the end," as he explained to Dana. Harte spent Christmas at the Trübners' home in St. John's Wood and New Year's Eve at the annual Tenants' Ball at Bestwood Lodge. Back in London on January 4, he visited George Eliot at her home. "She said many fine things to me about my work, and asked me to come again to see her," as he reported to Anna. At the Rabelais Club that week, too, he met Thomas Hardy ("a singularly unpretending-looking man") and saw Henry James for the first time since the memorable dinner at Howells's home in Cambridge nine years earlier ("he looks, acts, and thinks like an Englishman, and writes like an Englishman, I am sorry to say"). Harte returned in mid-January to Nottingham to spend a week with his so-called "English cousins" at Newstead Abbey.

Back in London on January 20, he wrote his old friend John Hay, who had succeeded Seward as assistant secretary of state, to press for a transfer if not a promotion: "I have been a pretty fair officer for nearly two years, have not embezzled any public moneys, but have sent considerable to the Treasury above my fees." Hay replied after Harte returned to Crefeld on January 27 that the season was too far advanced to move him to a "southerly station." Harte rejoined that he was "not asking for a change of latitude nor of temperature, but only a change from the excessive *dampness* of this place," and he bluntly asked Hay to be appointed U.S. ambassador to Spain, France, or Great Britain. Given Harte's notoriety, such a prestigious job was plainly out of the question, but Hay promised to do what he could. In late March Harte was finally nominated to be U.S. consul in Glasgow—he read the news in the London *Times* for March 22 before he was formally notified by the department. As Hay wrote Joaquin Miller at the time, "We have got Glasgow for Bret Harte. It cost me friends, too, to do it, but I do not regret it."

On balance Harte was pleased, though scarcely ecstatic. "I hear it is a rather *expensive* place," he allowed, and the "change is not all that I would seek in the way of a climate." Still, it was a promotion to a full consulate in the second-largest city in Great Britain at an annual salary of $3,000 and "other emoluments which make it [worth] at least $4000." And it was a mere express-train ride to London. Still, if only between the lines, his note of thanks to Hay betrayed his irritation: "I believe you have had to work as hard and as conscientiously for this Glasgow Consulship, as if it had been a Mission to the Hague

or Lisbon" or other such appointments as he would have preferred. In any event, the British papers hailed his nomination. The
London *Globe* editorialized that Harte "will receive a warm welcome in North Britain, and, indeed, in England generally." The
London *Telegraph* similarly predicted that he would be given a
"cordial welcome" like those extended to other diplomats "when
they come to us with literary genius to recommend them." If
Harte remained in good health and political grace, he might even,
"within a few years, be appointed a Minister Plenipotentiary, or at
least Secretary of Legation, to some European court."

Before he could be confirmed by the Senate, however, there
was a potential crimp in the best-laid plans: news of his heavy
drinking was printed in a Berlin newspaper in late March and
widely copied in the German press. According to this "adom-
inable and filthy slander," Harte's passion for *Feuerwasser,* or
brandy, was so well known he had been sent by his government
to Germany, where it was hoped that he might be cured.
"Imagine a man addicted to drinking sent to this land of swilling
sots for a cure!" he wailed to Anna. He retained a Berlin lawyer
and demanded a retraction before he filed suit for libel, and at
his request his doctor in Düsseldorf "wrote an indignant letter
to the *Kölnische Zeitung,*" one of the papers that had reprinted
the "infamous lie," to insist "that I not only *was not* but never
could *have been* a drunkard, &c. &c." The Berlin paper issued
the requisite apology and other papers "copied the retraction—
and so the matter ended. I triumphed," Harte crowed, though
he suspected "*that slander came from America,*" more specifically that it originated with Clemens. Their feud still smouldered.

Coincidentally, Harte learned of his nomination to Glasgow
shortly before he was scheduled to return to Great Britain for a
series of appearances. He left Crefeld on April 19 and lectured
on the "Argonauts of '49" at Oxford, Cambridge, and Norwich
over the next several days. Lewis Carroll, who heard the lecture
in Oxford on April 21, remarked on its "quiet humour" in his
diary. Though Harte reported to Schneider that "the lectures
were a success," as usual he also reported to Anna that they
were "not profitable; my expenses in traveling . . . equalled my

very small fee." He visited William Black at his home in Brighton for a few days, and then he attended the Royal Academy dinner at Burlington House in London on May 1. The painter William Frith had approached Harte while he was in London in January to ask whether he was interested in delivering the reply to the "Toast to Literature" at the Royal Academy dinner that spring, and he acceded when Sir Frederick Leighton wrote him in early April with a formal invitation. Such "swells" as Froude, Arthur Sullivan, Robert Browning, T. H. Huxley, Anthony Trollope, Lawrence Alma-Tadema, W. E. Gladstone, the archbishop of Canterbury, and the Prince of Wales "toasted me very kindly," he reported to Anna, and he "made a neat little speech—not bad and not very good" on American humor. In fact he read his "Toast" with his head bent over the manuscript and as usual mumbled his words. The final two pages of his text were not transcribed in news reports of the dinner and, like Harte's lecture on "American Humor," they are now lost. Nevertheless, the prince asked to be introduced to him afterwards, and "I've had no end of invitations and a general kind of patronage from every body." He spent a day reconnoitering in Glasgow ("very smokey, very damp") before leaving on May 12 for a week in Paris en route back to Crefeld "to pack up my traps," as he put it.

There he negotiated one more complication to his nomination. As a trustee of the government, Harte was expected to file a bond guaranteeing the United States against losses through malfeasance in office. His brother-in-law David Cooper, Callie's father, had signed his Crefeld bond, but for a couple of weeks in the spring of 1880 Harte feared he would lose his commission for lack of signatories to his Glasgow bond. Both Dana and Thomas Musgrave refused to sign it, much to Harte's dismay, though Hay finally intervened on his behalf. On June 16 he left Crefeld forever, much as he had earlier left San Francisco and Newport and New York. Though he would reminisce in letters to Schneider and his wife Clara until the end of his life about "the dear old days of Crefeld" and "our gossiping chats and the sympathy that was always ready for me" there, he would never return even for a visit.

On June 21, pausing in London en route to his new post, Harte lectured on the "Argonauts" at Steinway Hall, a charitable event in support of the Victoria Hospital for Children. With "rustling silks and laces inside and rattling carriages and bawling footmen outside . . . I dont think any one came really to *hear* me," he admitted. Most of the audience

> were my "society" friends and they nodded their heads at me and shook their faces and smiled graciously and chatted with each other and came to enjoy apparently "a very good time." I managed finally to frown them into silence, and then they all pretended to be vastly interested, and applauded in the wrong places, and said, in loud stage whispers, to each other "O isnt it perfectly charming! Really, how delicious! You know! The idea! you know!" At last they got me to laughing too—and so the lecture ended.

However peculiar the occasion, the *London Daily News* commended Harte's "quaint and abundant humour." As if finally to retire the lecture, he published a version of it as the introduction to an edition of his collected writings issued by Chatto and Windus in 1880 and in German translation under the title "Aus Kaliforniens fruhen Tagen" in *Deutsche Rundschau* later the same year.

Harte finally took charge in Glasgow on July 20 and promptly ran away for two weeks to Paris "as soon as I could to get one ray of blessed sunshine." He privately complained about the climate in Scotland (no surprise) to friends and family from his very first days there. "I dont know yet whether I can stand this perpetual gloom," he wrote Schneider as early as August 4. "My transfer from Crefeld on account of my health resolves itself into a ghastly farce," he added to Anna on August 7. Three months later, he was despondent: "It is a hundred times worse than Crefeld—more *depressing,* and poisonous from chemical fumes from the factories." He would never lose the sense "that I am living by gas light in a damp cellar with an occasional whiff from a drain, from a coal heap, from a mouldy potatoe bin and from dirty wash tubs." Worse yet, when he arrived the consulate was barely functional, or so he claimed; he compared it to "Mr. Micawber's office at the time of his unsuccessful coal brokerage" in a letter to Hay. However, he escaped the miasma of the city every evening by commuting to Innellan, "a lovely little watering place on the Clyde" an hour and a half away by boat. Fortunately, too, he retained the services of his predecessor's vice-consul, William Gibson, "a hard headed Scotch lawyer" and "an upright man" who reorganized the office. Like Schneider in Crefeld, in fact, Gibson would do most of the consular work in Glasgow during Harte's five-year tenure there.

At first, if only to get up a good reputation, he remained "at my post pretty regularly" despite the weather. "As a *seaport* Consulate is a new thing to me," he explained near the end of his first year in Glasgow, "all my time, when I am not laid by my heels in this wretched climate, has been taken up by my official duties." The consulate annually certified invoices amounting to some ten million dollars in exports. To his credit, Harte intervened on behalf of several crew members of the American bark *Bessie Wittich* who had quit their brutal captain (and later recreated the experience in his story "Young Robin Grey"). He received a handsome letter of thanks from the chief signal officer of the War Department for some meteorological reports he submitted. He also persuaded his superiors at the State Department to erect a stone monument on the island of Iona to honor nineteen American seamen who had died in the wreck of the *Guy Mannering* off the coast of Scotland in 1865. As the *Glasgow Herald* reported, the memorial would not have been built save for "the exertions of the distinguished Consul at Glasgow, Mr. Bret Harte," and Harte gleefully reported to Anna that he had been "repeatedly thanked by the Department" for "the performance of a thoughtful little diplomatic courtesy outside of my usual routine." "In fact I'm *rather* a good Consul," he bragged. Even when he was away from Glasgow, he reviewed all consular reports and documents "and I telegraph often twice a day."

Still, he was the target of a cadre of sniping journalists who caricatured him unmercifully. According to their columns, he had been denationalized by the "adulations which he has received from literary and aristocratic people in Great Britain," and he took every opportunity to escape the fogs of Glasgow. The gossip intensified after Harte was injured in a hunting accident in mid-September 1880—an overloaded gun recoiled and cut his mouth in three places, and the wound required a few stitches. Though at first he reported to his family that the cuts were "trifling" and "very slight," he complained a month later that his "lip was still swollen and stiff, and as I lost a good deal of blood, I'm yet far from strong." Another month later, he was nearly incapacitated, "scarcely able to sign my name to official documents, going to my office in a cab, and often being able to stay there only an hour at a time. The Doctors say my condition is owing to loss of blood, 'shock,' and, hardest of all, the attempt to acclimatize myself here in Glasgow." He canceled an appearance in Edinburgh on November 6, a dinner in honor of James Russell Lowell, to recuperate at Newstead Abbey with the Webbs, as he explained in a telegram read aloud at the dinner. The news was increasingly distorted in the press (e.g., the New York *World* reported ten days later that Harte lay "seriously ill" at Newstead). Hay read in another paper that he planned to resign his station in Glasgow for health reasons. Harte denied the rumor: "Who is the paragraph fiend who continually pursues me so?"

Not that he was without his defenders. Hay remarked in an interview a few weeks later that "Harte met with an accident last summer, about which nothing was said, but it disabled him for a while. . . . He makes a good consul." Privately, Hay wrote Harte that he wondered "what Heaven meant by creating so few men like Clarence King and you." The author of a letter to the editor of the *New York Tribune,* dated March 21, 1881, from Paris and merely signed "H." (perhaps Hay, but more likely his friend Lord Houghton) exonerated Harte on all counts: He "has done and is doing great honor to the country which he represents," and while he "has received some very marked attentions" from British gentry he is "under all circumstances a loyal, even an aggressive American." And, the letter went on,

while he may be compelled for reasons of health "to make frequent brief visits to the country," the Glasgow consulate, "from
all trustworthy reports, is one of the best administered in the
kingdom."

Lest his job in Glasgow seem too stable and secure, he was
again quick to discourage Anna from thoughts of reuniting the
family. Not only might his fortunes shift overnight with a change
of administrations in the election of 1880, he could scarcely
afford the cost of bringing the whole family over for only a few
months. Were he to lose his government job, "I could not make
enough money by mere literary work in England to support my
family. I should be obliged to return to America at once," so
better they remain there. Should the Republicans be reelected,
"I may expect not only to be retained but promoted" to
another station, where his family might join him later. For over
twenty years, as Geoffrey Bret Harte observed, his grandparents
"maintained across three thousand miles of ocean a polite correspondence and the fiction of re-union in the near future. This
fiction found expression in my grandfather's letters in an ever
green plan to return to the United States." After Garfield's
assassination in July 1881, Harte abruptly canceled his plans to
vacation in the United States—"Guiteau's bullet not only stopped
my visit" to his family "but kept me in England," as he wrote
Clara Schneider in Crefeld. He was also advised "as a matter of
selfish wisdom" to stay at his post to quiet the rumors about his
many absences. "There are many office-seekers hungering for
my place, and telling all sorts of lies," he reasoned.

His private life became, in truth, much more complicated
after his appointment to Glasgow. During a visit to the Trübners
in St. John's Wood in 1878, he had met their neighbors the Van
de Veldes—Arthur, chancellor of the Belgian legation in
London; his "high-minded intellectual wife," daughter of the
Italian ambassador in Berlin; and their many children. Harte
first dined with the Van de Veldes in their house at 15 Upper
Hamilton Terrace on February 18, 1881—"they have all been
devoted to me ever since I first met them when I first came to
Europe," he boasted to Anna. Rather than visit the United States

after Garfield's assassination, he spent over a month with the Van de Veldes at their summer home in the resort town of Bournemouth (where he would eventually meet Robert Louis Stevenson). "We all live here very simply and as members of a large family," he wrote Hay. Whenever he was in London he stayed in the Van de Velde home, too—"I have a room there always known as mine, and always containing something of mine summer or winter," as he explained—a continual temptation to spend even less time in Glasgow. In fact he became a type of permanent guest in the Van de Velde home in London on September 20, 1881, when he had his trunk delivered there upon his return from Bournemouth. Harte hardly wrote to pay his rent in the manner of a Grub Street hack if only because he literally had no rent to pay. The Van de Veldes "adopted me into their family,—Heaven knows how or why—as simply as if I had known them for years."

To be sure, the exact nature of their friendship soon became the subject of rumor and gossip. As Harte cryptically recorded in his diary in early November 1881—a diary transcribed entirely in Mme Van de Velde's hand and perhaps edited by her—he discovered some "mischief and innuendos" had "originate[d] with Mrs Trübner" and had written her "to demand [an] explanation." Because "her answer [was] unsatisfactory," he had "inform[ed] her that our acquaintance is at an end." Later the Van de Veldes broke with Frank Miles and his wife, "who support the Trübners view of our friendship." As Harte wrote Anna, he was forced to give up Trübner when his wife "got to quarrelling with my other friends." Axel Nissen has detailed the likely reasons the Van de Veldes were so hospitable: Madame was a woman with a past, a first husband she may never have divorced, and nine children fathered by a man to whom there is no evidence she was legally married. Though they posed as "a genteel and even titled family," and "despite their wealth and culture," Nissen explains, "in high society terms, the Van de Veldes were strictly nobodies." As Harte's hosts, however, they enjoyed respectability and entrée to polite literary and social circles. Through his agency, the "charming woman" (as Dana called Mme Van de

Velde) became an occasional London correspondent of the New York *Sun* and society correspondent of the London *World,* for example, and she hosted the Duchess of St. Albans and Lady Airlie at tea.

Beyond a doubt, Harte was smitten with Hydeline de Seigneux Van de Velde, who was three years his elder, from the first months of their acquaintance. Fluent in three languages, a facile translator, a "woman of wit and singular charm" and "a brilliant hostess," as his grandson Geoffrey remembered, "she was also possessed of tremendous energy and determination." Or as her grandson Hubert van Zeller explained in a family history, "She particularly disliked motor cars, the Liberal Party, the smell of camphor, scenes of any sort, continental hotels, and criticism of Bret Harte." Frank Harte, who met her in 1884, praised her without stint in a letter to a cousin: she was "a very bright woman about forty eight years old I should judge—very tall and stately impressing me at first as being cold—but she is quite the woman—she is full of fun and like nonsense too. Her conversational prowess is truly remarkable—she speaks with quite a foreign accent which rather enhances her charms than deducts from them . . . and she dresses beautifully." Though several of the books Harte inscribed to Mme Van de Velde over the years have survived, no original letters they exchanged are extant— she apparently destroyed both sides of their correspondence after Harte's death. She did permit Pemberton, in his 1903 biography, to reproduce the texts of two innocuous letters Harte had written her (in the first, dated September 1880, he jokes with her about "Scotch lassies" who walk about "without stockings"), and she supplied the frontispiece to his book—a photo of Harte taken in Düsseldorf in 1879 that he sent her in September 1880). Otherwise, most of the details of their relationship are forever lost in a biographical blind spot.

So clubbable a fellow as Harte predictably enjoyed the opportunity to mingle in polite society from his first weeks in Great Britain. He was pleased that his old friends—the Webbs at Newstead Abbey, the Duke and Duchess of St. Albans, the Van de Veldes, the Froudes, William Black—were "still loyal and

Bret Harte in 1879. Photo by Overbeck, Düsseldorf. (Pemberton, *The Life of Bret Harte* [1903])

true," but his social circle was by no means limited to this group. An avid theatregoer and dinner companion, he was also active in the Rabelais Club, whose membership included Hardy, Lord Houghton, and other men of letters such as Charles Leland,

Walter Besant, and Andrew Lang; the artist George du Maurier; Arthur Collins, the gentleman usher to Queen Victoria; and the actor Henry Irving. "We know nothing about Rabelais," Harte admitted, and "except drinking our one toast to the 'Memory of the Master,' it is considered bad form to speak of him." The charm of the club, so far as he was concerned, was "the utter irresponsibility of its members" at their dinners. He sometimes met Robert Browning socially, either at the Reform Club or at the home of the duchess. According to his diary and letters from this period, he socialized with such figures as Baron Rothschild; Sir William Harcourt; Herbert Gladstone; and Herbert Bismarck, son of the German chancellor, as well as such actors and playwrights as Barry Sullivan, Helena Modjeska, Arthur Wing Pinero, and Oscar Wilde. He was one of a select group Osgood managed to scare up for a dinner at the Hotel Continental in London on September 7, 1882—Aldrich, Hay, Howells, Henry James, Clarence King, Moncure Conway, Charles Dudley Warner, and Edwin Booth among them. "It was a most remarkable coincidence to find all these men together in London," he reported to Anna; indeed, "it would have been most remarkable for New York or Boston." His most vivid impression of Howells was that he had "grown fat." On his part, Howells remarked later that Harte resembled "a French marquis of the ancien regime" or "an American actor made up" for the role. It was the last time they would meet.

The allegations about Harte's absences dogged him throughout his tenure in Glasgow, not least because the rumors were true. Nissen fairly concludes on the basis of Harte's diary entries that "during the five years of his appointment to Glasgow, he spent no more than one fifth of his time at his post." In 1881, for example, he was in Scotland (though not necessarily in Glasgow or at the consulate) from January 1 to 5, a fortnight in early February, March 14 to 24, September 21 to October 30, and November 19 to 23. In 1882 he was there from January 24 to 31, February 2 to 15, May 6 to 24, and October 5 to November 3. His friend William Black privately compared him to a "globule of mercury" that ran and pooled unpredictably or to a "wandering comet. The only place he is sure not to be found is at the Glasgow Consulate." In January 1885, near the end of his diplomatic career, Harte vigorously defended his supervisory methods: "For the past five years I have never been without communication with the consulate—and even when I am in London for a holiday, or for *work* (I find it difficult to write in Glasgow), I always write *daily* and personally superintend—though at a distance—my consular work." George Stewart reported in 1931 that he had found 562 letters and telegrams from Harte to Gibson in the consular archives in Glasgow, which "makes certain" that the titular consul "must have been away from Glasgow an extraordinarily large proportion of the time."

Harte also went to elaborate lengths to conceal these absences. As Nissen explains, he dated "his America-bound letters," including those to Anna, from Glasgow—indeed, he often wrote them on official stationery—and sent them to Gibson to mail so they would have the correct postmark. Still, the rumors about his dereliction of duty were so persistent and widespread that the State Department informally asked Harte to reply to them in November 1882. He insisted that he could not document the exact dates of his approved absences because "I do not keep a diary" (a patent lie), and then he welcomed the opportunity to "utterly deny" the rumors of "inattention, negligence or delay" in the discharge of his duties. Save for approved leaves of absence, all "half holidays, local Fast-days and Sundays" and the whole of the summer, when "I found it beneficial to my health to follow the custom of the Glasgow merchants and businessmen" and vacation at the seashore, he had been on the job. "If an invoice has been delayed, a signature withheld, an interview denied or any duty unfulfilled through my absence," he insisted, "I have yet to hear of it."

So how *did* Harte fill his time? On the surface the early 1880s seem to be a fallow period in his literary career. He published only two stories ("Jeff Briggs's Love Story" and "A Gentleman of La Porte") in 1880, none in 1881, two stories ("Found at Blazing Star" and "Flip: A California Romance") and a tribute to Longfellow in 1882, and three stories ("At the Mission of San

Carmel," "In the Carquinez Woods," and "Left Out on Lone Star Mountain") in 1883. While these tales were undeniably popular, they were also mocked by the pecksniffian critics for the *Saturday Review* (Harte "burnt his heroine and drowned his hero in the most unnecessary way") and the *Spectator* ("he does not take the pains to finish off any of his characters very carefully; nor, indeed, are they, for the most part, worth the trouble"). And while Harte would often assert near the end of his life that he had never received a letter of rejection from an editor, in fact his story "Flip" was rejected by the Very Reverend Donald Macleod, chaplain to the king of Scotland and editor of *Good Words*. Macleod objected to the overt eroticism of Harte's serial novel, with its references to the heroine's "shapely limb," "tanned bare arms," "lithe, nymph-like figure," "bright flanks," and "childish bosom." Harte refused to rewrite the story or "restrict my work to the habits and tastes of a restricted and narrower class" of readers, so he arranged for "Flip" to appear serially in the *Glasgow Herald*. Whereas in Crefeld he had sent his consular salary in monthly drafts to Anna and lived on the income from his writing, during his first year or two in Glasgow he was ostensibly unable to supplement his salary with literary work due to poor health and drew his entire income from the consulate.

Then Mme Van de Velde became, if not quite a patron, an angel who took him under wing. She flattered him; wrote brief enconiums of him for *Belgravia* and the *Illustrated London News;* nagged him to curtail his drinking; translated several of his later stories into French for publication in *Figaro, Nouvelle Revue,* and elsewhere; sometimes served as his amanuensis; and collaborated with him on four plays, three of them based on his stories. After she "took him in hand," as the *New York Tribune* reported in 1883, he became "productive again." One of her grandsons remembered that she "lavished her devotion upon Bret Harte." His grandson Geoffrey recalled that "She laughed and talked and contradicted him with perfect composure as though they were equals, without trace of that deference, almost reverence that surrounded him on his visits to us. And he seemed to enjoy it!" Under her influence he once more became a bankable, if not a serious writer.

In mid-January 1882 they began to write a play together based on Harte's story "Thankful Blossom," set in Morristown during the American Revolution. Harte had dashed it off for the *Sun* in December 1876, in the interlude between the failure of *Two Men of Sandy Bar* and the disaster of *Ah Sin,* and while Clemens believed "it belongs at the very top of Harte's literature," it was generally scorned by reviewers when it first appeared. "It is wonderful how well and quickly it adapts itself to stage effect," he explained to Anna, "and its dialogue keeps it *understandable* by all audiences, while all the old cant about my *coarseness* and *slang* certainly cannot be used against [it]." While Harte had no idea "what *the play may be,*" whether it would ever be produced or not, he derived at least one satisfaction from writing it: "During the last two years I have done scarcely anything in the way of literary work," and he had begun "to fear that I had lost the power. It is with heartfelt gratitude that I find I can at least *seem* to do it." For the record, he informed Anna that he had "solemnly promised" not to divulge the name of his collaborator. He was remarkably discreet for someone who had nothing to hide.

Despite his earlier failures as a playwright, Harte was still keen to succeed in the genre. Plays could be "vastly more profitable" than stories, he repeatedly insisted. Whereas he always sold his tales for a lump sum, retaining only the right to reprint them in his books, a "good popular play" might easily earn three thousand dollars or more a year in royalties. He was also appalled that so many playwrights and actors, among them Bartley Campbell and Parsloe in *My Partner,* had made barrels of money by exploiting in stage productions the brand of western melodrama he had popularized in his fiction, sometimes even by plagiarizing him. Annie Pixley played the ingenue in a "vulgar" (Harte thought) theatrical adaptation of "M'liss" over two thousand times between 1878 and 1888 and earned a fortune, while the author of the original story received nary a cent. Harte sued Pixley in 1890 to enjoin the production of the play in England.

Joaquin Miller stole shamelessly from Harte's fiction in his script of '49, whose cast included a female lead who was "a weak reproduction of M'liss" and a comical figure reminiscent of "the drunken heroes of Bret Harte." After Elisha Bliss sold dramatic rights to his novel without so much as consulting its author in 1884, the actor McKee Rankin staged a dramatization of *Gabriel Conroy* with "a number of scenes transferred almost bodily from Mr. Harte's story." Such plays "draw what little money there is in my dramatic work, by the most unscrupulous and unskillful means," he complained to Anna, and he was determined to cash in, if possible, on his own reputation.

Unfortunately, he was unable to persuade any theatrical managers to stage *Thankful Blossom*. Bram Stoker of the Lyceum Theatre (and later, of course, the author of *Dracula*) expressed some interest, though nothing came of it; D'Oyly Carte wrote him "doubtfully" about the play; and Michael Gunn, Carte's partner, thought the script, given its subject, "more assured of success in America than here." The actress Lotta Crabtree, whom Harte had known in San Francisco twenty years before, asked to see the script but returned it a week later. His old friend Boucicault read it and recommended major structural changes. "I see the justice of all his suggestions," he admitted to Anna, "but the work will be nearly as great as writing another play."

He soon concluded that was exactly what he would do. Determined "to succeed with a play this season" and preferring to write "*a new one* rather than risk more on the old," he and Mme Van de Velde at Boucicault's urging began to collaborate in June 1882 on a peculiar dramatization of "The Luck of Roaring Camp." Harte summarized the plot later to Augustin Daly:

> The first act—or prologue as it really is—is an almost literal dramatization of my original story, except that the child is a girl instead of a boy. The two remaining acts . . . take place in Paris, where the girl, grown a young lady, has been placed at school by her rough but devoted fathers of Roaring Camp. . . . It is a comedy, naturally—the humorous situations dominate, but the rough element is never low comedy—nor is it ever obstusive or protracted. All my old characters appear:—Oakhurst, Stumpy, Kentuck and Skaggs.

The collaborators finished the script in Bournemouth, where Harte again spent the month of August with the Van de Veldes— "I came here ostensibly for my health but really to work at my new Play"—and he read the script aloud to Hay and King during their visit to London in early September. ("When is that play coming out?" Hay wrote from Paris in December. "I will come to London for that if I have strength enough to lie in a gutter and call for a coach.")

Harte and Mme Van de Velde freely adapted the original story for dramatic purposes, as in the opening act when Stumpy comments on the regeneration of the miners: "Since that yer baby was born they've let up a heap in the yellin and shoutin that gave a name to Roaring Camp. I reckon there ain't been a free fight or a six shooter fired in three days." Harte was disappointed three weeks later when Boucicault judged the two last acts "radically wrong in structure" and advised him to

> *begin it all over again.* You know how hard it is for me to write a play [he complained to Anna]; imagine how provoked and exasperated I feel at having lost my holiday in such ungracious work only to find it futile. Of course I shall not give it up—but it means that I must turn my leisure now to writing some little story *for money* to keep the pot boiling before I can go on with the larger work which is to pay me better in the end.

Harte's "larger work" was not more ambitious or more artistic than his potboilers, of course; it was simply better paid. His standard of value, whether he was writing stories or plays, was not aesthetic but commercial.

Though he asked the American playwright Bronson Howard, another neighbor in St. John's Wood, for advice about dramatic structure, he was never able to transfer his talent as a western local colorist from fiction to drama: "It seems I can write dialogue like an angel, draw character like a heaven born genius, but I cant make *situations* and *plots.*" The London theatrical managers were "more or less afraid to risk" a production of *The Luck* with "English actors and English audiences," he learned, and in New York his friend Daly also rejected it. While he wasted months on these scripts, he also conceded he would rather "have them failures in *MS* than before the footlights." Charles Frohman eventually agreed to produce *The Luck* at the Madison Square Theatre in New York in 1884 for a royalty of fifteen dollars per performance, ceasing at ten thousand dollars, though Frohman soon thought better of the deal (the script "must be almost entirely rearranged and rewritten before it can appear"). Harte was predictably discouraged, though he still hoped to "get a thousand dollars or two out of it." He collected a small forfeiture, no more than five hundred dollars, which likely went to pay some old debts. David Belasco proposed in June 1885 to "rewrite and supervise the production of the play" in New York, paying Harte an advance of five hundred dollars and "one third of all royalties on said play," though nothing came of the proposal. The comic actor and theatrical manager John L. Toole offered to stage the play, "that long-travailing infant," in 1886, but Harte withdrew the script when he decided that "either the pathetic or the farcical" element in the play "must be dominant; that I could not blend them, and that either Toole or the audience must be disappointed."

Finally, in 1890, after protracted negotiations, Harte authorized Boucicault to dramatize the story—in effect, he sold dramatic rights to the title and characters to him for fifteen pounds weekly so long as the play kept the stage. Boucicault began to write the adaptation but died before it was completed—yet another unfortunate twist of Harte's financial fate. The fragment—the first act of a projected three-act play—was briefly staged as a curtain raiser by Frohman at the Empire Theatre in New York in May 1894. Despite his contract, Harte received no royalties from the production because Boucicault's supposed collaborator claimed he had done all the writing.

Harte and Mme Van de Velde cowrote two more plays, adaptations of Edmond About's salacious novel *Germaine*, a convoluted tale of extramarital affairs, doubtful paternities, and marriages of convenience among the French aristocracy, and Harte's own "A Blue Grass Penelope." At the suggestion of Arthur

Sullivan, he also outlined a libretto based on "At the Mission of San Carmel." None of these projects bore fruit. The actress Genevieve Ward read the script of *Germaine* and "would have taken it" but for "the sudden squeamishness of the 'Censor of Plays,'" J. W. Pigott, who "highly disapprove[d] of its morality," "refuse[d] to license it," and instead "suggested alterations and difficulties." Lester Wallack agreed in early 1884 to produce the play and pay Harte a royalty of $125 a week, though in the end he paid a forfeiture fee of $200 instead. (When the *Brooklyn Eagle* reported that the fee was $1,000, Harte joked that "it won't hurt to let people *think* so—but I wish I had the money.")

Lawrence Barrett visited Upper Hamilton Terrace in June 1884 to hear *Penelope* read aloud and to offer suggestions, and Harte subsequently tried to interest both Lillie Langtry and William Kendal in the play, but to no avail. The actress Fanny Mary (Mrs. Bernard) Beere liked the script so much she told Harte that "if she had a theatre of her own she would produce" it—but she did not have a theatre of her own. In truth, Mme Van de Velde was arguably the more gifted playwright of the two. Her adaptation of F. C. Philips's novel *As in a Looking Glass,* starring "the divine Sarah" Bernhardt, was briefly staged at the Théatre des Variétés in Paris and the Lyceum Theatre in London in 1889. On his part, Harte was nothing if not persistent. "You may wonder why I work so hard at a thing thus far so unprofitable," he wrote Anna in June 1884. The reason was simple. A successful play "would take the place of my consulate in ekeing out my income."

He would need to replace his consular income soon enough. The long-simmering rumors about his absences from Glasgow were brought to a boil by a paragraph in the *New York Tribune* for August 26, 1883:

> Bret Harte resides in St. John's Wood, London, with the Chancellor of the Belgian Legation, Mr. Vandervelde, a cultivated man whose wife seriously set herself to work to regulate Mr. Harte, of whose genius she had a high idea. He held the American consulate at Glasgow, but was there irregularly and yet he did not produce any

literary work. She discovered that he required surroundings and conditions to stimulate his powers, of which meantime, a great variety of result-killing society people were getting amusement at dinner parties. Mrs. Harte lives in this country upon her husband's consular salary, not being able to provide the conditions, as aforesaid, to decoy his fancy forth.

Anna Harte enclosed without comment a copy of this paragraph clipped from the *Tribune* in her next letter to her husband, who was appalled. He tried to mollify her, despite its "wanton fling at you" and "intimation that I do not live at Glasgow and have always been irregular there." As before, Harte continued to insist that he was the target of "reports" and "jokes" but no "complaints": "I am always there when wanted." The Glasgow merchants "naturally prefer to do their purely clerical business with my Vice Consul—their own countryman—who is one of the best and most efficient lawyers in Glasgow. *They* dont complain. *The Department* dont complain of inattention. Who does?"

Harte nevertheless used the paragraph in the *Tribune* to rationalize his decision not to return to the United States for a visit in the summer of 1883, despite the grant of a leave of absence by the State Department. Were he to return, "what may not be said when the pen is sharpened by envy or malice"? Besides, his old creditors had not "abated a single jot of their claims," and he worried that "when it is known that I have returned for a leave of absence, they will all make a dead set at me—*at once.*" He had anticipated liens against the royalties he hoped to earn by his plays in the United States by making them "payable to my *collaborateur* here who is not an American," much as he "protected myself with publishers in America by getting the money [for his stories] *in advance.*" He worried, too, that his fortunes might change for the worse were he to leave England for even a few weeks: "I have been *singularly lucky while I have been here in Europe.* My affairs have prospered; I have a market for my wares; I am not dependent upon publishers whims or caprices." Anna replied that he was a "strange man"—a point

Harte readily conceded, with the caveat that he was "trying to be a more practical one than I have ever been."

The rumors of Harte's inattention to duty in Glasgow were compounded in the spring of 1885 when he was forced to fire Peter Forgie, the chief clerk he had inherited from his predecessor. Forgie had ignored for years past some State Department regulations about the certification of invoices, though he had not been detected in the practice. Harte expressed to his superiors in the State Department his "mortification" at the "apparent disregard" of government instructions. His clerk had "behaved so dishonestly," Harte admitted privately, that he could have been arrested and jailed; instead, Harte simply dismissed him. Forgie retaliated by alleging that Harte had paid him only part of the salary to which he was entitled and pocketed the difference—much as Harte had been accused in 1872 of skimming from the contributors to the *Overland*—and the State Department investigated the charge. Harte convinced the American consul in Belfast to accept his explanation for his lapse of supervision: he had been on leave of absence. Though cleared of any wrongdoing, Harte was scarcely exonerated: his letter of explanation and apology was forwarded to the State Department auditor.

The imbroglio could hardly have happened at a worse moment, moreover. Since the inauguration of Grover Cleveland, a Democrat, in March 1885, Harte had retained his office through the good graces of the new president. With good reason, he expected to be replaced in office at virtually any moment. "Except by some extraordinary intercession I do not imagine I will be kept in my place by a Democratic administration," he had confided to Anna in a note scribbled the day after the election, "and it is even doubtful if the Republicans will retain me in the service, so that I am quite ready for any emergency." "I know nothing of the intentions of the present Administration regarding me," he added in late May 1885. His friends Hay and Dana, among others, "are doing all they can to keep me here, and all write to me that the Government does not look upon my appointment as a *political* one—like the others. But I shall be surprised at nothing."

If, in the words of the old saw, forewarned is forearmed, then Harte wisely anticipated his dismissal and took precautions. Before he could be turned out of office, he hired the literary agent A. P. Watt to represent him. Their agreement was instrumental to the commercial success Harte enjoyed over the last eighteen years of his life. With Watt's help, for which he received the standard 10 percent commission, Harte began to write for a living again. "Until authors know a little more about business, and are less likely to feel that it interferes with that perfect freedom essential to literary composition," he observed in his first extant letter to Watt, in May 1885, "it seems better that they should employ a *business man* to represent them with those other *business men,* the publishers." Similarly, Henry James wrote to his brother William of "the relief & comfort of having [Watt] take all the mercenary & selling side off one's mind." Harte also reported to Anna in November 1886 that Watt "looks after my interest" and "relieves me from all the horrible torments of being obliged to offer my *MSS* personally to publishers, as I used to do in America. It takes away half the pains of authorship." As Stewart explained, in Watt's hands "a story was a piece of goods to be sold to the highest bidder, so that without emotional disturbance he could peddle it among possible buyers until he had got the best price." The exact date Watt began to represent Harte formally is unclear; certainly it was no later than July 11, 1884, when Harte referred to "my agent A. P. Watt Esq." in a note to Baron Tauchnitz. Watt had earlier handled the sale of "In the Carquinez Woods" to the newspaper syndicates in mid-1883, though Harte was still contacting publishers on his own as late as November 1883.

In any event, Harte's productivity increased dramatically after Watt began to represent him. By Nissen's estimate, it quadrupled between 1884, when he wrote only two stories ("A Blue Grass Penelope" and "Sarah Walker"), and 1885, when he published three stories in his "more condensed style" ("A Ship of '49," "An Apostle of the Tules," and "Snow-Bound at Eagle's") and the serial novel *Maruja,* with a corresponding jump in his literary income from about $3,615 to $9,680. (Two of these tales

contained "flagrant caricatures" of women he remembered
from the old days in California: Sarah Walker was modeled on
one of Anna's friends, Sarah Hunter, and the heroine of *Maruja*
was based on Alejandra Atherton, an "awful flirt" formerly of
Menlo Park, since married to the consul general in Paris.) He
reported to Anna in mid-March 1885 that he was working
"breathlessly to make the most of advantageous offers that do
not occur everyday, and to avoid being stranded hopelessly
here, in case I shall not be able to keep my office." He wrote
Clara Schneider two weeks later that he had been "quite over-
whelmed with literary work for the last six months." "Except
when I was in the Mint in San Francisco and edited the *Overland* at the same time," he reiterated to Anna, "I do not think I
ever worked so hard."

In fact, he would publish at least one new collection of stories
every year between 1884 and 1903, virtually all of them originally
published more or less simultaneously in magazines and newspapers on both sides of the Atlantic. He credited Watt in 1886
not only with increasing his share of the literary market but with
increasing the rate of payment he received: "I am quite convinced that *the commission I pay you has been fully returned by the
appreciation of the market value of my work through your efforts,*
to say nothing of the saving of time and trouble to me." Six
years later, he could say no more: "I am delighted to find nothing
that I would alter of the full praise I gave you then, and nothing
that our later continued relations have not fully endorsed and jus-
tified." His arrangement with Watt, which coincided with the
rise of the literary syndicates in the United States and England,
was one last stroke of good fortune of the kind that punctuated
his career.

The growth in his income from the magazines and newspapers more than compensated, and none too soon, for the loss of
his government salary. His fate as a diplomat was sealed one day
in the spring of 1885 when an inspector from the State Department called at the Glasgow consulate without warning and
asked for the consul. Gibson explained that "Harte is never here.
He lives in London and devotes himself to literature." Had he

known the purpose of the stranger's visit, Gibson later protested, he would have cabled Harte in London "and he'd been
here [the next] morning." The guillotine finally fell in mid-July.
Much as he had read of his transfer to Scotland in the London
Times in 1880, he read in the *Times* for July 18, 1885, that "a new
Consul was appointed to Glasgow." Though he had been steeled
for the news, he was "quite unprepared for the excuse that I was
removed for 'inattention to duty,' and this gratuitous insult
galls me." He claimed later that he had simply been fired to
make room for another appointee. In any event, the joke soon
made the rounds in Glasgow that the only man who did not
know the location of the U.S. consulate had been the U.S. consul.
Ironically, Clemens had warned in 1878 that Harte's selection to
a diplomatic post would end badly, perhaps even in his disgrace.
He had been right, if for the wrong reasons.

Three years later, upon the election of the Republican presidential candidate Benjamin Harrison, Harte wrote Hay to explore
the possibility of another consular appointment. "I believe my
record in the State Department is a good one," he volunteered,
"although a travelling Assistant Secretary of State, I am told,
did not find me at home one day." Hay was initially sympathetic: he wrote Joaquin Miller that Harte had been "a first-rate
Consul, square, accurate and efficient in all his work" and that
he expected him to be reinstated in a diplomatic post by the
new administration. However, the new secretary of state, James
G. Blaine, deflated the trial balloon. The Consular Bureau, he
reported to Hay, regarded Harte as "the worst consul thus far
recorded." There was no repairing such a reputation. Like a
trail of crumbs that leads to a cliff, Harte's diplomatic career
came to an abrupt halt in the summer of 1885.

CHAPTER 6

Tailings from the Claim

HARTE no longer needed to remain in Britain after his successor arrived in August. He might have returned to his family in New Jersey. But he chose to stay in London with his adopted family rather than resume a life he had shed, like a snake its skin, over seven years before. "I shall remain here" to "finish some more literary work" and "make the most I can of the English demand" for his stories, he announced to Anna. The Van de Veldes had invited him to their new seaside country house in Hampshire when he left Glasgow for good and all, and "after that—we shall see." His dismissal, he wrote Clara Schneider, "will not affect—at least at present—my remaining in Europe. I can pursue my literary work, which has been gradually increasing each year, much more *profitably* here than in America." He replayed this refrain often in his letters over the next few months. "I have never stood so well in regard to the *market value* of my works in any other countries as here," he noted in mid-August. "I remain in England because I have the best market there," he reiterated in January 1886.

His point gradually evolved into an argument for international copyright—and a regret that he could never return to his native land except perhaps for a visit of a few weeks until such a law was enacted. His family could not join him in England even for a brief visit without vastly overtaxing his income, inasmuch as he had no home save for a room in the Van de Velde mansion. "To make your visit here in London what it should be," he averred, "would cost more than I could afford." (He admonished them not to be so selfish.) To Anna's repeated entreaties that his children needed their father, he merely replied that his work as the family breadwinner "keeps us apart." Never mind that his son Griswold had written him only two letters in five years. He performed his parental duties much as he had discharged his consular ones—by proxy.

Lest he seem to enjoy his continuing exile, he assured Anna that his life was "quiet" and "very uneventful" and "very monotonous" and that there was little "in it to interest you." True to his word, he spent much of his time pinned to his desk with his "wretched pen" in hand—Nissen estimates that he published an average of about ninety thousand words per year between 1885 and 1891. Before 1885 he wrote slowly and painstakingly, no more than a few hundred words per day. After 1885, entirely dependent on his pen for a livelihood, he routinely wrote upwards of a thousand words a day, Sundays included, not that he could maintain such a pace or average more than a few hundred words daily over a period of weeks. In 1886 alone he wrote the juvenile novel *The Queen of the Pirate Isle* for publication by Houghton Mifflin in the United States and Chatto and Windus in England; the novella "Struck at Devil's Ford" for the *Sun* syndicate in the United States and the Central News Agency in England; the serial "A Millionaire of Rough-and-Ready" for holiday issues of *Harper's Bazar* and the *Illustrated London News;* and much of the serial novel "The Crusade of the Excelsior" for *Harper's Weekly* and the *Illustrated London News.*

All but the first were written under contract, targeted at a certain class of readers and tailored to a certain length. "Just now in England there is no one who can fill a certain want as I can—or as the English publishers *think* I can," he explained to Anna in October 1886, though he worried that were he to leave for even a brief visit to the United States they might "find out that they could do without me. I would like to *fill* the market for a few months, by work ahead," and then "return before they knew I was gone. If I lose the hold I have upon them here, Heaven knows what would support us." Or as he complained to Anna in November 1887, "I see nothing ahead of me but my habitual work—as long as opportunity and strength suffice."

To be sure, he did not necessarily work every day—"the pump is dry" or "works a little slowly at times," he sometimes admitted—though he was usually puttering with a manuscript. Merely to silhouette Harte's regimen of writing, on November 3, 1886, Watt received an offer from the *Illustrated London News* for a serial novel to commence publication in January 1887. Harte began to draft "The Crusade of the Excelsior" on November 11. Watt had to prod him for copy on December 30, when the first installment went to press. Harte finished the story, which was over seventy thousand words in length, on March 28, 1887. Five days later he began "A Drift from Redwood Camp" and finished it, some thirty thousand words, a month later. In late May he began "A Phyllis of the Sierras" for the *Illustrated London News*. He loitered over the manuscript most of the summer—he had drafted only five thousand of the thirty thousand words by early August—and finished it on September 11. A week later he began "The Argonauts of North Liberty" for William F. Tillotson's syndicate, finishing the tale on November 24. On December 18 he began yet another serial novel, "Cressy," for *Macmillan* (Oscar Wilde would pronounce it "one of his most brilliant and masterly productions," which "will take rank with the best of his Californian stories").

Meanwhile, he declined offers from Tillotson to write a weekly syndicated letter for an annual payment of £500 pounds and from the London *Globe* to write thirteen articles for a total of £250. "For the last two years I have worked harder and more continuously" than "at any time of my life except when I was quite young," he wrote Clara Schneider in October 1888. "I dont know how long the demand for my kind of work will last." Or as he wrote her in October 1891, "I have been *very hard at work* for the past ten years; they have really been my most industrious ones." He would have welcomed a salaried editorial job, one that allowed him the same autonomy as the consulate—but none was offered. Without a government sinecure, entirely dependent on his own resources for a livelihood for the first time since he fled his creditors in 1878, Harte was anxious to avoid any drastic misstep that would compel him to abandon his station in British society and return to the United States. His letters to Anna until the end of his life are filled with worry about his uncertain income, and the gamblers and prospectors who struggle for their livelihood in his western stories from these years seem to betray his concern for his own precarious fortunes.

To his credit, Harte expanded his repertoire beyond his "monotonous romances," as he called them, by turning to dialect poetry, a genre he had ignored since 1878, and by experimenting with both theatrical farce and new forms of fiction. Like the entrepreneurial Buffalo Bill Cody, he reinforced a popular if sensational mythology about the American West that he had helped to invent a generation before. (When Cody brought his Wild West Show to London for the first time in 1887, in fact, Harte attended at least two performances at Earl's Court and occasionally dined with the showman.) While he was not so versatile with a pen as Cody with a six-shooter, he was careful not to alienate his readers. "I do not quite know whether, after these years, the gentle muse [of poetry] will again visit me, for I fear I have let her know that she is too expensive and exacting a flame for my old age," he worried. Still, "if I can successfully woo the muse again it might *pay* me—but never as well as prose." Lest he seem to abandon his distinctive brand of western writing, he reassured Anna that his new poetry "is coming from the same spring as my prose only the tap is nearer the fountain—and filtered." He resurrected Truthful James, who describes the latest bilking of Jim Nye in "The Thought-Reader of Angels," published in the Christmas 1886 issues of the *Illustrated London News* in Britain and *Harper's Weekly* in the United States. The same magazines also printed such "characteristic verses" from his pen as "Artemis in Sierra," "Jack of the Tules," and "'Crotalus'/Rattlesnake Bar, Sierras." He earned £60 for a lyric, "The Mission Bells of Monterey," which the composer Charles Gounod set to music.

In the spring and summer of 1886 he collaborated with John L. Toole on a two-act western comedy, never produced and now lost, entitled "Furnished by Bunter." "I am still working at my 'Farce,'" he wrote his wife in August, though the term seemed

"almost ironical" given "the laborious matter-of-fact performance it has become in my weary hand." He feared he was merely
wasting time on it "that I ought to employ in story-writing for
my bread-and-butter." A month later he reported that he had
heard nothing from Toole, "to whom I sent the play" that "has
cost me so much worry and labor. It will be too late for the
Season now, if it appears at all, and I suppose I must put it
among my failures." At least the collapse of one more pipe
dream enabled him to rationalize his decision to delay (again)
his visit to the United States: "I cannot go now until I have
done some more work and made some more money." Ironically, he earned at least $6,800 from the sale of his stories in
1886, and his annual income was publicly estimated the next
year at between $8,000 and $10,000.

Meanwhile, some of the western stories he wrote for his bread
and butter during these months, such as the allegorical "Crusade
of the Excelsior," betrayed his political sympathies. This novella
had "an original idea as its foundation," he explained to Anna.
In the most immediate sense, the plot is Harte's gloss on the
labor strikes and demonstrations that rocked London in 1886–87—
the same civil unrest that inspired Henry James's novel *The
Princess Casamassima*. "I have seen the English upper classes
shaken in their firm belief in their own superiority and eternal
power," he wrote in February 1886.

> I have seen them brought face to face, through their own plate
> glass windows, with the howling, starving mob they and their
> fathers have trodden upon and despised for all these years, and they
> have grown pale, as the plate glass shattered around them. For once
> their sacred police could do nothing! For once they saw these ter-
> ribly famished creatures, whom they had patronized in workhouses,
> petted in hospitals and kept at a distance generally with good
> humored tolerance, absolutely breaking their bounds, and clam-
> oring for Heaven knows what! You will read all these accounts in
> the papers—but you will never understand it until you see these
> people as I have seen them—of both classes!—and learn how hope-
> less is the ditch that has been dug between them by centuries of
> class government.

"I like these people very much," he conceded later, "but Heaven help them when the day of reckoning comes." He indicted both halves of the house divided—both "the usual one-idead stupidity of the governing classes, and the feeble revolutions of Trafalgar Square, which like the English thunderstorms, thicken, without clearing the air"—in a letter to John Hay shortly after the publication of "Crusade."

Onto its dystopian plot of class warfare in a fictional Mexican village ironically named Todos Santos (All Saints), Harte grafted a thinly disguised anti-imperialist subplot about the American filibuster William Walker, who had briefly established colonial governments in Sonora and Nicaragua over thirty years before. For good measure he tossed into the mix a character modeled upon the infamous actress and poet Adah Isaacs Menken, who had starred in the melodrama *Mazeppa* clad only in flesh-colored tights in San Francisco in 1863. Though "Crusade" was one of Hay's favorite novels, the *Boston Transcript* sniffed at its "cheap devices, tricks smelling strongly of the amateur domestic drama"; the London *Times* concluded it was "unsatisfactory as a whole"; the *Athenaeum* pronounced it Harte's "first complete failure"; and the author admitted he was "rather disappointed in it, myself."

In the end Harte labored over his manuscripts at a distinct disadvantage: he was a writer whose stories were normally set in the American West but who had fled the region in 1871 and never returned. Little wonder that he repeatedly evoked in his fiction the faded memories of people he had known there long years before. He was no literary realist in these stories. In fact, his failures of verisimilitude or *vraisemblance* were often the subject of comment, as when Charles S. Green lampooned him in a parody of "Plain Language from Truthful James" published in 1898 in the very magazine Harte had helped found in 1868:

> Which I wish to impart,
>   And I hopes not in vain,
> That I think that Bret Harte
>   Should come back again

> To the land that is called California,
>> And the reasons I now will explain.
>
> Which he says that the woods
>> On the Carquinez grow,
> And he likewise alludes
>> To Mendocino
> As being just north of Bonita,—
>> Oh Bret, you knew better than so!
>
> But what kills me plumb dead
>> Is to see where he's writ
> That our poppies is red,—
>> Which they ain't red a bit,
> But the flamingest orange and yellow,—
>> Oh Bret, how could you forget?

Harte may have been the father of western American fiction, but his children were careful to deny his influence. Bailey Millard, the book editor of the *San Francisco Chronicle,* told Rudyard Kipling during his visit to the Bay Area in 1889 that "Bret Harte claims California, but California don't claim Bret Harte." "I have great faith in the possibilities of San Francisco and the Pacific Coast as offering a field for fiction," the novelist Frank Norris observed a few years later, but not "the fiction of Bret Harte . . . for the country has long since outgrown the 'red shirt' period." So far as Norris was concerned, Harte, with his precious plots and bathetic endings and "shilling-shockers," epitomized everything that was wrong with western fiction. When Harte found his brand of "local color fading from the West," Mary Austin observed in the *Atlantic* in 1902, "he did what he considered the only safe thing, and carried his young impression away to be worked out untroubled by any newer fact." Similarly, the Harvard philosopher Josiah Royce, the son of a '49er, remarked in 1909 that "as a Californian, I can say that not one childhood memory of mine suggests any social incident or situation that in the faintest degree gives meaning or confirmation to Bret Harte's stories." Harte depicted California,

according to Royce, "in distinctly provincial terms." Little wonder
that Wallace Stegner joked that Harte's popularity "was always
greatest in direct proportion to the reader's distance from and
ignorance of the mines."

Especially in his late stories, Harte imag(in)ed San Francisco
as a rough-and-tumble boomtown at the height of the gold rush.
Such stories as "The Secret of Telegraph Hill" (1889) and "The
Ward of the Golden Gate" (1890) are rich in picturesque details
specific to their midcentury San Francisco setting, such as the
semaphore telegraph that gave Telegraph Hill its name, the
gambling saloons along the Barbary Coast, and the house on
Sansome Street that had been erected on a foundation of tobacco
crates. These details notwithstanding, the setting of the stories
resembles a city of shadows, of dimly remembered, half-imag-
ined streets and alleyways. That is, to compensate for his stale
memories Harte constructed a fictional California with a romantic
past that appealed to his middlebrow European audience.

Perhaps the best way to illustrate the point is to consider a
recurring trope in these tales. First, a slice of local history: the
ship *Niantic,* after delivering its cargo of 248 miners to San
Francisco in July 1849, was run on shore near the foot of Clay
Street and converted into a storeship. The San Francisco fire of
May 1851 left it little more than a charred hull. The Niantic
Hotel was then erected on its ruins. According to local legend,
a boarder in the early 1850s hid in the hotel a large cache of
stolen money that was never recovered. When the hotel was
finally razed in 1872, the year after Harte left town, several cases
of champagne and other articles from the old ship were discovered buried in the sand beneath it. Harte transformed such
banalities into the stuff of popular romance; indeed, the Niantic
Hotel is perhaps the most picturesque of all the sites in old San
Francisco that he appropriated in his late fiction. In his memoir
"Bohemian Days in San Francisco" (1900), he remembered
that in the 1860s the hotel was infested with rats that "had
increased and multiplied to such an extent that they fearlessly
cross the wayfarer's path at every turn." In the first chapter of
"Trent's Trust" (1901), the young hero arrives in the city on the

boat from Stockton (very much like Harte himself in 1860) and in his "feverish exaltation" spies "the hull of a stranded ship already built into a block of rude tenements." And in "A Ship of '49," he embellished the legend of a lost treasure secreted somewhere aboard the ship-hotel, here renamed the Pontiac. Predictably, the rats that infest the old hotel are mentioned only once, briefly, and in passing.

To be sure, like a cobbler repairing old shoes Harte occasionally tried to dress up his fiction with new material. He set the final chapter of "A Phyllis of the Sierras" (1887) in an old English country house like Newstead Abbey and "treaded lightly upon English country life," for example, and "The Ghosts of Stukeley Castle" (1890) recounts the spooky dream of a self-styled "Western Barbarian" and longtime expatriate in England. "Two Americans" (1897) was based in part on the experiences of his musical cousin Gertrude Griswold, who lived with her mother in London until October 1886 and often visited Harte at Upper Hamilton Terrace. Eventually, Harte even tried to weave his own experiences in Glasgow into a series of four tales that feature an unnamed American consul in the Scottish city of St. Kentigorn—"The Heir of the McHulishes" (1893), "Young Robin Grey" (1894), "A Rose of Glenbogie" (1894), and "The Desborough Connections" (1898). Harte tailored the first of these stories to the requirements of *Century* magazine, in stark contrast to his refusal to revise "Flip" for *Good Words* eleven years before. In ordering the story, the editor of *Century,* Robert Underwood Johnson, urged Harte to consider "very carefully the limitations under which a writer [must labor] who contributes to a family magazine." That is, Johnson wanted Harte to omit any erotic or other titillating elements from the story.

While the St. Kentigorn tales were more artistically successful than his German sketches, they proved in the end to be neither particularly popular nor lucrative. Harte readily allowed that, as an American and a foreigner, he "could not depict English character truthfully." He had little more than a tourist's knowledge of Scottish scenery and culture, and he asked his friend and illustrator Alexander Boyd to correct "any outrages in Scotch dialect or Scotch customs that, as an ignorant foreigner," he may have inadvertently described. In the end, the St. Kentigorn stories were anomalies in Harte's career which merely demonstrate that he could write fiction other than formulaic westerns, much as "O Captain! My Captain!" proves that Whitman could write poetry with rhyme and regular meter.

Though no longer a public official, Harte nevertheless remained prominently in the public eye. "I have met him at all sorts of gatherings—Bohemian and Belgravian," Justin McCarthy once observed, "and no one can meet him without being the happier." Harte began to frequent the salon of Florence Henniker, younger daughter of Lord Houghton and a distinguished author in her own right. (She collaborated with Thomas Hardy on the story "The Specter of the Real," and in 1892 she would dedicate her novel *Bid Me Goodbye* to Harte.) In March 1887 he joined the Kinsmen Social Club, whose members included William Black, Edmund Gosse, and Henry James, and over the next few months he accepted invitations to become a member of the New American Club and an honorary member of both the British Authors Association and the Devonshire Club. Harte was outraged when the London *Star* for June 21, 1888, called him a "lion in society," however. As he wrote Anna, "A half-dozen nice people—or, as they call them here, 'smart people'—have always been very polite to me. As they all happen to be 'titled' folk, it is quite enough for the average American to assume that I am a 'lion' in consequence and in fashionable society."

Rather than a lion, Harte preferred to be a dandy, to judge from the impression he left on several new acquaintances. The writer George Newell Lovejoy thought him "a charming man to meet," though one "somewhat given to fads" such as wearing stockings that matched his cravat. The theatrical producer John D. Williams also remembered his "rather large, curiously knotted scarlet cravat." Gertrude Atherton saw him at a reception at the U.S. embassy in London and described him later as a "dapper dandified little man, who walked with short mincing steps, as if his patent leather shoes were too small for him." C. Lewis

Hinds met him at a literary luncheon and noted "the glint of wax on the moustache" and his "manicured fingernails." Interviewing Harte for the *Idler*, George B. Burgin noted his "fashionably cut morning-suit of grey cloth" and the "delightfully polished man-of-the-world air about him." He seemed to be "an individual who was equally at home in a wigwam or a palace." The author and editor Jerome K. Jerome remembered that Harte "lived with great swells named Van der Velde. . . . He was a slight dapper gentleman, courteous and shy, with a low soft voice. It was difficult to picture him ruffling it among the bloodstained sentimentalists of Roaring Camp and Dead Man's Gulch." Harte sold many of his old suits—"the finest styles of tweeds, cassimeres, of good value, and impeccable cut from the best West End tailors"—to used-clothing stores in London, or else offered them to his sons. "I could point out to you certain faultless tweeds," he wrote in a jocular (?) vein to his younger son Frank, "in which you could travel from one end of England to the other without paying your bills."

Harte cut so public a figure that he attracted, as usual, more than his share of gossip and snide criticism. "I was a little surprised the other day," he reported to Anna in December 1887, to learn that some American tourists had spread gossip in London, at their hotel and at the U.S. embassy, "to the effect that you were left in such poverty by me that you were obliged to borrow money to keep yourself and children from want." It was "hard to exile myself here at hard work" supporting his family and yet "be met by such gratuitous falsehoods." (In fact, Anna had borrowed a hundred dollars the previous July from Sam Barlow, a lawyer friend on Long Island, to pay some unexpected family expenses and had begged her benefactor "to keep the matter *strictly confidential*.")

Harte also was profoundly embarrassed in October 1888 by an item in the St. Louis *Globe-Democrat*, reprinted in the *Boston Herald*, detailing his expensive and careless habits, more specifically "alleging that I was a ruined spendthrift living in England 'on money I borrowed from my English friends,' and that I would probably stay abroad as long as I could borrow money

Bret Harte, June 8, 1885. Photo by Elliott and Fry, London. (Bret Harte Collection, Clifton Waller Barrett Library, Special Collections Department, University of Virginia Library)

from them." Worse yet, the piece was written in an "air of affected regret and commiseration over the decadence of a once brilliant 'overpraised,' but now 'played out' and 'broken down' hack." At his earnest request, Dana issued a rebuttal in the New York *Sun:* When some irresponsible newspaper correspondents have "nothing else to write about they write about Bret Harte," Dana began, "and the stories they sometimes tell are astounding." The item in the St. Louis and Boston papers, for example, "was entirely destitute of truth." Harte's "mode of life" in London "is perfectly moderate, his labors most methodical, and his income almost as steady as if it were derived from cash investments" because of the "steady excellence of his productions."

To be sure, he was nothing if not methodical, "a militant creature of habit," as he once wrote Anna. He was "generally so worn out after my daily work at my desk that I loathe the sight of a pen," he said. He was "tired of work, and what is worse— empty of material and vapid as the public will soon find out." He wrote Florence Henniker in February 1890 that "my writing lately has revealed to me hitherto unknown depths of weariness and stupidity." He echoed the point in a note to his wife: "Sick or well, in spirits or out of spirits I must work, and I do not see any rest ahead." "In the last two or three years," he later added, "whenever I have begun a piece of work I have lived in nervous terror lest I should fall ill and be unable to finish it." Like a tailor with a backlog of unfilled orders, he scarcely "finished one piece of work when I am obliged to set down to another."

Despite a siege of pneumonia that laid him up for several weeks in the spring of 1890, he published a poem and twelve stories totaling some 230,000 words in 1889–90, a pace he maintained only by adhering strictly to his formula. Revising the usual complaint about the family resemblance of all Harte's romances, M. Crofton argued in *Once a Week* that, on the contrary, the "secret of his success lies in the fact that he has never varied the background of his pictures." "I have only one jar to dip into," as he told an interviewer in 1901. Virtually every western tale Harte wrote late in his career opens with a mise-en-scène, a detailed description of the California climate and landscape in the tints he remembered through the veil of nostalgia. Many of these stories contain an ensemble of recurring characters; e.g., Judge Beeswinger, introduced in *Gabriel Conroy,* reappears over twenty years later in "Clarence" (1894) and "A Ward of Colonel Starbottle" (1901); the lawyer Calhoun Bungstarter, first mentioned in the *Atlantic* story "The Romance of Madroño Hollow," appears again in "Colonel Starbottle's Client" (1891); the good-natured drunk Whiskey Dick surfaces in both "Struck at Devil's Ford" (1886) and "Three Partners" (1897); and Abner Dean, who debuted in "A Monte Flat Pastoral" and *Ah Sin,* appears as well in "Cressy" (1888). Harte began to write sequels centered on the same cast of characters (e.g., "Barker's Luck" and "Three Partners" in 1895–97) and even trilogies of tales (e.g., "A Waif of the Plains," "Susy," "Clarence" in 1889–94 and "Chu Chu," "The Devotion of Enriquez," "The Passing of Enriquez" in 1894–98).

Four characters introduced in Harte's earliest western stories were particularly overworked. The physician Dr. Duchesne, who made his first appearance in "M'liss," figures in a total of fourteen stories, ten of them written after 1885, including "The Chatelaine of Burnt Ridge," "The Youngest Prospector in Calaveras," and "Mr. Bilson's Housekeeper." The blustering lawyer Colonel Starbottle, first mentioned in the *Overland* story "Brown of Calaveras," appears in the play *Two Men of Sandy Bar* and a total of twenty stories, ten of them after 1885, including "Captain Jim's Friend," "A First Family of Tasajara," and "What Happened at the Fonda." The stage driver Yuba Bill first appears in the *Overland* tale "Miggles" and then in fifteen subsequent stories, eight of them after 1883, including "Dick Spindler's Family Christmas" and "A Niece of Snapshot Harry's." The gambler Jack Hamlin, first mentioned in the *Overland* story "The Idyl of Red Gulch," appears in twenty stories, thirteen of them after he dies of consumption in *Gabriel Conroy* (1876), including "A Sappho of Green Springs," "Mr. Jack Hamlin's Mediation," and "A Mercury of the Foothills." "I do not usually *begin* with a *plot,*" he once explained, "but,—having a few characters and a situation in my mind,—I let *them* work out the plot in *their* own lives and generally find they do it better than I can!" He told Pemberton that he "did not always see the end" of a story when he began it, but "I do know what my characters are" and he trusted them to "work their own conclusion."

Though sticking to a literary formula enabled him to maintain his production and so sustain his income, Harte was anxious to escape the "treadmill" or "grind," as he put it: "Like the old Californian miner who works 'for grub,' I have always the hope of 'striking something'—in a play perhaps—that may lift me out of this drudgery." In June 1889, hoping to copy Annie Pixley's theatrical success, he began to collaborate with the author and journalist Joseph Hatton on a dramatization of "M'liss" to feature Hatton's daughter Bessie in the title role. The project "looks more practical than my other ventures of the kind," he confided to Anna. A successful play, paying regular royalties, "seems to me my only hope of getting some relief to this perpetual grinding out of literary copy which is exhausting me, and no doubt the public." After they completed a draft of the script in November, he and Hatton tried to recruit the actor Edward Willard to play the schoolmaster. Hatton invited Willard to meet Harte at lunch, at which the men tarried over a fine Mumm. Willard became hostile and arrogant under the influence of the champagne, as Hatton remembered later. "He never had good manners; they were damned bad on this occasion. He spoke as if he had never had any intention of considering the play— M'liss—though I had talked the part over with him and he had read it. . . . Harte was very indignant, never forgave him, thought him a boor and impertinent." Though Harte tinkered with the script as late as April 1890, and though Hatton still hoped as late as November 1890 to find a producer for it, in the end the project collapsed like a house of cards, like almost all of Harte's other dramatic ventures. Hatton wrote Pemberton after Harte's death that he treasured the memories of their collaboration, "though the play still lies on my shelves unacted."

Unfortunately, Harte was no more successful a father than he was a playwright. His sons Frank and Griswold had attended a commercial college in New York during the first years of his exile, though neither of them seemed very bright or ambitious.

Frank had visited his father in Scotland and England for seven weeks in the autumn of 1884 and spent the Christmas holiday with him in 1888—his first physical contacts with any member of his family since sailing from New York in 1878. Frank had flirted with a theatrical career and had, in fact, spent four seasons performing with the companies of Lawrence Barrett, Dion Boucicault, and Edwin Booth. Griswold, the elder son, had canceled out of the trip in 1884 at the last moment, ostensibly to work— he earned $7 a week as a clerk—and from all indications was estranged from his father during the final ten or fifteen years of his life. He worked as the business manager of *Town Topics,* a New York society magazine, in the fall of 1885, though he had lost the job by the spring of 1886. He then founded and edited a weekly newspaper, the *Greene County Advertiser,* in Cairo, New York, though the paper soon failed and a hotel there sent an unpaid board bill for $68 to Harte in London. (The sins of the father?) Dana eventually hired Griswold at the New York *Sun,* at least partly as a favor to his father.

About Frank's prospects Harte harbored little hope: "After four years of stage experience, under exceptional advantages and patronage—advantages that many a striving young actor, of more than Franks ability, would have deemed himself blessed to have—with even the possible advantages of his fathers name and his fathers friends to make his apprenticeship light," Frank had finally decided he did not want to be an actor after all. He has "very foolish ideas of what makes or constitutes success" and "not the least conception of what is good for him" and he "lives in a world of the feeblest expediencies and makeshifts." He had become infatuated with a rich young English widow with two sons who, despite her annual income of over five thousand dollars, "holds him in debt for $10,000!" (They would be married in 1893.) At least Griswold "has clung to the newspaper work" into which "the poor boy stumbled. . . . I have more hope for him than Frank." While he did not "think that Wodie ever will make a great newspaper writer," it was possible "he may make a successful *journalist*." He certainly anticipated no support from his sons in his infirmity: "I have nothing but this

Francis King Harte, ca. 1887. (Courtesy of Cathy Gardner and Paul Deceglie)

wretched hand of mine—already growing weaker by age—to support us year by year and none of my children are likely to help me," he complained to Anna in June 1892.

Meanwhile, his status in his adopted family was becoming increasingly ambiguous. Arthur Van de Velde fell ill with influenza in December 1891 at the height of an epidemic in London and lingered for six weeks before "passing in his checks" on February 7, 1892. (By a strange coincidence, Mme Van de Velde's father, the Count de Launay, had died in Berlin a few hours earlier.) "The end was very unexpected," Harte wrote Clara Schneider, for his host "was always a miracle of health and activity, a great lover of out-door sports and exercise, without ills or ailments." His death "was a terrible blow to poor Madame." At first Harte assumed that his friend's death would require a change in his domestic arrangements. "It was a sad breaking up of the household," he wrote Anna with the news two weeks later. "His kindness and almost brotherly friendship did so much to make a possible home for me here so long among strangers."

Socially, it was one thing to live respectably as a guest in the home of Monsieur and Madame Van de Velde; it was quite another to cohabitate in the same house with the widow. In the short run, Harte was left in charge of the Van de Velde children still at home while she went to Berlin to settle the count's affairs. Upon her return, as Harte wrote Anna at the time, "I do not know what will be the disposition of the family," though he guessed they "will still remain in England." In April, a month after Madame's return, he wrote Anna that "I still remain with the Van de Veldes, until they move to a new house." He spent the summer "in the country, *alone,* at small hotels," as he assured his wife, and the following January he reported that the Van de Veldes "are still looking for a new house; when they make the change I shall, in all probability, leave them and go elsewhere to live, but where I do not yet know." By June 1893 he had decided "to go *temporarily* with the V de V" to their new house rather than "find myself lodgings elsewhere." In August, as he lamely explained to Anna in passive voice, "my things were moved" to the new Van de Velde home at 109 Lancaster

The Van de Velde mansion at 109 Lancaster Gate West, London, 1998.
(Courtesy of Bob and Esther Fleming)

Gate West and so "I came here also, and shall remain, at present, whatever I may do *later on*."

In the end, of course, Harte and Madame "went to housekeeping without the aid of a Justice of the Peace" much like Tennessee and his partner's wife. He moved with Madame and her children to their new mansion ("her salon looks like a German drawing room!" he excitedly reported to Clara Schneider), and he regularly summered with her at Arford House, "her new country home—a little cottage in a very rural but very delightful part of Hampshire." Their unconventional living arrangements prompted a more definite break with Anna, as George Stewart tactfully notes. Though Harte continued to support her to the end of his life, the letters he enclosed with the monthly

drafts became more and more perfunctory. If "the old arrangement seemed strange, perhaps equivocal, the new one must have
seemed to the man of the world—unequivocal. Mrs. Harte could
probably have gained a decree in any divorce court."

Read in this context, moreover, many of the passages in
"Susy," the novella Harte composed in the spring and summer
of 1892, seem transparently autobiographical. After the untimely
death of his patron Judge Peyton, the hero prepares to leave the
ranch where he has lived ("this quiet foreign household has
become quite an American ranch," Harte wrote from the Van
de Velde house in July 1887) but first confesses his love to the
judge's widow: "I loved you when I came here,—even when
your husband was alive. Don't be angry, Mrs. Peyton; *he* would
not, and need not, have been angry." On the final page of the
romance, despite her fears of what "the world [will] say," Mrs.
Peyton collapses into the hero's arms. Fifteen years later, in his
autobiographical dictation, Clemens gleefully repeated gossip he
had heard in London: that Harte had been "kept" by the widow.

For their feud, like a dump fire, still smouldered. In September 1895, while in Australia on a round-the-world lecture tour,
Clemens foolishly criticized his former friend by name. In an
interview with the *Sydney Morning Herald,* he remarked, "Bret
Harte I consider sham and shoddy, and he has no pathos of the
real, true kind." He echoed and elaborated the point in an
interview the same day with the *Melbourne Argus:*

> I detest him, because I think his work is "shoddy." His forte is
> pathos, but there should be no pathos which does not come out of
> a man's heart. He has no heart, except his name, and I consider he
> has produced nothing that is genuine. He is artificial. That opinion,
> however, must be taken with some allowance, for, as I say, I do not
> care for the man.

Not only did Clemens's comments provoke a hailstorm of rejoin-
ders to the editors of these papers, Harte replied in an aggrieved
tone in a subsequent interview published, ironically, in his old
nemesis the New York *World:*

I always considered that we were friends until that trip of his to
Australia, and there, it appears, he attacked me in a most savage and
unprovoked manner—denounced me as a feeble sentimentalist, and
altogether gave it to be understood that Art and I were strangers.
I've never been able to understand his sudden change of attitude. It
was foolish of him, too, for I have a great many friends in Australia,
and it was inevitable that all this should come to my ears.

In fact, Clemens may have simply retaliated for a subtle though
no less public barb Harte had aimed his way two years earlier.

In "An Ingénue of the Sierras" (1893), Harte dramatized an
embarrassing if little-known episode in Clemens's early career.
In December 1870, soon after the publication of "Plain Language
from Truthful James" and at the height of Harte's popularity,
there appeared in the pages of the *Buffalo Express,* co-owned at
the time by Clemens, a poem entitled "Three Aces" in transparent imitation of Harte and signed "Carl Byng." The poem
was widely copied from the *Express,* sometimes with the signature "Mark Twain." Thomas Bailey Aldrich, in fact, complained
in *Every Saturday* for January 7, 1871, that "Mark Twain's versi-
fied story of 'Three Aces' seems to be a feeble echo of Bret
Harte." A week later, Clemens wrote Aldrich to demand a public
apology and retraction: "I did not write the rhymes referred to,
nor have anything whatever to do with suggesting, inspiring, or
producing them. . . . I am not in the imitation business."
Another week later, he again wrote Aldrich to ask him not to
publish his first letter, that it would simply draw attention to the
allegation that he had imitated Harte. By then, however, his
first letter was already in press, so Aldrich offered to "withdraw
his apology"—to which Clemens replied with a letter in which
he expressed regret for his first, overhasty disclaimer. Two years
later, Clemens equivocated on the question whether he was the
author of "Three Aces" when John Camden Hotten issued an
edition of his writings that included the doggerel poem. In a
letter to the London *Spectator,* Clemens merely complained
that "there is no affliction in this world that makes a man feel so
down-trodden and abused as the giving him a name that does

not belong to him." The letter was something less than an unqualified denial of authorship.

Whether or not Clemens was the author of "Three Aces," Harte certainly believed he was. "An Ingénue of the Sierras" features a notorious highwayman, Ramon Martinez, who poses as a bill collector named Charley (or Charles, the English equivalent of Carl) Byng, the alias under which Clemens allegedly masqueraded in writing "Three Aces" in pale imitation of Harte. Even the villain's real name, Martinez, suggests Mark Twain—they share six letters in sequence. (For the record, there is only one other character surnamed Martinez in Harte's oeuvre—a malcontent in "The Crusade of the Excelsior" who rails against the Catholic Church and spouts the natural-rights philosophy of Thomas Paine.) That is, Harte represents Clemens in his tale as a road agent who plunders stagecoaches and sails under false colors. "Handsome and even cultivated-looking, he assuredly was" with his dark mustache, Harte wrote. "But there was a certain half-shamed, half-defiant suggestion in his expression" coupled "with a watchful lurking uneasiness." Fortunately, his reign of terror was nearing an end. The Martinez gang was "about played out," not "from want of a job now and then, but from the difficulty of disposing of the results of their work." At the most literal level, Martinez could no longer fence his swag, much as Clemens, who had recently had trouble foisting the potboilers *Merry Tales* and *The American Claimant* off on readers, was nearing bankruptcy. In the shorthand of Harte's story, Martinez had "lately been robbing ordinary passengers' trunks" just as Clemens had begun to trade on his popularity. Ironically, "An Ingénue of the Sierras" as well as "A Protégée of Jack Hamlin's," both originally published in 1893, were critically acclaimed. Written in a more economical style reminiscent of his early *Overland* tales, they were, according to Stewart, "his best stories in nearly twenty years."

Harte was never more popular or commercially successful or in vogue than in the early to mid-1890s, moreover. According to contemporary estimates, he earned about $16,000 in 1891, though Axel Nissen calculates his income that year more realistically at

$8,545, or slightly more than half what was publicly reported. His income would climb to nearly $11,000 in 1895, more than he had received under contract to Osgood in 1871–72. So long as he received his standard rate of payment, he was not picky about its source; e.g., he sold "The Homecoming of Jim Wilkes" (1892) to Lever Brothers for use as a publicity gimmick for Sunlight Soap. "I have enough work on hand" or ordered in advance, he wrote Anna in April 1893, "to keep me continuously employed" for a year and a half. Four months later, he wrote Clara Schneider that "I have always work enough to do, and work enough ordered to keep my hands full." Not that he regarded such stories as "The Reformation of James Reddy" (1893) or "The Sheriff of Siskiyou" (1894) or "A Yellow Dog" (1895) as singular achievements: "I have scarcely dared to read what I have written—lest I should destroy it in disgust."

But so long as he was busy Harte had no time to visit his family in the United States; and, on the other hand, had he the leisure to make the trip he might have pled poverty and postponed the trip to save money. Though he admonished Anna not to believe the news reports about his income, from all indications he was flush. He joined the Royal Thames Yacht Club on Albemarle Street in 1893, and he hobnobbed with such luminaries as Lord Compton, who occasionally hosted him at his ancestral estate, Compton Wynyates ("a most wonderful house, far beyond my conception of it"), one of the most famous Tudor mansions in England, as well as the Earl of Crewe, Florence Henniker's brother, who sometimes invited him to Fryston Hall in Yorkshire.

In early January 1895 Harte received an overture from his old Birmingham friend T. Edgar Pemberton, who had read his latest romance in the *Pall Mall Magazine*, to adapt it to the stage. "The Judgment of Bolinas Plain" was of a piece with much of Harte's other sensational fiction of the period: a sexually frustrated ranch wife, Sue Beasley, runs off with a circus acrobat (no subtlety here) and fugitive from the law. Her crippled (and impotent?) husband, Ira, kills a deputy trailing the fugitive whom he mistakes for his wife's lover. Eventually captured, the acrobat is tried and found guilty of the murder when suddenly the old rancher appears in court and announces that he killed the deputy for seducing his wife—justifiable homocide under the "primal law," it would seem. The judge dismisses all charges and old Ira and Sue are reconciled.

At first, and to his credit given his own abysmal track record with plays, Harte tried to discourage Pemberton from trying to dramatize the tale. "There is always the doubt if what is dramatic in ordinary *prose narrative*," he noted, "is equally dramatic in *theatrical representation*. The story is but a single *episode*, and I am afraid that much would have to be imported into it that might weaken its dramatic intensity!" Still, if Pemberton persisted in his plan, Harte offered to collaborate with him. "Perhaps we could *together* make something out of it, or I could at least make some suggestions regarding it," he proposed. He certainly did not want yet another dramatist to make a fortune on his material unless he also had a stake in the project. He had recently been angered by the unauthorized production of Boucicault's script of *The Luck* in New York. ("Its a miserable affair," he had complained to Anna, "and a mixture of *deceit* and downright swindling and robbery, which I am unfortunately accustomed to in my dealings with my countrymen ever since I left America.") Harte initially downplayed Pemberton's proposal to write and produce a melodrama based on his story: "It is one of my old illusions," but "I do not hope *much*, and shall not be disappointed."

They immediately went to work on weekends and holidays at Pemberton's home in the village of Broadway and were well advanced on a draft of a three-act script of *Sue* in April, when Harte suggested that they "*read* over and *talk* over the *MSS, together*, until it is *complete* in a rough draft; *then* I propose that we should *each* go over it in typewritten copy, and make our emendations and corrections." They had nearly finished a draft in late May, when he wrote Anna he hoped to make enough from it "to get out of this terrible daily grind for a while." So amoral a story could not be literally enacted on the Victorian stage, so Harte and Pemberton revised the plot slightly to omit the murder of the deputy, who is merely presumed dead and who miraculously reappears during the trial in act 3. "As there is now no 'killing'—the end need not be so grim," Harte explained. He had also "made the Judge more of a character—and really the symbol of the reckless, illogical but sincere Lyncher." With its overuse of soliloquies and asides, the finished script betrays many of the faults of inexperience, but the authors were satisfied their time had not been wasted. As soon as they completed a draft of *Sue,* they began another play together—*Rushbrook,* adapted from Harte's story "A Maecenas of the Pacific Slope," which Sir Charles Wyndham briefly considered staging.

Meanwhile, Harte and Mme Van de Velde slipped away from England separately and rendezvoused in Switzerland in August 1895 for a holiday together. Harte was careful to cover his tracks; he could scarcely maintain the polite fiction that he was a mere house guest in the Van de Velde home, even in the family summer home, if he vacationed alone with Madame on the continent. He wrote Anna on August 3 that he hoped "to go somewhere, out of England, for a holiday" on his doctor's orders. "I may go to Switzerland or the Black Forest but I do not know yet where," he explained, and urged her to write him through his club. Madame started for the continent in early August, and Harte left London on August 16 for Folkestone, where his son Frank had moved with his wife Aline and their sons. He wrote Clara Schneider from his hotel in Folkestone on August 17 that he would arrive in Cologne two days later to meet his friend Arthur Collins for a Rhine cruise and that he hoped "to see you and your family while I am in Germany." Though he arrived in Cologne as planned, and though the Schneiders sent a telegram to his hotel, Harte as usual temporized. He spent the next three days with Collins in Cologne, Rudesheim, and Bonn, only an hour or two by rail from Crefeld and the friends he had not seen in fifteen years. "We basked in the sun, and the *sauerkraut,* and the dear old smell of pipes and dregs of beer glasses," he wrote his friend Mary Boyd. Harte eventually worked some of the details of this sentimental journey into his last two stories set in Germany, "The Indiscretion of Elsbeth" (1895), a trivial farce, and "Unser

Karl" (1897), both a gloss on the Dreyfus affair in France and a spy tale with a tricked-up, O. Henry–like surprise ending.

On August 22 Harte received a telegram from Madame summoning him to Switzerland, and the next day he parted from Collins "in the garden of the dear old Grand Royal Hotel" in Bonn "and I escaped by night over Strassburg and Bale" to Villeneuve on Lake Geneva. He apologized to Clara Schneider but promised to pass through Germany in a few weeks en route back to England "and then I hope to see you all together and we can be together a little longer than is possible for me just now." He failed to return to England by way of Germany, however, so he never saw the Schneiders again. On August 25 he wrote Anna to remind her to contact him through his club because the Van de Velde house at Lancaster Gate "will be closed while the family are visiting their relatives in Belgium and Berlin." He gave no hint in this letter, of course, that he was in Switzerland with Madame.

For six "light-hearted" weeks, until their return to London in mid-October, Harte and Mme Van de Velde traveled at leisure, free of all social obligations, without apparently arousing any suspicions among family or friends. They visited Vevey, Montreux, and Chillon; Lausanne and Neuchâtel; Geneva and Caux and Berne. They cruised around Lake Leman and railed to Territet and Glion and "up to Rochers de Naye, about six thousand feet!" They enjoyed "unclouded sunshine, unsurpassed sunsets, absolutely balmy nights, when you can sit out all night without a thought of imprudence—where going to bed seems the only thing stupid, and even improper!" "The weather here is lovely—almost *too* lovely and luxurious to be bracing," he wrote Pemberton, and "the views beautiful—almost too beautiful." From their Geneva hotel Harte could see "Mont Blanc, thirty or forty miles away, framing itself in a perfect vignette," though he professed again to prefer western American to Swiss topography: "I wouldn't give a mile of the dear old Sierras, with their honesty, sincerity, and magnificent uncouthness, for a hundred thousand kilometers of this picturesque Vaud!" Still, if only for the sake of propriety, a few weeks after their return to London Harte moved into a bachelor flat at 74 Lancaster Gate, a few doors down from the Van de Velde mansion. "It has been of course a little more expensive to me since I have left Madame Van de Veldes home," he assured Anna with characteristic cheekiness, "although I have now much more freedom and independence than when I was in a private family."

During the summer of 1895, too, Pemberton sent the script of *Sue* to the impresario Daniel Frohman and, the following spring, persuaded Frohman's brother Charles, who was in London on business, actually to produce it. Harte reported to Anna in May 1896 that he and his collaborator had finalized a contract "with an *American Manager.*" They were surprised that the play would premiere in the United States rather than in England, "but we thought it advisable not to lose the offer. . . . I *hope* something may come of it to relieve me of this continuous strain." Five days later he received his copy of the contract and a check for twenty-five pounds from Pemberton: "It quite startled me to find 'Sue' actually *born* and alive to *that* extent!" After so many failures and disappointments, Harte had finally cowritten a script that had earned money other than a forfeiture fee. Frohman was intent on its success, moreover, and hired the thirty-two-year-old American actress Annie Russell, well known as a stage ingenue, to star in the title role.

Sue opened its four-week run at Hoyt's Theatre on Broadway on September 15 with predictable fanfare. Frohman cabled Pemberton that the play was "well received, acting fine, press praises." It was puffed, on the one hand, by the New York *World* ("almost a great play"), by C. W. Taafe in *Collier's* ("a delightfully fascinating drama"), by Arthur Hoeber in *Illustrated American* ("cleverly-drawn characters, witty speeches"), and by James Stetson in *Life* ("'Sue' won't do. She's too good"). On the other hand, it was panned by the New York *Evening Post* ("exceedingly silly and mawkish stuff"), the *New York Tribune* ("three hours of chatter, melodrama, and farce"), the New York *Sun* (the sort of play "which we are disposed to relegate to the Bowery"), the *New York Times* ("must go into the limbo of soon-forgotten plays"), the *New York Dramatic*

Mirror ("curiously inexpert"), by Vance Thompson in the New York *Commercial Advertiser* ("anti-climax raced with absurdity"), and by Beaumont Fletcher in *Godey's* ("so bad that it might be almost taken as a model of how not to write a play"). Howells, arguably the most influential of all turn-of-the-century drama critics, figuratively held his nose, too. The melodrama, he wrote in *Harper's Weekly,* was "almost as bad in structure and false in motive as a play could very well be. It is so bad and so false that I wonder it is not a hurricane of success with the class that mainly forms our play-going public."

Still, even the harshest critics reserved a few lines of praise for Annie Russell. Howells thought she played Sue "with the subtle insight and the beautiful art which have given her a unique reputation." The *New York Clipper,* a theatrical newspaper, declared that Russell "gave a performance never to be forgotten. It is doubtful if anyone else could be found who would so perfectly portray the role." Even the ascerbic Thompson applauded "Beautiful Annie Russell," whose art "is as reticent and subtle as the touch of a butterfly's wing. . . . Perhaps the highest encomium one can pass is that her winsome creation of Sue made one forget at times the dislocated absurdity of Bret Harte's play."

On his part, Harte professed disinterest in the verdicts of the New York drama critics. (Would but he had ignored them twenty years before, after the premiere of *Two Men of Sandy Bar!*) "I am quite content if the papers abuse the play as long as the audience like it, and the thing pays," he insisted to Anna, who wrote her husband that she thought it was a "perfect play." Under the circumstances, Harte could afford to be magnanimous: "I am even quite willing that my *collaborateur* Mr Pemberton should receive *all* the praise for its success—as he has worked very hard upon it, and it is *he* who succeeded in placing the play with Frohman, who, I dare say, would not have looked at it in *my* hands—nor would any other American manager have troubled himself about it." The critics may even be correct "in pointing out the anticlimaxes of the latter portion of the play," he conceded, and had the playwrights attended the rehearsals they doubtless "could have arranged" a "more satisfying" denouement.

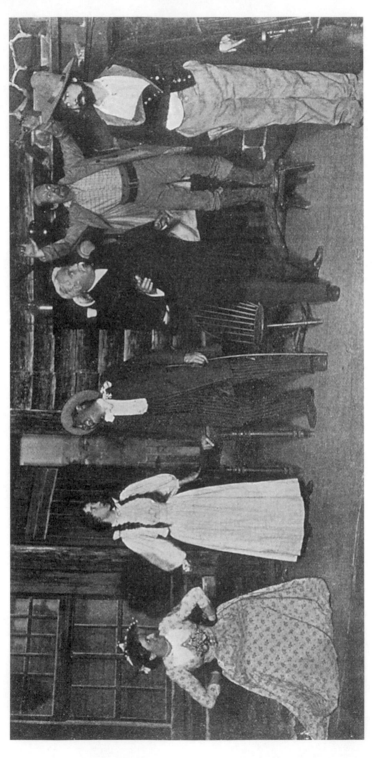

The cast of *Sue* on stage at Hoyt's Theatre, New York, September 1896. Annie Russell second from left. (*Illustrated American,* October 24, 1896, p. 567)

Harte hoped Frohman would produce the play in London "with as good an actress as Miss Russell"—if so, "*we* could make the alterations *ourselves* and see to the rehearsals *ourselves!*"

Meantime, Frohman had decided to take the play on tour with its original cast after it closed in New York. His plan "is a fair augery of success, and the evidence that Miss Russell has made a 'hit' in the character is strongly corroborative," Harte wrote Pemberton on October 4. Between mid-October and the end of November, *Sue* was staged in Brooklyn ("a play which has aimed for the highest artistic rank and just missed attaining it," according to the *Brooklyn Eagle*), Pittsburgh, Chicago, Toledo, St. Louis, and Philadelphia. It then moved to the Boston Museum for the last four weeks of 1876 ("a series of incidents unevenly strung," according to the *Boston Herald*). Even the juvenile novelist Horatio Alger, Jr., who was certainly no snob, thought the plot faulty and the play on the whole something less than a success after he saw it performed in Boston. From there *Sue* traveled to Providence, Washington, Brooklyn again, Harlem, Bridgeport, Lowell, Newport, Brockton, Lynn, Hartford, and Buffalo before closing on February 13, 1897. Frohman wrote Pemberton that "she is no good for the smaller provincial towns" and had "exhausted" the larger cities.

Despite its apparent popularity, Harte received only modest royalty payments from Frohman. As he reported to Anna, "I get occasional cheques from my share in the play"—a typical one in October 1896 was for fourteen pounds, about as much as he was paid per thousand words of fiction by the newspaper syndicates, which was "not much though I am very grateful for it—even that little!" He wrote Pemberton in early January that the last week of the Boston run had not "been very successful and I do not think Frohman would feel like continuing the tour on houses that dropped below $2000 per week. Their expenses must be nearly that!" Certainly his income from the play was not sufficient to permit him to retire even temporarily from the daily grind of writing fiction. In the end, Frohman claimed the play was a financial failure, though Harte disputed his judgement: "one can hardly call a play 'a failure' which has made the amount

of money that 'Sue' has. Still we do not know what *expenses* the
Frohmans had in *advertising* &c &c. which they certainly did
not stint." The play was later revived in the United States at
least three times: in San Francisco in October 1897, Denver in
August 1898, and Pittsburgh in November 1900. "Good old
Sue!" Harte wrote Pemberton when he received a small royalty
check for one of these revivals. "She has such a charming way of
cropping up when we least expect it!"

Harte still hoped the play would be staged in England. "It
should have a better hearing here than in my own country," he
figured, because "the London audiences and critics are not
afraid of being thought *vulgar* if they like to hear of 'common'
people or American subjects." The British actress Annie Hughes,
who had seen Annie Russell's performance in America, offered
to play *Sue* in London "*if* she can get a theatre," he wrote Anna
in September 1897, but nothing came of this plan. Harte was
confident "it would make a good *provincial* play," even if no
London manager would stage it, "and we might try it—failing
other arrangements—in Birmingham! Then we could see it
rehearsed," as he proposed to Pemberton. Frohman eventually
agreed to an experiment: a "matinee first performance" of the
play with Annie Russell again in the title role at the Garrick
Theatre in London on June 10, 1898. Harte attended at least one
rehearsal—when Russell flung her arms in the air and collapsed
from exhaustion just as the curtain fell at the end of the second
act he mistakenly thought it was part of her performance and
murmured, "Great climax, real acting, wonderful scene!" As he
wrote his son Frank later, Russell

> is very charming; I can quite understand her popularity in America,
> and certainly there is no *ingenue* on the *English* stage comparable
> to her. But at the rehearsal, I was pleased to see that other American
> actors were equally good in their *roles,* and while the play has cer-
> tain inherent defects it is by no means as bad as the American critics
> made it. The Lynch trial was wonderfully good.

He was confident, given "what I know of English audiences,"
that the sensational final act "will 'go' with them."

For once, he seemed prescient. Frohman's matinee experiment succeeded beyond expectations, and *Sue* seemed destined to be a hit. At the close of the performance the audience called the authors to the stage, though Harte "had just left the theatre," as one reviewer noted, and "Pemberton very wisely objected to take the call alone." The London correspondent of the *New York Dramatic News* remarked that "I have seldom heard a group of playgoers and critics leave a theatre giving off such unanimous expressions of approval and delight." The play was favorably reviewed in the *Academy* ("seldom has so good an all-round representation been witnessed on the London stage"), the *Speaker* ("delights by its very artlessness"), the *Athenaeum* ("admirably played"), the London *Times* ("plenty of entertainment"), the *Daily Mail* (Russell was a "peerless gem"), and the *Pall Mall Gazette* ("the performance of 'Sue' should be an object-lesson to our own actors and actresses"). Harte was particularly pleased by Clement Scott's notice of the play in the London *Daily Telegraph,* which pronounced him "a born dramatist. He possesses every gift for the art which he so strangely and unaccountably neglected." Harold Frederic, the London correspondent of the *New York Times,* noted in his next dispatch that the play was praised "with all the superlatives at the critics' command." The melodrama was so successful, in fact, that Frohman booked it into the Garrick Theatre for a four-week run beginning June 29—the only block of time his actors, including Russell, were available to perform it.

Unfortunately, while *Sue* was a critical success in London, the financial returns to the playwrights again were very disappointing. Though the theatre was usually full, the producers apparently papered the house with complimentary tickets. As usual, Harte found a scapegoat: the newspapers, which had published detailed synopses of the play. As he reported to Anna in early August, he had been

> once more cruelly disappointed; in spite of the praises of press and audiences; in spite of the attractions of a perfect actress, like Annie Russell, and a splendid company—in spite of everything that goes

to make the success of a play—*it never paid!* I cannot understand it—the manager, Mr. Frohman, is equally bewildered and confounded, although he is much more *satisfied* with the money he has undoubtedly *lost,* and the artistic success the play has gained, than we are. I need not tell you how *for six weeks* I had hoped to delight and astonish you with news of a good fortune that would spare me all the trials and troubles I have had lately over my literary work—and how deeply disappointed I have been!

Under the circumstances, there seemed but one alternative open to the authors: try, try again. May their next play be "a greater success!" Harte adjured Pemberton. He was dismayed when an adaptation of "Tennessee's Partner" by the playwright Scott Marble—yet another melodrama based on his writings that paid him no royalties—began an American tour; and he complained that Clyde Fitch's popular play *The Cowboy and the Lady* was nothing more than "a very clumsy imitation of my work, and distinctly an outcome of 'Sue.'"

Harte and Pemberton had, in fact, been toying with several new scripts, all of them adapted from Harte's recent stories. Unfortunately, they still knew next to nothing about dramatic structure. "The greatest trouble we have," Harte admitted to his collaborator, "is that our experience of 'Sue' has been so utterly confusing, conflicting and astounding that it *teaches* us nothing by way of example" and so "we have absolutely nothing to go upon by way of guide to our other ventures!" Still, they finished a draft of *Clarence,* based on Harte's novella about the American Civil War, which he considered "an infinitely better play" than *Sue.* "I think we should have no difficulty in placing 'Clarence,'" he wrote Pemberton, and indeed they submitted it to the Frohmans. In the end, however, the producers declined it on the ground that "war plays were over done." *Clarence* had been anticipated by William Gillette's "Secret Service," which opened in London in May 1897, and "*two* American plays on nearly the same lines wouldn't succeed." Harte and Pemberton dusted off their old scenario of *Rushbrook,* a fragment of which survives among Pemberton's papers in the Beinecke Library at Yale. Charles Frohman also rejected it in the fall of 1897, and although he "*promised* to do his best" to place both scripts with other theatrical managers, he failed to deliver on the promise. "I expected nothing better from Frohman," Harte groused in October 1897. "He has acted like the speculating manager throughout, and his 'opinions' or 'suggestions' have always been subordinate to what was his present use and necessity, and good for his syndicate or his monopoly." Frohman and his ilk were "truly 'a law unto themselves.'"

Nevertheless, at Frohman's suggestion Harte and Pemberton worked up a dramatic version of Harte's tale "Snow-Bound at Eagle's," which they entitled *Held Up*. "I dont believe I am over-sanguine when I say that, as it stands now, it is very original and *striking*, and I cannot conceive of any actor or manager thinking otherwise," Harte insisted in November 1897 upon reading a draft of the second act. "I am more sanguine of 'Held Up' than I have been of any of our other plays." Once again, however, Frohman rejected the script because, he said, the situation lacked novelty. As late as January 1900 Harte still harbored the hope it might eventually make a hit. "I think that audiences are beginning to be sick of the erotic and neurotic—and all the other 'rotic'—plays, and would welcome something strong and vital" such as western melodrama. Arthur Bourchier, the manager of the Criterion Theatre in London, eventually staged *Held Up*, albeit at the Worcester Theatre fifteen months after Harte's death and for only one performance. A copy of the script survives in the New York Public Library. "We are, if we consult the notices and critiques of 'Sue,' the authors of a highly successful and much talked of play—even a distinctly 'novel' one," Harte griped to Pemberton in November 1898, "yet we couldn't draw a paying audience for that one, nor can we get an order for another from actor or manager—or know precisely what was the matter with the last. Verily a dramatists life is not a happy one!"

Unfortunately, too, Harte's income from the sale of his poems and stories had begun to slip. Although he was "doing my usual amount of work my agent has had some delay in disposing of it," he explained to Anna in March 1897. "It would not be strange if, after all these years, people should not be quite as keen to buy or read B.H's stuff as ten or twenty years ago!" He had always sold his literary "wares" outright, like a line of shirts, so when the rate per word he was paid began to decline, he had no reserves on which to draw. (This method of sale also deprived his heirs of an income from reprints of his stories after his death.) He began a long sequel to his Zolaesque story "The Ancestors of Peter Atherly," apparently never finished and certainly never published, which is now lost. Much as he had exploited the popularity of "Plain Language from Truthful James" by approving an illustrated chapbook edition of it in 1871, he tried to cash in on it again with a new poem, "Free Silver at Angel's," narrated by Truthful James and again featuring Ah Sin. In no way could this satire be misconstrued as anti-Chinese propaganda, however: Harte ridiculed the silver plank in the 1896 Democratic party platform. But neither did it strike a chord with readers; indeed, the poem was virtually ignored.

His scale of payment also declined: he earned only £50 from Chatto and Windus for all rights to his collection *Some Later Poems* (1898), for example, and only £50 from *Youth's Companion* for his semiautobiographical essay "How I Went to the Mines" (1899). Whereas he had normally earned £14 per thousand words in the early 1890s, the McClure syndicate cut his pay to as little as £5 per thousand words for such stories as "The Man at the Semaphore" (1897), "Salomy Jane's Kiss" (1898), and "Mr. Bilson's Housekeeper" (1899). Despite his increasing production, Harte earned on average less than £1,350 or $6,800 a year between 1896 and 1899, according to Nissen's estimates. He began to draw small advances from Watt in April 1897, in turn assigning some of his copyrights to his agent as security. His income slowly fell behind his expenses—in May 1898 he owed Watt about £375, a year later about £520.

He also anticipated a reduction in Anna's living costs. He reduced her monthly allowance to £30, or about $150, when their older daughter Jessamy—by all accounts a great beauty, with dark curls and "an exquisitely molded figure"—married the recently divorced Henry Milford Steele, an art editor for

Scribner's, in the summer of 1898. "My daughters engagement and marriage came to me as a surprise," he wrote Clara Schneider in August 1898. "I could not think of her except as the *child* I had left in America. She has married a man much older than herself—but it is a love match!" In the wake of the London box-office flop of *Sue,* he had no heart to write Jessamy "regarding her affairs, and even now I can only congratulate her upon finding a husband who can take the place of her father and his precarious fortunes." A talented artist and aspiring writer and musician, his daughter had published an essay in the *Ladies Home Journal* in 1892, exhibited some of her drawings at the Columbian Exposition in Chicago in 1893, and worked as a magazine illustrator. At the time Harte had resisted his wife's entreaties to send her to France to finish her education. "If Jessamy can already turn her talent to profit in America, why should she come to Paris, where she cannot earn a penny" and "where it will cost her more than either you or I can afford to teach her to do something else in Art"? With Jessamy's marriage five years later, he no longer had to support her at all. Harte's niggardliness seemed to have paid off.

He could not have foreseen what happened next. As a result of his daughter's marriage and his consequent reduction in Anna's allowance, his wife and their younger daughter Ethel one day in mid-December 1898 boarded a ship for England, where their younger son had promised them a home with his family in Caversham. "I am greatly surprised," Harte wrote Frank on December 14, "as your mother never intimated to me her intention of coming to England, nor have you ever told me you were sending for her or intended to send for her." In any event, he divorced himself from their plans. "I can only hope and wish that the arrangements you have thus made may prove perfectly satisfactory to you all, and that in being able to share your house with your mother and sister you may have all the pleasure you have looked forward to." Not that their domestic economies would relieve any more stress on his own budget: "Until the last year I have regularly sent $3000 a year to support your mother, Ethel and Jessamy,—three people—and a decrease of that sum brings your mother here in debt!" Upon her arrival in England, probably via the White Star liner *Majestic* on December 19, Anna sent her husband a letter to the effect that she and Ethel were in good spirits. Harte replied a few days later that he had "very little time to myself," given the press of his writing schedule, but "I shall run up for a day—or at least *part of day* very soon." Even after a separation of over twenty years, he was in no hurry to see her again.

CHAPTER 7

Epilogue

Played Out

THEIR reunion was more stiff and formal than poignant. Geoffrey Bret Harte remembered years later that his father Frank's attempt to reconcile his grandparents "by importing my grandmother to England aroused at first a stormy protest" from his grandfather. Before "these two irreconcilables" could meet Anna Harte "had to be carefully coached in self control and in the avoidance of any dangerous topic of conversation," specifically no doubt his status in the Van de Velde household. Their occasional visits over the months—there were no more than five or six—"were almost as relaxing as sitting on a powder keg watching the fuse slowly burning, and waiting for the bang which would blow them all sky high. The entire family was on tenter-hooks and the sigh of relief which all members breathed when the ordeal was over was heartfelt." On his part, Harte agreed to visit his wife with the clear understanding, according to his grandson, that "should a single repetition of the old flare-ups occur, he would never cross our threshold again."

Like many of the salient events in his life, Harte's reunion with Anna, "a woman of striking appearance" according to the San Francisco *Argonaut* in 1894, still imperially "slim and tall with slender hands and feet" as her grandson remembered, eventually became grist for the fiction mill. In his story "The Reincarnation of Smith" (1901), Harte described the mixed emotions of a man who sees his wife from "the States" after long years of separation: "Her profile he certainly remembered, but not with the feeling it now produced in him. Would he have ever abandoned her had she been like that? Or had *he* changed, and was this no longer his old self?—perhaps even a self *she*

Bret Harte and Francis King Harte, ca. 1900. (Courtesy of Cathy Gardner and Paul Deceglie)

would never recognize again? . . . The years had certainly improved her; he wondered with a certain nervousness if she would think they had done the same for him."

In truth, now well past the age of sixty, he was in failing health. He had been a heavy drinker and smoker most of his life—

Howells and Annie Fields, among others, had remarked on his vices in the early 1870s, and while he curbed his drinking after he came under Mme Van de Velde's influence, he never curtailed his tobacco use. His friend Alexander Boyd sketched him in March 1892 with a cigarette in his mouth), and he admitted seven years later that "I smoke so much that I only can use *very mild* cigars." His bad habits took their toll. He begged off a dinner invitation at the Boyds' home on February 1, 1897, pleading a bad throat and cough, early symptoms of the throat cancer that would eventually kill him. "I have suffered dreadfully from neuralgia in my face and jaws," he complained to Anna two months later, and he anticipated "a siege with the dentist" to relieve the pain. The following October, even as they persevered in their playwriting, he admitted to Pemberton that "my cough is troublesome at night" and "my catarrh still remains." To the end of his life he punctuated his letters to family and friends with reports of his poor health.

Hamlin Garland, who had favorably reviewed *A Millionaire of Rough-and-Ready* for the *Boston Transcript* in 1887, met Harte at Joseph Hatton's home and visited him in his flat at Lancaster Gate in May 1899 and afterwards described his appearance in detail. Like most people who knew him only by reputation, Garland was first surprised by Harte's gaudy dress: he wore "gray-striped trousers, a cutaway coat over a fancy vest," "lavender spats" over "polished shoes," and a monocle, and he carried "a pair of yellow gloves." His pose "was almost precisely that of the typical English clubman of the American stage" or "an elderly fop whose life had been one of self-indulgent ease." But even more alarmingly he "looked old and burnt out," his rheumy eyes "clouded with yellow," "his skin red and flabby." To judge by his appearance Harte had "lived hard and fast," Garland thought. He was "an exile, an expatriate, old and feeble and about to die. . . . He was poor and the subject of gossip" to the effect that he was a kept man "living on the bounty" of Mme Van de Velde. (On his part, Harte was fond of quoting with "quiet scorn" the motto of the Earls Mareschal of Aberdeen: "They say. What say they? Let them say!") William Alden,

Sketch of Harte by A. S. Boyd dated March 18, 1892. (*Idler* 4 [January 1894], 552)

who had known Harte in New York in the 1870s, met him in London about this time and was also shocked to see how "old and apparently feeble he had grown." Justin McCarthy, too, who had known Harte in San Francisco, thought he looked "outworn and prematurely old." Unfortunately, Harte's cancer was diagnosed only after it became inoperable. As his grandson later explained, his life might have been "considerably prolonged and much suffering prevented had his doctors been more competent. The almost incredible fact remains that they never discovered what was wrong until it was far too late."

Harte understood full well in 1899–1900 that he was in bad shape, though he did not yet know he was terminally ill. During these months he soldiered on, often reminding Anna that her income was no more certain than his fragile health. "I have cried 'Wolf' so often that it has got to be a familiar warning. Yet it is at the door now," he laconically observed early in 1899. Not that he exactly stinted himself. He sometimes escaped the "black, poisonous, smoky fog" of London "that makes every inhalation a smart" for the resort in Southsea, and he frequented the Red House, Madame Van de Velde's new country home near Camberley. He lived "in London just as little as possible," he told an interviewer with the New York *World* in December 1901, and instead loved "to come down and meander in these country lanes."

He continued to write, even at reduced rates, in a vain attempt to build a nest egg on which he might retire and/or his widow might live. "I am working very hard now," he wrote Pemberton from Camberley in August 1900, "even in the country house on holiday." And he continued to accept new orders for work—"A Jack and Jill of the Sierras" for the Christmas 1899 issue of the *Graphic*, "How Reuben Allen 'Saw Life' in San Francisco" for *Frank Leslie's Popular Monthly*, "The Mermaid of Lighthouse Point" for the *Illustrated London News*. He contributed to the *Saturday Evening Post* a new series of condensed novels, comparable to the burlesques he had written for the *Californian* thirty-five years earlier, parodying a entire new generation of writers, among them Arthur Conan Doyle, Hall Caine, Rudyard Kipling, and Marie Corelli. In "A Niece of Snapshot Harry's," serialized in the *Graphic* in March 1900, he alluded to his new hobby of amateur photography. Like Jack Hamlin bluffing in a game of high-stakes poker, he told the London *M.A.P.* in August 1901 that he thought he was "doing my best work" in his old age: "I have more skill and confidence than when I was in callow youth; I have now a command over my instrument which I had not then."

Bret Harte, ca. 1900. Photo by Walter Shaw, Camberley. (Bret Harte Collection, Clifton Waller Barrett Library, Special Collections Department, University of Virginia Library)

Much as he had tailored "The Heir of the McHulishes" for publication in *Century* in 1893 at the insistence of Robert Underwood Johnson, he again submitted to certain restrictions on his style laid down by Richard Watson Gilder, its new editor. Gilder cautioned Harte in late June 1900 to avoid "the kind of thing that you are aware an American 'family magazine' has to be careful about," to omit whatever would "too greatly 'shock the proprieties.'" Harte agreed to "accept the commission from Mr. Gilder with the proviso mentioned" and soon sent the squeamish editor a tepid and entirely satisfactory coming-of-age romance entitled "Trent's Trust." In a later memoir of the author, in fact, Gilder allowed that he "always found Harte quite ready to revise any work and use the criticism of others as far as it was serviceable to him." Similarly, J. Lever Tillotson of the British syndicate Tillotson and Son cautioned Harte in February 1902 "to avoid anything that might reasonably be open to objection. The American purchaser we have in view has very strict ideas on all points relating to morals."

In all, Harte published twenty-seven stories in 1900–1901 and earned by Nissen's estimate about seventeen thousand dollars during these two years. Despite his forebodings about the future, late in 1900 he even agreed to raise Anna's monthly allowance to thirty-seven pounds so that she could take Ethel to Paris for private voice lessons, much as Gertrude Griswold had studied there over twenty years before. He did not expect his daughter "to become a great singer but I shall be content if she picks up some knowledge and experience" which would enable her to teach music later, he explained. He worried she would fall victim to the same exaggerated expectations "in the prosecution of *her* profession of signing" that had befallen her mother "when you were engaged in the choir, in our younger days." In any event, he wrote Anna, "I know you will keep your promise to keep your expenses within the limits we spoke of." He sometimes had to borrow the additional seven pounds he sent her, and he reminded her in May 1901 that his income was "continually becoming more and more uncertain." He urged her again to "consider how precarious is the living I am making."

Ethel Harte, ca. 1902. (Courtesy of Cathy Gardner and Paul Deceglie)

For in the end he could merely postpone the inevitable, not escape it. By January 1901, still convinced he was simply suffering from a protracted case of laryngitis, he was able to swallow only so-called "spoon victuals," or "slops, soups, and jellies." His doctor and dental bills were exorbitant, or so he thought. "My wretched body is scarcely worth the sum I am spending on it," he wrote Anna from the Red House on February 1. "I should not hesitate at any expense that could procure me a day and night free from pain and discomfort," he admitted to Frank in April. (In "The Convalesence of Jack Hamlin," written for newspaper syndication about this time, the title character at one point suddenly awakens "with a delicious sense of freedom from pain, and of even drawing a long breath without difficulty.") By then Harte's diagnosis was an "ulcerated sore throat with swollen tonsil" or a "derangement of the whole mucous membrane."

Still, he accepted every commission and job offer that came his way. As he wrote Anna on July 29, 1901, he had promised Gilder that he would finish "Trent's Trust" for the *Century* by August 1, and "I am now working on it night and day." He began to write the libretto of *The Lord of Fontenelle*, a western light opera based upon his story "The Strange Experience of Alkali Dick" for the Austrian composer Emmanuel Moör. The first stanza of one of his lyrics, "The Buffalo Bill Rider," betrays the banality of the project as a whole:

> Whether in Lone Prairie where buffaloes roam,
>   In London, or Paris, or Berlin, I stray,
> In the shade of St. Paul's, or St. Peter's big dome,
>   I gallop and gallop and gallop away.

In October 1901 he contracted to write a three-thousand-word introduction to a new edition of Dickens's *Martin Chuzzlewit*, to be delivered within a year, for twenty-six pounds. As late as February 1902, he accepted a commission from the Tillotson syndicate for three stories, not to exceed five thousand words each, to feature Colonel Starbottle.

Under the circumstances, Harte was predictably outraged to
learn in mid-September 1901 that Anna had secretly been giving
part of her allowance to their older son and his family in Brooklyn.
In effect, she was sending Griswold money he had had to borrow
to send her. Though Griswold earned about forty dollars a month
as a writer for the *Sun,* he was also the object of his mother's
charity. "I returned from my brief holiday" in Camberley, Harte
fumed in perhaps the angriest letter he ever wrote to Anna,

> to find that wretched batch of lying, begging letters which you had
> forwarded to me in explanation of your again sending money to
> America, and diverting a part of the sum which I can only get with
> difficulty for *your own* needs, to other purposes. I need not say that
> the letters are utterly unconvincing. Fraud and Incompetency are
> written all over them in letters large enough for the most self-
> blinded and doting mother to read! I cannot believe that even *you*
> were deceived by them! If you believed in them, and that it was
> your mission to sacrifice yourself and others for Wodie, you would
> never have left America, where, with the money I sent you, you
> could have easily taken Wodie into your house and looked after
> him—instead of now expecting the father of *over sixty years,* in his
> old age to support a son of *nearly forty!* You would not have wished
> to add a dubious grandchild to my decreasing income and increas-
> ing years.

Were she "a rich woman and able to support yourself" or had
she "saved anything out of the $60,000 I have sent you in the
last twenty four years," he raged, she might freely share her
money with their son,

> But you are still in debt after spending that money. . . . For the last
> 7 or 8 years I have been warning you of my decreasing income, and
> my ill health. A months illness would stop your income, three
> months incapacity for work would be more apt to make *me* a sub-
> ject for charity and the hospital than it would Wodie!
>   When you came to England, without my knowledge or consent,
> I was told by Frank that you expected in that way to reduce your
> expenses by living with him, and *that* I conceived to have been his
> reason for advising you to such a rash and expensive step, and

becoming himself responsible for it. But that expectation has not been realized. You found it *necessary* for Ethel to study in Paris, and although I finally consented to it, I must tell you frankly, now, that I couldnt afford it, and had to get money advanced on my work to do it—and am by no means certain that it ever was a *necessity!*

He was particularly incensed that Anna had complained to Griswold

that "I had reduced your income"! This is hardly the way to express *my* diminished income but even then it is not quite correct as *to the facts*. I had during many years sent you £50 per month—when the children were younger, and the family larger; it was only at about the time of Jessamys marriage that I reduced it—through necessity—to £30. I never "reduced your income" even after my own *regular* income—the only one I had here—as Consul, was taken away.

The letter widened the rift between the Hartes, of course. They apparently exchanged no letters for over three months afterwards. Harte's outburst was also a type of valediction. His son Griswold died unexpectedly of consumption at his home in Brooklyn on December 11, less than three months later.

Meanwhile, his own health continued to decline. Publicly, he put on a brave face, insisting that he merely suffered from advancing age. "Except for a little cold," he told a reporter, "I have no ailments or complaints. While I am getting to be a pretty old man . . . there is life in the old dog yet." He then lit a cigar "so large it would have done credit to any of his Poker Flat friends." He denied published reports in the United States that he was "dangerously ill"; rather, he claimed to be "in perfect health." Privately, however, he told a different story. "I have been oscillating between the Doctor and the Dentist, and suffering painfully from neuralgia," he wrote Frank on December 1. "I have had teeth pulled out and operated upon to no purpose, and have been taking quinine till I am dizzy. The Doctor sends me to the Dentist and *vice versa,* till I am quite worn out and miserable." He was "scarcely able to work more than an hour or two a day." He had six more teeth extracted in the weeks before Christmas 1901, and he was "so distracted with pain and sleeplessness" that he felt "quite helpless." When Anna volunteered to nurse him, he protested that she "would have had an invalid on your hands! My principal trouble now is a very sluggish *sore-throat* (ulcerated,) which puzzles the Doctor with its slowness of improvement, although he says now it is mending."

He spent a few weeks that winter at Southsea, but he failed to rally in the change of climate. He was by turns worried and indignant: "It has been a very protracted case, and I cannot help thinking a very much mismanaged case from the beginning." A physician in Southsea insisted "the case was serious enough to have the tonsil out!" He wrote Frank on February 1, 1902, that he had been unable to work at all "since the 4th of December, and I have had to borrow the money" for Anna's monthly draft. "Tell your mother this and impress upon her the necessity of being careful of the little I am still able to give her. Tell her I will write to her again when I know what the specialist says, and what must be done. I should only bother her now with my fears and depressions." The only subsequent letters from his pen known to survive are addressed to Watt, his agent, and Pemberton, his friend and biographer.

A throat specialist he consulted in London at last diagnosed the cancer. In March his physician hastily performed an operation which failed to slow the advance of the disease. He accepted "his sentence of death" stoically, according to his obituaries, and "in the intervals of poignant suffering he continued his literary work." No less than six of his stories appeared in such magazines as *Harper's, Cosmopolitan,* and the *Saturday Evening Post* during the first four months of 1902. On April 12, 1902, in the last letter he is known to have written, he reported to Pemberton that he was feeling "very poorly; everything is against me—even this smileless, joyless 'sere and yellow' spring! I get no stimulus from it. I can scarcely write a letter. The grasshopper is indeed a burden!" He borrowed the quoted phrase from Shakespeare's *Macbeth:* "My way of life / Is fall'n into the sear, the yellow leaf / And that which should accompany old age, / As honor, love, obedience, troops of friends, / I must not look to have."

"My grandfather's death was marked by courage and simple dignity," Geoffrey Bret Harte reminisced forty years later. He spent most of his final weeks at the Red House with Mme Van de Velde. There on April 17 he began a new story, "A Friend of Colonel Starbottle's," one of the tales he had contracted in February to write for the Tillotson syndicate. He visited his son's family in Richmond for a few days and saw a specialist in London on April 26 before returning to Camberley. At about three in the afternoon of May 5, as his grandson later wrote, "he suffered a sudden hemorrhage. He rose and, asking that nobody should assist him, went slowly up the stairs to his room. He refused to [be] put to bed and spent his last moments in prayer. A short time after, there came a second hemorrhage." In the "very brief moments which elapsed" between these attacks he was "surrounded only by intimate friends (one myself)," Mme Van de Velde wrote the next day, and he "passed away without struggle or pain." He died at about six P.M., officially from heart failure caused by exhaustion.

Anna Harte and Mme Van de Velde met for the first and only time at the funeral at Frimley Church, Surrey, on May 8. The day was stormy, with rain and hail. Harte was buried in the churchyard with little ceremony, and his grave remained unmarked for several months until Madame had a slab placed on the site. Etched into one side of the granite was a line from Harte's poem "The Reveille," which he had written in San Francisco in 1863 to honor martyrs to the cause of Union: "Death shall reap the braver harvest." On the other side, in testimony to her esteem, were engraved these words: "In faithful remembrance M. S. Van de Velde." The grave has been neglected since Mme Van de Velde's death in 1913, at the age of eighty, at her Lancaster Gate mansion in London.

After his death, Harte's reputation was up for grabs, his legacy contested as never before. Whereas the London *Spectator* insisted in May 1902 that he had "probably exerted a greater influence on English literature than any other American author," the New York *Nation* editorialized the next month that during his long and prolific career Harte apparently never "received a

Bret Harte's grave. (Pemberton, *The Life of Bret Harte* [1903])

new impression" or "made a new observation." Like Herman Melville, he had outlived his fame. The *Washington Post* asserted in its obituary "that nine-tenths of his fellow countrymen did not know whether he was alive or dead." Similarly, such old or former friends as Clemens ("his pen pictures of California camps and mountain scenery have seldom been equaled and never surpassed") and Howells ("one of the most refined and delicate of artists") paid public tribute to his memory within days of his death. Privately, however, they were more circumspect. "He was bad, distinctly bad; he had no feeling, and he had no conscience," Clemens remarked in February 1907. Similarly, Howells admitted to Clemens in December 1903 that he "could have written things [about Harte] that would have left blisters on his fame." Harte's early biographer Henry C. Merwin conceded to Ernest Knaufft, Harte's nephew, in 1911 that he omitted "a good deal of the truth" about his life "because it would be injurious to his reputation and would hurt the feelings of his relatives. You must have noticed that I have said nothing about the immorality of his life."

Harte died intestate, but no matter: as he had repeatedly warned Anna, he had little money. His worldly goods were valued at only £360 or about $1,800, a sum less than half what he had paid in 1871 for a summer rental in Newport. As the executor of his father's estate, Frank was instructed by solicitors in January 1903 to distribute all available funds "amongst the Creditors of the estate prorata"—that is, at his death Harte's assets did not equal his debts. In a letter to John Hay in July 1902, Mme Van de Velde privately noted "what a failure our friend's domestic life" had been, how he had worked "to meet the exhaustive claims made on his resources, too chivalrous and generous to repudiate them even when flagrantly excessive." She was only slightly less pointed in a memoir published after his death in which she speculated that he had never created "a perfectly noble, superior, commanding woman" in his fiction because "such a model had never offered itself to him, or because other memories clouded his perception of womanly excellence."

As he had often predicted, his widow and daughter Ethel fell on hard times soon after his death. Ethel tried to earn a meager living by singing on the London stage, just as her father had feared, until her health broke under the strain. In July 1905 several prominent British authors, among them George Meredith, Arthur Conan Doyle, and Hall Caine, organized the "Bret Harte Assistance Fund" to "permanently benefit Miss Ethel Bret Harte" and no doubt her mother. The fund collected nearly £1,000 from about five hundred subscribers, which enabled Anna to purchase a small annuity and Ethel to set up a Typewriting Bureau on Baker Street in London. Anna outlived her husband by eighteen years; she died senile, from gangrene, in Hove, England, in 1920, at the age of eighty-five. Ethel returned to the United States a few years later and died of heart disease in 1964, in Ojai, California, at the age of eighty-nine.

In fact, none of Harte's survivors led a charmed life. Jessamy, his older daughter, separated from Henry Steele after a few years of marriage and, in 1907, was living in the almshouse in Portland, Maine. (Clemens made national news by refusing to contribute to a fund on her behalf.) She divorced Steele in 1910 on grounds of extreme cruelty—he had been physically abusive—and in 1915, after a failed career as a cabaret singer, she was admitted to the mental ward of a hospital in Islip, New York. Two years later she was transferred to the St. Lawrence State Hospital in Ogdensburg, New York, where she died forty-seven years later, in October 1964, at the age of ninety. Frank Harte died in 1917, aged fifty-two, in Monte Carlo. Frank's wife Aline died of pneumonia in England in October 1920. Their older son Richard married and divorced a pupil of Isadora Duncan in the early 1920s and, despondent over a love affair, committed suicide in Paris in 1925. His death was reported on the front page of the *New York Times*, which had buried on page nine the news of his grandfather's death a generation before. Geoffrey Bret Harte, who edited his grandfather's *Letters* for Houghton Mifflin and served as his last literary executor, drowned in Mexico in 1956 at the age of sixty-one.

Ironically, the family fortunes were rebuilt early in this century by several successful theatrical and motion-picture adaptations

of Harte's writings. The play *Salomy Jane,* based on Harte's story
"Salomy Jane's Kiss," scripted by Paul Armstrong and starring
Eleanor Robson, was a Broadway hit in 1907 and earned Harte's
heirs a royalty variously described as "handsome" and "substantial" after they sued the producers for infringement of copyright. This horse opera in turn inspired two early silent film
westerns, the first in 1914, the second starring Jacqueline Logan,
a former Follies girl, in 1925. In fact, Harte's writings became
the basis of at least twenty-four feature films produced between
1909 and 1955, including *The Lily of Poverty Flat* (1915), starring
Beatriz Michelena; *The Half Breed* (1916), based on "In the
Carquinez Woods," starring Douglas Fairbanks; *M'liss* (1918),
starring Mary Pickford; no less than three versions of *The Outcasts of Poker Flat* (a silent version in 1919 directed by John Ford
and talkies in 1937 and 1952, the latter starring Dale Robertson
and Anne Baxter); and a loose adaptation of *Tennessee's Partner*
(1955), starring Ronald Reagan, John Payne, and Rhonda Fleming.

The negotiations with motion-picture companies for dramatic
rights to Harte's stories, especially in the teens and 1920s, the
heyday of the movie western, were complicated by disagreements
among the heirs and especially by the conditions of Jessamy's
confinement. As Geoffrey Bret Harte once explained to Ferris
Greenslet of Houghton Mifflin, "Mrs. Steele . . . is insane and
therefore a committee would have to be appointed" to represent her interests in the sale of any rights. In 1921 Jessamy asked
the staff of the asylum in Ogdensburg "to bring action against
several moving picture companies" she claimed had "used her
father's stories on the screen without paying royalties due her,"
and in 1927 she contacted a lawyer to demand an accounting
from Houghton Mifflin. Even a quarter century after Harte's
death, that is, his heirs were at odds over the money his stories
still earned. In death as in life, Harte remained a creature of the
market.

Like wing tips and wide ties, the "Bret Harte" brand of western
American fiction falls in and out of fashion every few years. In
1925–26, after his manuscripts and other literary remains became
prized collectibles, his heirs sold over four hundred of his letters

at auction for a total of about six thousand dollars. His commodification in the 1920s occurred even as Tuolumne and Calaveras Counties began to be touted in travel magazines as "Bret Harte country," and with the construction of State Highway 108 the small town of Twain-Harte, near Sonora and Angels Camp, became a popular tourist destination with an annual Bret Harte Pageant. As early as 1923, a roadside monument to Harte was erected on Mount Diablo, and in 1927, according to *Time*, his stories about the gold rush so enchanted Joseph Stalin that the Soviet leader began to encourage mass migration to the Siberian "frontier." "Of all the Californias that men have invented for their delight or their profit," the travel writer Mildred Adams mused in 1930, "Bret Harte's is the most charming."

By any reasonable criteria, Harte deserves to be resurrected from the footnote. Not only did he mentor the original contributors to the *Overland Monthly*, he was a literary pioneer who surveyed the American West and helped develop a formula, including an ensemble of characters, to which western writers have subscribed ever since. While he founded no literary school, he set a standard for such twentieth-century imitators as Damon Runyon and O. Henry, the so-called "Bret Harte of the City." Above all, he epitomized the man of letters as a man of business during the Gilded Age of American commerce. If Herman Melville was a "divine amateur," then Bret Harte was a type of "profane professional" whose career silhouettes the inner workings of the Anglo-American literary marketplace during the final decades of the nineteenth century. Whatever his personal peccadillos, moreover, Harte was not a moral monster, as Samuel Clemens alleged. No less than the calculating gamblers and scheming miners who people his best stories, he deserves our respect if he does not inspire our affection.

Sources

THE following guide to primary and secondary materials I consulted in the preparation of this biography should establish a baseline of sources for the reader interested in more detailed information about Harte's life and career. This commentary should address most questions related to the subject. As I also note in the preface, however, I have deposited a fully documented manuscript of the biography in the University of New Mexico English Department library for scholars who wish to verify the accuracy of any of my specific statements.

Though Harte's name nowadays has roughly the same resonance among literary critics that the administration of Millard Fillmore inspires among presidential historians, his career can be reconstructed in detail because he was so well known during his life. Over 2,000 letters from his hand survive, the largest numbers of them in the Alderman Library, University of Virginia (672 letters, including all of those to Florence Henniker and the Schneiders); the UCLA Research Library (243 letters, most of them to family members); the National Archives (192 diplomatic dispatches dated between 1878 and 1885); the Bancroft Library, University of California, Berkeley (191 letters, including all 11 extant letters written to Clemens); the Beinecke Rare Book and Manuscript Library, Yale University (104 letters, 82 of them written to Pemberton between 1895 and 1900); the Huntington Library (54 letters, many to his publishers Fields and Osgood); the Berg Collection of English and American Literature, New York Public Library (50 letters); the Humanities Research Center, University of

Texas, Austin (49 letters); the John Hay Library, Brown University (33 letters, including 28 written to Hay between 1871 and 1897); the Houghton Library, Harvard University (29 letters, including all of those to Howells, Longfellow, and Lowell); the Manuscripts Division, Library of Congress (24 letters); Bobst Library, New York University (22 letters, including 6 to F. H. Mason); and the Princeton University Library (11 letters). Among other valuable manuscript sources of biographical data are the diaries of Annie Fields at the Massachusetts Historical Society. The records of A. P. Watt, Harte's literary agent, repose in Wilson Library, University of North Carolina at Chapel Hill. Harte's great-grandson John Bret-Harte owns some two dozen holograph letters retained by the family as well as an unpublished family history written by Geoffrey Bret Harte in 1941, and Harte's great-grandniece Cathleen F. Gardner also owns about thirty letters, most of them written by Harte to his sister Eliza Knaufft, as well as a collection of family photographs.

Several collections of Harte's letters have been published over the years, most significantly *The Letters of Bret Harte,* edited by Geoffrey Bret Harte (Boston: Houghton Mifflin, 1926); Bradford Booth's "Unpublished Letters of Bret Harte," *American Literature* 16 (May 1944): 131–42, and "Bret Harte Goes East: Some Unpublished Letters," *American Literature* 19 (January 1948): 318–35; Brenda Murphy and George Monteiro's "The Unpublished Letters of Bret Harte to John Hay," *American Literary Realism* 12 (Spring 1979): 77–110; and *Selected Letters of Bret Harte,* edited by Gary Scharnhorst (Norman and London: University of Oklahoma Press, 1997).

Two of Harte's diaries survive, the one covering the period from October 1857 to March 1858 in the Bancroft Library at Berkeley, the other, entitled "Things That Happened," covering the period 1881–88, in the Berg Collection, New York Public Library.

Harte rarely granted interviews, and only three significant ones were published: "Bret Harte Interviewed," Washington

Capital, October 1, 1876, p. 4; Henry J. W. Dam, "A Morning with Bret Harte," *McClure's* 4 (December 1894): 38–50; and "Kate Carew's 12-Minute Interview on 12 Subjects with Bret Harte," New York *World* 22 (December 1901): 5. At least one early biographical sketch was written, if not by Harte, at least with his assistance: "Francis Bret Harte/A Sketch of His Life by the San Francisco Correspondent of the Topeka Record," reprinted in the *Chicago Tribune,* November 20, 1870, p. 6. Other important nineteenth- and early twentieth-century newspaper clippings survive in the Willard S. Morse Collection, UCLA Research Library.

All of Harte's known publications are listed in Gary Scharnhorst's *Bret Harte: A Bibliography* (Lanham, Md.: Scarerow Press, 1995); this volume also includes production dates of his plays and itineraries of his lecture tours and lists reviews of both his plays and lectures. The most comprehensive list of published responses to Harte's writings is Linda Diz Barrett's *Bret Harte: A Reference Guide* (Boston: G. K. Hall, 1980).

In addition to the standard collected editions of Harte's writings, a number of volumes gather published works otherwise lost to scholarship: *Sue,* with T. Edgar Pemberton (London: Greening and Co., 1902); *The Lectures of Bret Harte,* edited by Charles Meeker Kozlay (Brooklyn: privately printed, 1909); *Stories and Poems and Other Uncollected Writings,* edited by Kozlay (Boston and New York: Houghton Mifflin, 1914); *Sketches of the Sixties,* edited by John Howell (San Francisco: Howell, 1927); *Ah Sin: A Dramatic Work,* with Mark Twain, edited by Frederick Anderson (San Francisco: Book Club of California, 1961); and *Bret Harte's California: Letters to the Springfield Republican and Christian Register, 1866–67,* edited by Gary Scharnhorst (Albuquerque: University of New Mexico Press, 1990). One of Harte's most important essays, never reprinted, is available only in its original publication: "The Rise of the 'Short Story,'" *Cornhill Magazine* 7 (July 1899): 1–8.

Harte has also been the focus of several solid book-length bio-
graphies, including T. Edgar Pemberton's authorized *The
Life of Bret Harte* (New York: Dodd, Mead, 1903). Henry
Childs Merwin's *The Life of Bret Harte* (Boston and New
York: Houghton Mifflin, 1911) is also useful for its docu-
mentation of Harte's early life. George Stewart's *Bret Harte:
Argonaut and Exile* (Boston: Houghton Mifflin, 1931) was
for many years the standard reference. However, Richard
O'Connor's *Bret Harte: A Biography* (Boston and Toronto:
Little, Brown, 1966) is derivative and contains no new information. Gary Scharnhorst's *Bret Harte* (New York: Twayne,
1992) is a critical biography. Nils Axel Nissen's *Prince and
Pauper: The Life and Literary Career of Bret Harte* (1996), a
doctoral dissertation submitted to the faculty at the University
of Oslo, is a detailed record which cites a wealth of information about Harte that has surfaced over the past sixty years;
it is also thesis ridden, its analysis marred by its search for
evidence of homoeroticism in Harte's life and writings.

Harte was the subject of a surprising number of memoirs pub-
lished during the last years of his life or immediately after his
death. Among the sketches by his friends and associates in
San Francisco in the 1860s are Noah Brooks's "Bret Harte
in California," *Century* 58 (July 1899): 447–51, "Harte's
Early Days," *New York Times Saturday Review of Books,*
May 24, 1902, p. 350, and "Bret Harte: A Study and an
Appreciation," *Book Buyer* 24 (June 1902): 358–62; Joaquin
Miller's "Foppish Bret Harte," *San Francisco Examiner,*
July 7, 1895, p. 25, and "Reminiscences of Bret Harte," *New
York Times Saturday Review of Books and Art,* May 31, 1902,
p. 360; Josephine Clifford McCrackin's "A Letter from a
Friend," *Overland Monthly* 40 (September 1902): 222–25,
and "Reminiscences of Bret Harte and Pioneer Days in the
West," *Overland Monthly* 67 (December 1915): 7–15; Charles
Warren Stoddard's "Early Recollections of Bret Harte,"
Atlantic Monthly 78 (November 1896): 673–78, reprinted in
Exits and Entrances (Boston: Lothrop, 1903), "Francis Bret
Harte," *New York Times Saturday Review of Books,* August

2, 1902, p. 516, and "In Old Bohemia," *Pacific Monthly*, 19 (March 1908): 261–73; Jessie Benton Frémont's *Souvenirs of My Time* (Boston: Lothrop, 1887); and Ina Coolbrith's "An Introduction" to *Plain Language from Truthful James* (San Francisco: Nash, 1934), iv–xii.

Among the other valuable memoirs of Harte's years in the East or in Europe are the following: Mary E. W. Sherwood's *An Epistle to Posterity* (New York: Harper, 1897), and "Bret Harte," *New York Times Saturday Review of Books*, May 10, 1902, p. 308; Richard H. Clark's "Francis Bret Harte," *Atlanta Constitution*, May 12, 1895, p. 2; W. D. Howells's *Literary Friends and Acquaintance* (New York: Harper, 1910), 289–305; S. H. M. Byers's *Twenty Years in Europe* (Chicago and New York: Rand, McNally, 1900), 170–87, and "Bret Harte in Switzerland," *Overland Monthly* 42 (October–November 1903): 291–97, 426–32; sketches by Richard Watson Gilder, Henry Mills Alden, and Walter H. Page in "Francis Bret Harte: A Symposium," *Boston Transcript*, May 10, 1902, p. 18; Donald Macleod's "Reminiscences of the late Mr. Bret Harte," *Good Words* 43 (July 1902): 532–33; S. R. Elliott's "Glimpses of Bret Harte," *Reader* 10 (July 1907): 122–27; and M. S. Van de Velde's "Francis Bret Harte," *Belgravia* 45 (August 1881): 232–36, reprinted in *Potter's American Monthly* 17 (October 1881): 306–309, and "Bret Harte: First and Last Tales of the Argonauts," *Gentleman's Magazine* 195 (December 1903): 535–44.

Less reliable though no less interesting are Clemens's effluvia about Harte dictated in 1907 and published in *Mark Twain in Eruption*, edited by Bernard DeVoto (New York and London: Harper, 1940), 254–92. The vexed relations between Harte and Clemens are fully documented in a number of primary sources: *Mark Twain-Howells Letters*, edited by Henry Nash Smith and William M. Gibson, 2 vols. (Cambridge: Belknap, 1960); Bradford Booth's "Mark Twain's Comments on Bret Harte's Stories," *American Literature* 25 (January 1954): 492–95; George Peirce Clark's "Mark

Twain on Bret Harte: Selections from Two Unpublished Letters," *Journal of English and Germanic Philology* 57 (April 1958): 208–10; Francis Murphy's "The End of a Friendship: Two Unpublished Letters from Twain to Howells about Bret Harte," *New England Quarterly* 58 (March 1985): 87–91; and Gary Scharnhorst's "The Bret Harte-Mark Twain Feud: An Inside Narrative," *Mark Twain Journal* 31 (Spring 1993): 29–32. Margaret Duckett's *Mark Twain and Bret Harte* (Norman: University of Oklahoma Press, 1964) is a first-rate study, unfortunately undervalued because of its prolix style, disorganization, and tendency to blame both writers, but especially Clemens, for their estrangement. Some details about Harte's life and career appear in the following specialized articles: Helen I. Davis, "Bret Harte and His Jewish Ancestor, Bernard Hart," *Publications of the American Jewish Historical Society* 32 (1931): 99–111; Ernest R. May, "Bret Harte and the *Overland Monthly*," *American Literature* 22 (November 1950): 260–71; William J. Scheick, "William Dean Howells to Bret Harte: A Missing Letter," *American Literary Realism* 9 (Summer 1976): 276–79; Stanley T. Williams, "Ambrose Bierce and Bret Harte," *American Literature* 17 (May 1945): 179–80; and James Harvey Young, "Anna Dickinson, Mark Twain, and Bret Harte," *Pennsylvania Magazine of History and Biography* 76 (January 1952): 39–46. Harte's years in Humboldt County, California, are covered in detail by Charles A. Murdock in "Francis Bret Harte," *San Francisco Examiner*, February 24, 1889, p. 10, "Francis Bret Harte," *California Writers Club Quarterly Bulletin* 2 (June 1914): 1–3, and his autobiography *A Backward Glance at Eighty* (San Francisco: Elder, 1921). See also "Three Lost Years in the Life of Bret Harte," *San Francisco Examiner*, January 24, 1926, part 2, pp. 1–2; Sophia Whipple Root's "Three Lost Years of Bret Harte's Life," *Overland Monthly*, 90 (October 1932): passim; and Lynwood Carranco's "Bret Harte in Union (1857–1860)," *California Historical Society Quarterly* 45 (June 1966): 99–112. On Harte's diplomatic service in Crefeld and his popularity among German

readers, see Lewis Rosenthal, "Bret Harte in Germany,"
Critic 21 (February 1885): 85–86; Eugene F. Timpe, "Bret
Harte's German Public," *Jahrbuch für Amerikastudien* 10
(1965): 215–20; and Ward B. Lewis, "Bret Harte and
Germany," *Revue de Littérature Comparée* 54 (April–June
1980): 213–24. The special Bret Harte issue of the *Overland
Monthly*, 40 (September 1902), includes brief reminiscences
by Brooks, Howells, Hay, Anton Roman, and others.
Harte figures prominently in the letters of some of his contem-
poraries, as the following editions will attest: *The Letters of
Jessie Benton Frémont*, edited by Pamela Herr and Mary Lee
Spence (Urbana: University of Illinois Press, 1993); the multi-
volume *Mark Twain's Letters* (Berkeley, Los Angeles, London:
University of California Press, 1988–); *If Not Literature:
Letters of Elinor Mead Howells*, edited by Ginette de B. Merrill
and George Arms (Columbus: Ohio State University Press,
1988); and *W. D. Howells: Selected Letters*, 6 vols. (Boston:
Twayne, 1979–83).
Among the most provocative critical essays on Harte's writing
are a series of them published by Duckett in the 1950s:
"Bret Harte's Portrayal of Half-Breeds," *American Litera-
ture* 25 (May 1953): 193–212; "Bret Harte and the Indians of
Northern California," *Huntington Library Quarterly* 18
(November 1954): 59–83; "Plain Language from Bret Harte,"
Nineteenth Century Fiction 11 (March 1957): 241–60; and
"The 'Crusade' of a Nineteenth-Century Liberal," *Tennes-
see Studies in Literature* 4 (1959): 109–20. Of course many
other critical books and articles contain biographical infor-
mation, including Patrick Morrow's *Bret Harte: Literary
Critic* (Bowling Green, Ohio: Bowling Green State Uni-
versity Popular Press, 1979), and "Parody and Parable in
Early Western Local Color Writing," *Journal of the West* 19
(January 1980): 9–16. Luther S. Luedtke and Patrick
Morrow's "Bret Harte on Bayard Taylor," *Markham Review*
3 (May 1973): 101–105, is also a significant contribution to
Harte studies. The special Harte issue of *American Literary
Realism*, 8 (Fall 1973), includes Jeffrey F. Thomas's "Bret

Harte and the Power of Sex," 91–109; Roscoe L. Buckland's "Jack Hamlin: Bret Harte's Romantic Rogue," 111–22; Jack Scherting's "Bret Harte's Civil War Poems: Voice of the Majority," 133–42; and Donald E. Glover's "A Reconsideration of Bret Harte's Later Work," 144–51. In a subsequent article in the same journal, "The Outcasts of Literary Flat: Bret Harte as Humorist," *American Literary Realism* 23 (Winter 1991): 52–63, Harold H. Kolb, Jr., revises the conventional assessment of Harte's career. The following texts detail the circumstances of Harte's early publishing successes: Ella Sterling Cummins's *The Story of the Files* (San Francisco: World's Fair Commission of California, 1893); "The Overland Dinner," supplement to the *Overland Monthly* 1 (February 1883): 1–16; and Ellen B. Ballou's *The Building of the House: Houghton Mifflin's Formative Years* (Boston: Houghton Mifflin, 1970).

At Harte's death, lengthy obituaries (all dated May 7, 1902) appeared in such newspapers as the *New York Tribune*, p. 2, New York *Sun*, p. 2, *New York Times*, p. 9, San Francisco *Call*, p. 9, *San Francisco Examiner*, p. 3, and San Francisco *Chronicle*, p. 1.

Index